C# Data Structures and Algorithms

Explore the possibilities of C# for developing a variety of efficient applications

Marcin Jamro

BIRMINGHAM - MUMBAI

C# Data Structures and Algorithms

Commissioning Editor: Richa Tripathi
Acquisition Editor: Chaitanya Nair
Content Development Editor: Zeeyan Pinheiro
Technical Editor: Romy Dias
Copy Editor: Safis Editing
Project Coordinator: Vaidehi Sawant
Proofreader: Safis Editing
Indexer: Tejal Daruwale Soni
Graphics: Jason Monteiro
Production Coordinator: Shantanu Zagade

First published: April 2018

Production reference: 1170418

Published by Packt Publishing Ltd.
Livery Place
35 Livery Street
Birmingham
B3 2PB, UK.

ISBN 978-1-78883-373-8

www.packtpub.com

`mapt.io`

Mapt is an online digital library that gives you full access to over 5,000 books and videos, as well as industry leading tools to help you plan your personal development and advance your career. For more information, please visit our website.

Why subscribe?

- Spend less time learning and more time coding with practical eBooks and Videos from over 4,000 industry professionals

- Improve your learning with Skill Plans built especially for you

- Get a free eBook or video every month

- Mapt is fully searchable

- Copy and paste, print, and bookmark content

PacktPub.com

Did you know that Packt offers eBook versions of every book published, with PDF and ePub files available? You can upgrade to the eBook version at `www.PacktPub.com` and as a print book customer, you are entitled to a discount on the eBook copy. Get in touch with us at `service@packtpub.com` for more details.

At `www.PacktPub.com`, you can also read a collection of free technical articles, sign up for a range of free newsletters, and receive exclusive discounts and offers on Packt books and eBooks.

Contributors

About the author

Marcin Jamro, PhD, is an entrepreneur and researcher, as well as a developer and architect of various kinds of applications. He is the President of the Board at TITUTO Sp. z o.o. [Ltd.] in Rzeszów, Poland.

Marcin is interested in many aspects of computer science, including software engineering and project management. He is an author of two other books, namely *Windows Phone 8 Game Development* (2013) and *Windows Application Development Cookbook* (2017), both by Packt Publishing.

Marcin has published several papers, participated in many conferences, organized a few of them, and participated in two internships at Microsoft in Redmond, USA. He has the MCP, MCTS, and MCPD certificates.

About the reviewer

Dariusz Rzońca, PhD, received his BSc in Mathematics from the University of Rzeszow, Poland, in 2002, MSc in Computer Engineering from the Rzeszow University of Technology, Poland in 2004, and PhD in Computer Science at the Silesian University of Technology, Poland, in 2012. He has been working as an assistant professor in the Department of Computer and Control Engineering at Rzeszow University of Technology, Poland. Dariusz is the author or co-author of over sixty scientific papers.

Packt is searching for authors like you

If you're interested in becoming an author for Packt, please visit authors.packtpub.com and apply today. We have worked with thousands of developers and tech professionals, just like you, to help them share their insight with the global tech community. You can make a general application, apply for a specific hot topic that we are recruiting an author for, or submit your own idea.

Table of Contents

Preface

As a developer, you have certainly heard about various data structures and algorithms. However, have you ever thought profoundly about them and their impact on the performance of your applications? If not, it is high time to take a look at this topic, and this book is a great place to start!

The book covers many data structures, starting with simple ones, namely arrays and a few of their variants, as representatives of random access data structures. Then, lists are introduced, together with their sorted variant. The book also explains limited access data structures, based on stacks and queues, including a priority queue. Following this, we introduce you to the dictionary data structure, which allows you to map keys to values and perform fast lookup. The sorted variant of the dictionary is supported, as well. If you want to benefit from high-performance, set-related operations, you can use another data structure, namely a hash set. One of the most powerful constructs is a tree, which exists in a few variants, such as a binary tree, a binary search tree, as well as a self-balancing tree and a heap. The last data structure we analyze is a graph, which is supported by many interesting algorithmic topics, such as graph traversal, minimum spanning tree, node coloring, and finding the shortest path in a graph. There is a lot of content ahead of you!

Are you interested in knowing the influence of choosing a suitable data structure on the performance of your application? Do you want to know how you can increase the quality and performance of your solution by choosing the right data structure and accompanying algorithm? Are you curious about real-world scenarios where these data structures can be applied? If you answer positively to any of these questions, let's start reading this book to learn about various data structures and algorithms that you can use while developing applications in C#.

Arrays, lists, stacks, queues, dictionaries, hash sets, trees, heaps, and graphs, as well as accompanying algorithms—a broad range of subjects awaits you in the next pages! Let's start the adventure and take the first step toward your mastery of data structures and algorithms, which hopefully will have a positive effect on your projects and on your career as a software developer!

Who this book is for

This book is aimed at developers who would like to learn about the data structures and algorithms that can be used in C# in various kinds of applications, including web and mobile solutions. The topics presented here are suitable for programmers with various levels of experience, and even beginners will find interesting content. However, having at least a basic knowledge of the C# programming language, such as about object-oriented programming, will be an added advantage.

To easily understand the content, the book is equipped with many illustrations and examples. What's more, the source code for the accompanying projects is attached to the chapters. Thus, you can easily run example applications and debug them without writing the code on your own.

It is worth mentioning that the code can be simplified, and it can differ from the best practices. What's more, the examples can have significantly limited, or even no, security checks and functionalities. Before publishing your application using the content presented in the book, the application should be thoroughly tested to ensure that it works correctly in various circumstances, such as in the scenario of passing incorrect data.

What this book covers

Chapter 1, *Getting Started*, explains the very important role of using the right data structures and algorithms, as well as the impact it has on the performance of the developed solution. The chapter briefly introduces you to the topic of the C# programming language and various data types—both value and reference. Then, it presents the process of the installation and configuration of the IDE, as well as the creation of a new project, developing the example application, and debugging using breakpoints and the step-by-step technique.

Chapter 2, *Arrays and Lists*, covers scenarios of storing data using two kinds of random access data structures, namely arrays and lists. First, three variants of arrays are explained, that is, single-dimensional, multi-dimensional, and jagged. You will also get to know four sorting algorithms, namely selection, insertion, bubble sort, and quicksort. The chapter also deals with a few variants of lists, such as simple, sorted, double-linked, and circular-linked.

`Chapter 3`, *Stacks and Queues*, explains how to use two variants of limited access data structures, namely stacks and queues, including priority queues. The chapter shows how to perform `push` and `pop` operations on a stack, and also describes the `enqueue` and `dequeue` operations in the case of a queue. To aid your understanding of these topics, a few examples are presented, including the Tower of Hanoi game and an application that simulates a call center with multiple consultants and callers.

`Chapter 4`, *Dictionaries and Sets*, focuses on data structures related to dictionaries and sets, which make it possible to map keys to values, perform fast lookup, and carry out various operations on sets. The chapter introduces you to both nongeneric and generic variants of a hash table, the sorted dictionary, and the high-performance solution to set operations, together with the concept of the "sorted" set.

`Chapter 5`, *Variants of Trees*, describes a few tree-related topics. It presents the basic tree, together with its implementation in C#, and examples showing this in action. The chapter also introduces you to binary trees, binary search trees, and self-balancing trees, namely AVL and red-black trees. The remainder of the chapter is dedicated to heaps as tree-based structures, that is, the binary, binomial, and Fibonacci heaps.

`Chapter 6`, *Exploring Graphs*, contains a lot of information about graphs, starting with an explanation of their basic concepts, including nodes and a few variants of edges. The implementation of a graph in C# is also covered. The chapter introduces you to two modes of graph traversal, namely depth-first and breadth-first search. Then, it presents the subject of minimum spanning trees using Kruskal's and Prim's algorithms, the node coloring problem, and the solution to finding the shortest path in a graph using Dijkstra's algorithm.

`Chapter 7`, *Summary*, is the conclusion to all the knowledge acquired from the previous chapters. It shows a brief classification of data structures, dividing them into two groups, namely linear and nonlinear. Finally, the chapter talks about the diversity of the applications of various data structures.

To get the most out of this book

The book is aimed at programmers with various experience. However, beginners will also find some interesting content. Nevertheless, at least a basic knowledge of C#, such as about object-oriented programming, will be an added advantage.

Download the example code files

You can download the example code files for this book from your account at www.packtpub.com. If you purchased this book elsewhere, you can visit www.packtpub.com/support and register to have the files emailed directly to you.

You can download the code files by following these steps:

1. Log in or register at www.packtpub.com.
2. Select the **SUPPORT** tab.
3. Click on **Code Downloads & Errata**.
4. Enter the name of the book in the **Search** box and follow the onscreen instructions.

Once the file is downloaded, please make sure that you unzip or extract the folder using the latest version of:

- WinRAR/7-Zip for Windows
- Zipeg/iZip/UnRarX for Mac
- 7-Zip/PeaZip for Linux

The code bundle for the book is also hosted on GitHub at https://github.com/PacktPublishing/C-Sharp-Data-Structures-and-Algorithms. In case there's an update to the code, it will be updated on the existing GitHub repository.

We also have other code bundles from our rich catalog of books and videos available at https://github.com/PacktPublishing/. Check them out!

Download the color images

We also provide a PDF file that has color images of the screenshots/diagrams used in this book. You can download it here: https://www.packtpub.com/sites/default/files/downloads/CSharpDataStructuresandAlgorithms_ColorImages.pdf.

Conventions used

There are a number of text conventions used throughout this book.

`CodeInText`: Indicates code words in text, folder names, filenames, file extensions, pathnames, dummy URLs, and user input. Here is an example: "The class contains three properties (namely `Id`, `Name`, and `Role`), as well as two constructors."

A block of code is set as follows:

```
int[,] numbers = new int[,] =
{
    { 9, 5, -9 },
    { -11, 4, 0 },
    { 6, 115, 3 },
    { -12, -9, 71 },
    { 1, -6, -1 }
};
```

Any command-line input or output is written as follows:

```
Enter the number: 10.5
The average value: 10.5 (...)
Enter the number: 1.5
The average value: 4.875
```

Bold: Indicates a new term, an important word, or words that you see onscreen. For example, words in menus or dialog boxes appear in the text like this. Here is an example: "When the message **Installation succeeded!** is shown, click on the **Launch** button to start the IDE."

Warnings or important notes appear like this.

Tips and tricks appear like this.

Get in touch

Feedback from our readers is always welcome.

General feedback: Email feedback@packtpub.com and mention the book title in the subject of your message. If you have questions about any aspect of this book, please email us at questions@packtpub.com.

Errata: Although we have taken every care to ensure the accuracy of our content, mistakes do happen. If you have found a mistake in this book, we would be grateful if you would report this to us. Please visit www.packtpub.com/submit-errata, selecting your book, clicking on the Errata Submission Form link, and entering the details.

Piracy: If you come across any illegal copies of our works in any form on the Internet, we would be grateful if you would provide us with the location address or website name. Please contact us at copyright@packtpub.com with a link to the material.

If you are interested in becoming an author: If there is a topic that you have expertise in and you are interested in either writing or contributing to a book, please visit authors.packtpub.com.

Reviews

Please leave a review. Once you have read and used this book, why not leave a review on the site that you purchased it from? Potential readers can then see and use your unbiased opinion to make purchase decisions, we at Packt can understand what you think about our products, and our authors can see your feedback on their book. Thank you!

For more information about Packt, please visit packtpub.com.

Getting Started 1

Developing applications is certainly something exciting to work on, but it is also challenging, especially if you need to solve some complex problems that involve advanced data structures and algorithms. In such cases, you often need to take care of performance to ensure that the solution will work smoothly on devices with limited resources. Such a task could be really difficult and could require significant knowledge regarding not only the programming language, but also data structures and algorithms.

Did you know that replacing even one data structure with another could cause the performance results to increase hundreds of times? Does it sound impossible? Maybe, but it is true! As an example, I would like to tell you a short story about one of the projects in which I was involved. The aim was to optimize the algorithm of finding connections between blocks on a graphical diagram. Such connections should be automatically recalculated, refreshed, and redrawn as soon as any block has moved in the diagram. Of course, connections cannot go through blocks and cannot overlap other lines, and the number of crossings and direction changes should be limited. Depending on the size and the complexity of the diagram, the performance results differ. However, while conducting tests, we have received results in the range from 1 ms to almost 800 ms for the same test case. What could be the most surprising aspect is that such a huge improvement has been reached mainly by... changing data structures of two sets.

Now, you could ask yourself the obvious question: *which data structures should I use in given circumstances and which algorithms could be used to solve some common problems?* Unfortunately, the answer is not simple. However, within this book, you will find a lot of information about data structures and algorithms, presented in the context of the C# programming language, with many examples, code snippets, and detailed explanations. Such content could help you to answer the aforementioned questions while developing the next great solutions, which could be used by many people all over the world! Are you ready to start your adventure with data structures and algorithms? If so, let's start!

In this chapter, you will cover the following topics:

- Programming language
- Data types
- Installation and configuration of the IDE
- Creating the project
- Input and output
- Launching and debugging

Programming language

As a developer, you have certainly heard about many programming languages, such as **C#**, **Java**, **C++**, **C**, **PHP**, or **Ruby**. In all of them, you can use various data structures, as well as implement algorithms, to solve both basic and complex problems. However, each language has its own specificity, which could be visible while implementing data structures and accompanying algorithms. As already mentioned, this book will focus only on the C# programming language, which is also the main topic of this section.

The C# language, pronounced as "C Sharp", is a modern, general-purpose, strongly-typed, and object-oriented programming language that can be used while developing a wide range of applications, such as web, mobile, desktop, distributed, and embedded solutions, as well as even games. It cooperates with various additional technologies and platforms, including ASP.NET MVC, Windows Store, Xamarin, Windows Forms, XAML, and Unity. Therefore, when you learn the C# language, as well as getting to know more about data structures and algorithms in the context of this programming language, you can use such skills to create more than one particular type of software.

The current version of the language is C# 7.1. It is worth mentioning its interesting history with the following versions of the language (for example, 2.0, 3.0, and 5.0) in which new features have been added to increase language possibilities and to simplify the work of developers. When you take a look at release notes for particular versions, you will see how the language is being improved and expanded over time.

The syntax of the C# programming language is similar to other languages, such as Java or C++. For this reason, if you know such languages, you should quite easily be able to understand the code written in C#. As an example, similarly as in the languages mentioned previously, the code consists of statements that end with semicolons (;), and curly brackets ({ and }) are used to group statements, such as within the `foreach` loop. You could also find similar code constructions, such as the `if` statement, or `while` and `for` loops.

Developing various applications in the C# language is also simplified by the availability of many additional great features, such as **Language Integrated Query** (**LINQ**), which allows developers to get data from various collections, such as SQL databases or XML documents, in a consistent way. There are also some approaches to shorten the required code, such as using lambda expressions, expression-bodied members, getters and setters, or string interpolation. It is worth mentioning the automatic garbage collection that simplifies the task of releasing memory. Of course, the solutions mentioned are only the very limited subset of features available while developing in C#. You will see some others in the following parts of this book, together with examples and detailed descriptions.

Data types

While developing applications in the C# language, you could use various data types, which are divided into two groups, namely **value types** and **reference types**. The difference between them is very simple—a variable of a value type directly contains data, while a variable of a reference type just stores a reference to data, as shown as follows:

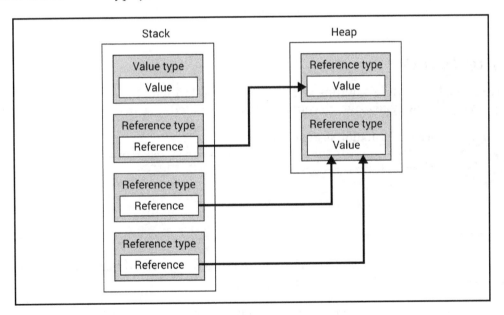

As you can see, a **Value type** stores its actual **Value** directly in the **Stack** memory, while a **Reference type** only stores a **Reference** here. The actual value is located in the **Heap** memory. Therefore, it is also possible to have two or more variables of a reference type that reference exactly the same value.

Of course, a difference between value and reference types is very important while programming and you should know which types belong to the groups mentioned. Otherwise, you could make mistakes in the code that could be quite difficult to find. For instance, you should remember to take care while updating the data of a reference type, because the change could also be reflected in other variables that are referencing the same object. Moreover, you should be careful while comparing two objects with the equals (=) operator, because you could compare the reference, not the data itself, in the case of two instances of a reference type.

The C# language also supports **pointer types**, which can be declared as `type* identifier` or `void* identifier`. However, such types are beyond the scope of this book. You can read more about them at: `https://docs.microsoft.com/en-us/dotnet/csharp/programming-guide /unsafe-code-pointers/pointer-types`.

Value types

To give you a better understanding of data types, let's start with the analysis of the first group (that is, **value types**), which could be further divided into **structs** and **enumerations**.

More information is available at: `https://docs.microsoft.com/en-us/dotnet/csharp/language-referenc e/keywords/value-types`.

Structs

Within structs, you have access to many built-in types, which could be used either as keywords or types from the `System` namespace.

One of them is the `Boolean` type (the `bool` keyword), which makes it possible to store a **logical value**, that is, one of two values, namely `true` or `false`.

As for storing **integer values,** you can use one of the following types: `Byte` (the `byte` keyword), `SByte` (`sbyte`), `Int16` (`short`), `UInt16` (`ushort`), `Int32` (`int`), `UInt32` (`uint`), `Int64` (`long`), and `UInt64` (`ulong`). They differ by the number of bytes for storing values and therefore by the range of available values. As an example, the `short` data type supports values in the range from -32,768 to 32,767 while `uint` supports values in the range from 0 to 4,294,967,295. Another type within the integral types is `Char` (`char`), which represents a single Unicode character such as `'a'` or `'M'`.

In the case of **floating-point values,** you can use two types, namely `Single` (`float`) and `Double` (`double`). The first uses 32 bits, while the second uses 64 bits. Thus, their precision differs significantly.

What's more, the `Decimal` type (the `decimal` keyword) is available. It uses 128 bits and is a good choice for monetary calculations.

An example declaration of a variable in the C# programming language is as follows:

```
int number;
```

You can assign a value to a variable using the equals sign (=), shown as follows:

```
number = 500;
```

Of course, declaration and assignment could be performed in the same line:

```
int number = 500;
```

If you want to declare and initialize an **immutable value,** that is, a **constant,** you can use the `const` keyword, as shown in the following line of code:

```
const int DAYS_IN_WEEK = 7;
```

 More information about the built-in data types, together with the complete list of ranges, is available at:
`https://msdn.microsoft.com/library/cs7y5x0x.aspx`.

Enumerations

Apart from structs, the value types contain **enumerations**. Each has a set of named constants to specify the available set of values. For instance, you can create the enumeration for available languages or supported currencies. An example definition is as follows:

```
enum Language { PL, EN, DE };
```

Then, you can use the defined enumeration as a data type, as shown as follows:

```
Language language = Language.PL;
switch (language)
{
    case Language.PL: /* Polish version */ break;
    case Language.DE: /* German version */ break;
    default: /* English version */ break;
}
```

It is worth mentioning that enumerations allow you to replace some *magical strings* (such as `"PL"` or `"DE"`) with constant values and this has a positive impact on code quality.

You can also benefit from more advanced features of enumerations, such as changing the underlying type or specifying values for particular constants. You can find more information at:
https://docs.microsoft.com/en-us/dotnet/csharp/language-referenc e/keywords/enum.

Reference types

The second main group of types is named **reference types**. Just as a quick reminder, a variable of a reference type does not directly contain data, because it just stores a reference to data. In this group, you can find three built-in types, namely `string`, `object`, and `dynamic`. Moreover, you can declare classes, interfaces, and delegates.

More information about the reference types is available at:
https://docs.microsoft.com/en-us/dotnet/csharp/language-referenc e/keywords/reference-types.

Strings

There is often the necessity to store some text values. You can achieve this goal using the `String` built-in reference type from the `System` namespace, which is also available using the `string` keyword. The `string` type is a sequence of Unicode characters. It can have zero chars, one or more chars, or the `string` variable can be set to `null`.

You can perform various operations on `string` objects, such as concatenation or accessing a particular char using the `[]` operator, as shown as follows:

```
string firstName = "Marcin", lastName = "Jamro";
int year = 1988;
string note = firstName + " " + lastName.ToUpper()
    + " was born in " + year;
string initials = firstName[0] + "." + lastName[0] + ".";
```

At the beginning, the `firstName` variable is declared, and the `"Marcin"` value is assigned to it. Similarly, `"Jamro"` is set as a value of the `lastName` variable. In the third line, you concatenate five strings (using the + operator), namely, the current value of `firstName`, the space, the current value of `lastName` converted to the upper-case string (by calling the `ToUpper` method), the string `" was born in "`, and the current value of the `year` variable. In the last line, the first chars from `firstName` and `lastName` variables are obtained, using the `[]` operator, as well as concatenated with two dots to form the initials, that is, `M.J.`, which are stored as a value of the `initials` variable.

The `Format` static method could also be used for constructing the string, as follows:

```
string note = string.Format("{0} {1} was born in {2}",
    firstName, lastName.ToUpper(), year);
```

In this example, you specify the **composite format string** with three format items, namely the `firstName` (represented by `{0}`), upper-case `lastName` (`{1}`), and the `year` (`{2}`). The objects to format are specified as the following parameters.

 More information is available at:
https://docs.microsoft.com/en-us/dotnet/csharp/language-referenc e/keywords/string.

It is also worth mentioning the **interpolated string,** which uses **interpolated expressions** to construct a `string`. To create a `string` using this approach, the `$` character should be placed before ", as shown in the following example:

```
string note = $"{firstName} {lastName.ToUpper()}
    was born in {year}";
```

More information is available at:
https://docs.microsoft.com/en-us/dotnet/csharp/language-referenc
e/keywords/interpolated-strings.

Object

The `Object` class, declared in the `System` namespace, performs a very important role while developing applications in the C# language because it is the base class for all classes. It means that built-in value types and built-in reference types, as well as user-defined types, are derived from the `Object` class, which is also available by using the `object` alias.

As the `object` type is the base entity for all value types, it means that it is possible to convert a variable of any value type (for example, `int` or `float`) to the `object` type, as well as to convert back a variable of the `object` type to a specific value type. Such operations are named **boxing** (the first one) and **unboxing** (the other). They are shown as follows:

```
int age = 28;
object ageBoxing = age;
int ageUnboxing = (int)ageBoxing;
```

More information is available at:
https://docs.microsoft.com/en-us/dotnet/csharp/language-referenc
e/keywords/object.

Dynamic

Apart from the types already described, the `dynamic` one is available for developers. It allows the bypassing of type checking during compilation so that you can perform it during the run time. Such a mechanism is useful while accessing some **application programming interfaces (APIs),** but it will not be used in this book.

More information is available at:
https://docs.microsoft.com/en-us/dotnet/csharp/language-referenc
e/keywords/dynamic.

Classes

As already mentioned, C# is an object-oriented language and supports declaration of classes together with various members, including constructors, finalizers, constants, fields, properties, indexers, events, methods, and operators, as well as delegates. Moreover, classes support inheritance and implementing interfaces. Static, abstract, and virtual members are available, as well.

An example class is shown as follows:

```csharp
public class Person
{
    private string _location = string.Empty;
    public string Name { get; set; }
    public int Age { get; set; }

    public Person() => Name = "---";

    public Person(string name, int age)
    {
        Name = name;
        Age = age;
    }

    public void Relocate(string location)
    {
        if (!string.IsNullOrEmpty(location))
        {
            _location = location;
        }
    }

    public float GetDistance(string location)
    {
        return DistanceHelpers.GetDistance(_location, location);
    }
}
```

The `Person` class contains the `_location` private field with the default value set as the empty string (`string.Empty`), two public properties (`Name` and `Age`), a default constructor that sets a value of the `Name` property to `---` using the **expression body definition**, an additional constructor that takes two parameters and sets values of properties, the `Relocate` method that updates the value of the private field, as well as the `GetDistance` method that calls the `GetDistance` static method from the `DistanceHelpers` class and returns the distance between two cities in kilometers.

You can create an instance of the class using the `new` operator. Then, you can perform various operations on the object created, such as calling a method, as shown as follows:

```
Person person = new Person("Mary", 20);
person.Relocate("Rzeszow");
float distance = person.GetDistance("Warsaw");
```

More information is available at:
https://docs.microsoft.com/en-us/dotnet/csharp/language-referenc
e/keywords/class.

Interfaces

In the previous section, a class was mentioned that could implement one or more **interfaces**. It means that such a class must implement all methods, properties, events, and indexers, that are specified in all implemented interfaces. You can easily define interfaces in the C# language using the `interface` keyword.

As an example, let's take a look at the following code:

```
public interface IDevice
{
    string Model { get; set; }
    string Number { get; set; }
    int Year { get; set; }

    void Configure(DeviceConfiguration configuration);
    bool Start();
    bool Stop();
}
```

The IDevice interface contains three properties, namely those representing a device model (Model), serial number (Number), and production year (Year). What's more, it has signatures of three methods, which are Configure, Start, and Stop. When a class implements the IDevice interface, it should contain the mentioned properties and methods.

More information is available at:
https://docs.microsoft.com/en-us/dotnet/csharp/language-referenc e/keywords/interface.

Delegates

The delegate reference type allows specification of the required signature of a method. The delegate could then be instantiated, as well as invoked, as shown in the following code:

```
delegate double Mean(double a, double b, double c);

static double Harmonic(double a, double b, double c)
{
    return 3 / ((1 / a) + (1 / b) + (1 / c));
}

static void Main(string[] args)
{
    Mean arithmetic = (a, b, c) => (a + b + c) / 3;
    Mean geometric = delegate (double a, double b, double c)
    {
        return Math.Pow(a * b * c, 1 / 3.0);
    };
    Mean harmonic = Harmonic;
    double arithmeticResult = arithmetic.Invoke(5, 6.5, 7);
    double geometricResult = geometric.Invoke(5, 6.5, 7);
    double harmonicResult = harmonic.Invoke(5, 6.5, 7);
}
```

In the example, the Mean delegate specifies the required signature of the method for calculating the mean value of three floating-point numbers. It is instantiated with the lambda expression (arithmetic), anonymous method (geometric), and named method (harmonic). Each delegate is invoked by calling the Invoke method.

More information is available at:
https://docs.microsoft.com/en-us/dotnet/csharp/language-referenc
e/keywords/delegate.

Installation and configuration of the IDE

While reading the book, you will see many examples presenting data structures and algorithms, together with detailed descriptions. The most important parts of the code will be shown directly in the book. Moreover, complete source code will be available to download. Of course, you can only read the code from the book, but it is strongly recommended to write such code on your own, and then launch and debug the program to understand how various data structures and algorithms operate.

As already mentioned, the examples shown in the book will be prepared in the C# language. To keep things simple, the console-based applications will be created, but such data structures could be used in other kinds of solutions as well.

The example projects will be created in **Microsoft Visual Studio 2017 Community**. This **Integrated Development Environment** (IDE) is a comprehensive solution for developing various kinds of projects. To download, install, and configure it, you should:

1. Open the website https://www.visualstudio.com/downloads/ and choose the **Free download** option from the **Visual Studio Community 2017** section just below the **Visual Studio Downloads** header. The download process of the installer should begin automatically.

2. Run the downloaded file and follow the instructions to start the installation. When the screen presenting possible options is shown, choose the **.NET desktop development** option, as shown in the following screenshot. Then, click **Install**. The installation could take some time, but its progress could be observed using the **Acquiring** and **Applying** progress bars.

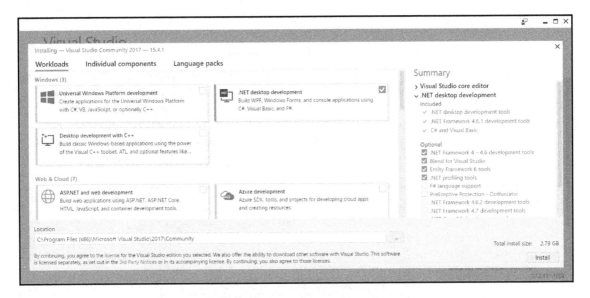

3. When the message **Installation succeeded!** is shown, click on the **Launch** button to start the IDE. You will be asked to sign in with the Microsoft account. Then, you should choose suitable **Development Settings** (such as **Visual C#**) in the **Start with a familiar environment** section. Moreover, you should choose the color theme from **Blue**, **Blue (Extra Contrast)**, **Dark**, and **Light**. At the end, click on the **Start Visual Studio** button.

Creating the project

Just after launching the IDE, let's proceed by creating a new project. Such a process will be performed many times while reading the book to create the example applications according to information provided in particular chapters.

To create a new project:

1. Click on **File | New | Project** in the main menu.
2. Choose **Installed | Visual C# | Windows Classic Desktop** on the left in the **New Project** window, as shown in the following screenshot. Then, click on **Console App (.NET Framework)** in the middle. You should also type a name of the project (**Name**) and a name of the solution (**Solution name**), as well as select location for the files (**Location**) by pressing the **Browse** button. At the end, click on **OK** to automatically create the project and generate the necessary files:

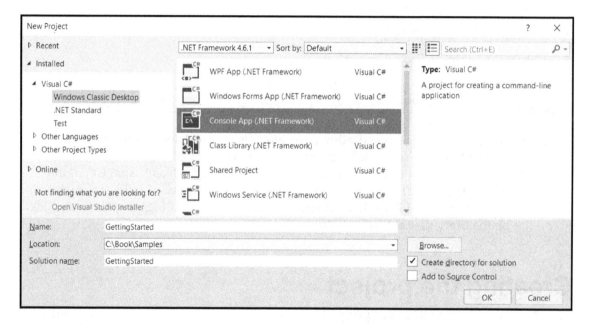

Congratulations, you have just created the first project! But what is inside?

Let's take a look at the **Solution Explorer** window, which presents the structure of the project. It is worth mentioning that the project is included in the solution with the same name. Of course, a solution could contain more than one project, which is a common scenario while developing more complex applications.

If you cannot find the **Solution Explorer** window, you could open it by choosing the **View | Solution Explorer** option from the main menu. In a similar way, you could open other windows, such as **Output** or **Class View**. If you cannot find a suitable window (for example, **C# Interactive**) directly within the **View** option, let's try to find it in the **View | Other Windows** node.

The automatically generated project (named `GettingStarted`) has the following structure:

- The **Properties** node with one file (`AssemblyInfo.cs`) that contains general information about the assembly with the application, such as about its title, copyright, and version. The configuration is performed using attributes, for example, `AssemblyTitleAttribute` and `AssemblyVersionAttribute`.
- The **References** element presents additional assemblies or projects that are used by the project. It is worth noting that you could easily add references by choosing the **Add Reference** option from the context menu of the **References** element. Moreover, you could install additional packages using the **NuGet Package Manager**, which could be launched by choosing **Manage NuGet Packages** from the **References** context menu.

> It is a good idea to take a look at packages already available before writing the complex module on your own because a suitable package could be already available for developers. In such a case, you could not only shorten the development time, but also reduce the chance of introducing mistakes.

- The `App.config` file contains the **Extensible Markup Language** (**XML**)-based configuration of the application, including the number of the minimum supported version of the .NET Framework platform.
- The `Program.cs` file contains the code of the main class in the C# language. You could adjust the behavior of the application by changing the following default implementation:

```
using System;
using System.Collections.Generic;
using System.Linq;
using System.Text;
using System.Threading.Tasks;

namespace GettingStarted
{
    class Program
    {
        static void Main(string[] args)
        {
        }
    }
}
```

The initial content of the `Program.cs` file contains the definition of the `Program` class within the `GettingStarted` namespace. The class contains the `Main` static method, which is called automatically when the application is launched. The five `using` statements are included as well, namely `System`, `System.Collections.Generic`, `System.Linq`, `System.Text`, and `System.Threading.Tasks`.

Before proceeding, let's take a look at the structure of the project in the file explorer, not in the **Solution Explorer** window. Are such structures exactly the same?

 You could open the directory with the project in the file explorer by choosing the **Open Folder in File Explorer** option from the context menu of the project node in the **Solution Explorer** window.

First of all, you can see the `bin` and `obj` directories, which are generated automatically. Both contain `Debug` and `Release` directories, whose names are related to the configuration set in the IDE. After building the project, a subdirectory of the `bin` directory (that is, `Debug` or `Release`) contains `.exe`, `.exe.config`, and `.pdb` files, while the subdirectory in the `obj` directory—for example—contains `.cache` and some temporary `.cs` files. What's more, there is no `References` directory, but there are `.csproj` and `.csproj.user` files with XML-based configurations of the project. Similarly, the solution-based `.sln` configuration file is located in the solution's directory.

 If you are using a **version control system**, such as **SVN** or **Git**, you could ignore the `bin` and `obj` directories, as well as the `.csproj.user` file. All of them can be generated automatically.

If you want to learn how to write some example code, as well as launch and debug the program, let's proceed to the next section.

Input and output

Many examples shown in the following part of the book will require interaction with the user, especially by reading input data and showing output. You can easily add such features to the application, as explained in this section.

Reading from input

The application can read data from the **standard input stream** using a few methods from the `Console` static class from the `System` namespace, such as `ReadLine` and `ReadKey`. Both are presented in the examples in this section.

Let's take a look at the following line of code:

```
string fullName = Console.ReadLine();
```

Here, you use the `ReadLine` method. It waits until the user presses the *Enter* key. Then, the entered text is stored as a value of the `fullName` string variable.

In a similar way, you can read data of other types, such as `int`, as shown as follows:

```
string numberString = Console.ReadLine();
int.TryParse(numberString, out int number);
```

In this case, the same `ReadLine` method is called and the entered text is stored as a value of the `numberString` variable. Then, you just need to parse it to `int` and store it as a value of the `int` variable. How can you do that? The solution is very simple—use the `TryParse` static method of the `Int32` struct. It is worth mentioning that such a method returns a Boolean value, indicating whether the parsing process has finished successfully. Thus, you can perform some additional actions when the provided `string` representation is incorrect.

A similar scenario, regarding the `DateTime` structure and the `TryParseExact` static method, is shown in the following example:

```
string dateTimeString = Console.ReadLine();
if (!DateTime.TryParseExact(
    dateTimeString,
    "M/d/yyyy HH:mm",
    new CultureInfo("en-US"),
    DateTimeStyles.None,
    out DateTime dateTime))
{
    dateTime = DateTime.Now;
}
```

This example is more complicated than the previous one, so let's explain it in detail. First of all, the string representation of the date and time is stored as a value of the `dateTimeString` variable. Then, the `TryParseExact` static method of the `DateTime` struct is called, passing five parameters, namely the string representation of the date and time (`dateTimeString`), the expected format of the date and time (`M/d/yyyy HH:mm`), the supported culture (`en-US`), the additional styles (`None`), as well as the output variable (`dateTime`) passed by reference using the `out` parameter modifier.

If the parsing is not completed successfully, the current date and time (`DateTime.Now`) is assigned to the `dateTime` variable. Otherwise, the `dateTime` variable contains the `DateTime` instance consistent with the `string` representation provided by the user.

While writing the part of code involving the `CultureInfo` class name, you could see the following error: `CS0246 The type or namespace name 'CultureInfo' could not be found (are you missing a using directive or an assembly reference?)`. This means that you do not have a suitable `using` statement at the top of the file. You can easily add one by clicking on the bulb icon shown in the left-hand margin of the line with the error and choosing the **using System.Globalization;** option. The IDE will automatically add the missing `using` statement and the error will disappear.

Apart from reading the whole line, you can also get to know which character or function key has been pressed by the user. To do so, you can use the `ReadKey` method, as shown in the following part of code:

```
ConsoleKeyInfo key = Console.ReadKey();
switch (key.Key)
{
    case ConsoleKey.S: /* Pressed S */ break;
    case ConsoleKey.F1: /* Pressed F1 */ break;
    case ConsoleKey.Escape: /* Pressed Escape */ break;
}
```

After calling the `ReadKey` static method and once any key has been pressed by a user, information about the pressed key is stored as the `ConsoleKeyInfo` instance (that is, `key`, in the current example). Then, you use the `Key` property to get an enumeration value (of `ConsoleKey`) representing a particular key. At the end, the `switch` statement is used to perform operations depending on the key that has been pressed. In the example shown, three keys are supported, namely *S*, *F1*, and *Esc*.

Writing to output

Now, you know how to read input data, but how can you ask questions to the user or present results on the screen? The answer, together with examples, is shown in this section.

Similarly as in the case of reading data, operations related to the **standard output stream** are performed using methods of the `Console` static class from the `System` namespace, namely `Write` and `WriteLine`. Let's see them in action!

To write some text, you can just call the `Write` method, passing the text as a parameter. An example of code is as follows:

```
Console.Write("Enter a name: ");
```

The preceding line causes the following output to be shown:

Enter a name:

What's important here is that the written text is not followed by the line terminator. If you want to write some text and move to the next line, you can use the `WriteLine` method, as shown in the following code snippet:

```
Console.WriteLine("Hello!");
```

After executing this line of code, the following output is presented:

Hello!

Of course, you can also use `Write` and `WriteLine` methods in more complex scenarios. For example, you can pass many parameters to the `WriteLine` method, namely the format and additional arguments, as shown in the following part of the code:

```
string name = "Marcin";
Console.WriteLine("Hello, {0}!", name);
```

In this case, the line will contain `Hello`, a comma, a space, a value of the `name` variable (that is, `Marcin`), as well as the exclamation mark. The output is shown as follows:

Hello, Marcin!

The next example presents a significantly more complex scenario of writing the line regarding the confirmation of a table reservation at a restaurant. The output should have the format `Table [number] has been booked for [count] people on [date] at [time]`. You can achieve this goal by using the `WriteLine` method, as shown as follows:

```
string tableNumber = "A100";
int peopleCount = 4;
DateTime reservationDateTime = new DateTime(
    2017, 10, 28, 11, 0, 0);
CultureInfo cultureInfo = new CultureInfo("en-US");
Console.WriteLine(
    "Table {0} has been booked for {1} people on {2} at {3}",
    tableNumber,
    peopleCount,
    reservationDateTime.ToString("M/d/yyyy", cultureInfo),
    reservationDateTime.ToString("HH:mm", cultureInfo));
```

The example starts with a declaration of four variables, namely `tableNumber` (A100), `peopleCount` (4), and `reservationDateTime` (10/28/2017 at 11:00 AM), as well as `cultureInfo` (en-US). Then, the `WriteLine` method is called passing five parameters, namely the format string followed by arguments that should be shown in the places marked with {0}, {1}, {2}, and {3}. It is worth mentioning the last two lines, where the string presenting date (or time) is created, based on the current value of the `reservationDateTime` variable.

After executing this code, the following line is shown in the output:

```
Table A100 has been booked for 4 people on 10/28/2017 at 11:00
```

Of course, in real-world scenarios, you will use read- and write-related methods in the same code. For example, you can ask a user to provide a value (using the `Write` method) and then read the text entered (using the `ReadLine` method).

This simple example, which is also useful in the next section of this chapter, is shown as follows. It allows the user to enter data relating to the table reservation, namely the table number and the number of people, as well as the reservation date. When all of the data is entered, the confirmation is presented. Of course, the user will see information about the data that should be provided:

```
using System;
using System.Globalization;

namespace GettingStarted
{
    class Program
```

```
{
    static void Main(string[] args)
    {
        CultureInfo cultureInfo = new CultureInfo("en-US");

        Console.Write("The table number: ");
        string table = Console.ReadLine();

        Console.Write("The number of people: ");
        string countString = Console.ReadLine();
        int.TryParse(countString, out int count);

        Console.Write("The reservation date (MM/dd/yyyy): ");
        string dateTimeString = Console.ReadLine();
        if (!DateTime.TryParseExact(
            dateTimeString,
            "M/d/yyyy HH:mm",
            cultureInfo,
            DateTimeStyles.None,
            out DateTime dateTime))
        {
            dateTime = DateTime.Now;
        }

        Console.WriteLine(
            "Table {0} has been booked for {1} people on {2}
             at {3}",
            table,
            count,
            dateTime.ToString("M/d/yyyy", cultureInfo),
            dateTime.ToString("HH:mm", cultureInfo));
    }
}
}
```

The preceding code snippet is based on the parts of code shown and described previously. After launching the program and entering the necessary data, the output could look as follows:

```
The table number: A100
The number of people: 4
The reservation date (MM/dd/yyyy): 10/28/2017 11:00
Table A100 has been booked for 4 people on 10/28/2017 at 11:00
Press any key to continue . . .
```

When the code is created, it is a good idea to improve its quality. One of the interesting possibilities associated with the IDE is related to removing unused `using` statements, together with sorting the remaining ones. You can easily perform such an operation by choosing the **Remove and Sort Usings** option from the context menu in the text editor.

Launching and debugging

Unfortunately, the written code doesn't always work as expected. In such a case, it is a good idea to start **debugging** to see how the program operates, find the source of the problem, and correct it. This task is especially useful for complex algorithms, where the flow could be complicated, and therefore quite difficult to analyze just by reading the code. Fortunately, the IDE is equipped with various features for debugging that will be presented in this section.

First of all, let's launch the application to see it in action! To do so, you just need to select a proper configuration from the drop-down list (**Debug,** in this example) and click on the button with the green triangle and the **Start** caption in the main toolbar, or press *F5*. To stop debugging, you can choose **Debug** | **Stop Debugging** or press *Shift + F5*.

You can also run the application without debugging. To do so, choose **Debug** | **Start Without Debugging** from the main menu or press *Ctrl + F5*.

As already mentioned, there are various debugging techniques, but let's start with breakpoint-based debugging, since it is one of the most common approaches offering huge opportunities. You can place a **breakpoint** in any line of the code. The program will stop as soon as the line is reached, before executing it. Then, you can see the values of particular variables to check whether the application works as expected.

To add a breakpoint, you can either click on the left-hand margin (next to the line on which the breakpoint should be placed) or place the cursor on the line (where the breakpoint should be added) and press the *F9* key. In both cases, the red circle will be shown, as well as the code from the given line will be marked with a red background, as shown in line **17** in the following screenshot:

```
Program.cs  ⊞ ✕
[C#] GettingStarted            ▼  ⚘ GettingStarted.Program      ▼  ⚙ Main(string[] args)             ▼
    10                    CultureInfo cultureInfo = new CultureInfo("en-US");        ⟰
    11
    12                    Console.Write("The table number: ");
    13               ▶|   string table = Console.ReadLine();
    14                        ⬤ table Q ▼ "A100"  ⇨
    15                    Console.Write("The number of people: ");
    16                    string countString = Console.ReadLine();
    17                    int.TryParse(countString, out int count);
    18
    19                    Console.Write("The reservation date (MM/dd/yyyy): ");
    20                    string dateTimeString = Console.ReadLine();
    21                    if (!DateTime.TryParseExact(|
    22                        dateTimeString,
    23                        "M/d/yyyy HH:mm",
    24                        cultureInfo,                                            ▼
 100 %   ▼ ◀                                                                  ▶
```

When a line with the breakpoint is reached while executing the program, it stops, and the line is marked with the yellow background and the margin icon changes, as shown in line **15** in the screenshot. Now, you can check the value of the variable by simply moving the cursor over its name. The current value will appear in the **ToolTip**.

You can also click on the pin icon located on the right-hand side of the **ToolTip** to pin it in the editor. Its value will then be visible without the necessity of moving the cursor over the name of the variable. Such a value will be automatically refreshed as soon as it has changed. The result is presented in the following screenshot.

The IDE could adjust its appearance and features depending on the operations performed currently. For example, while debugging, you have access to some special windows, such as **Locals**, **Call Stack**, and **Diagnostic Tools**. The first shows available local variables together with their types and values. The **Call Stack** window presents information about the following called methods. The last one (namely **Diagnostic Tools**) shows information about memory and CPU usage, as well as events.

Moreover, the IDE supports conditional breakpoints that stop execution of the program only if the associated Boolean expression is evaluated to `true`. You can add a condition to a given breakpoint by choosing the **Conditions** option from the context menu, which is shown after right-clicking on the breakpoint icon in the left-hand margin. Then, the **Breakpoint Settings** window appears, where you should check the **Conditions** checkbox and specify the **Conditional Expression**, such as the one shown in the following screenshot. In the example, execution will stop only when the value of the `count` variable is greater than 5, that is, `count > 5`:

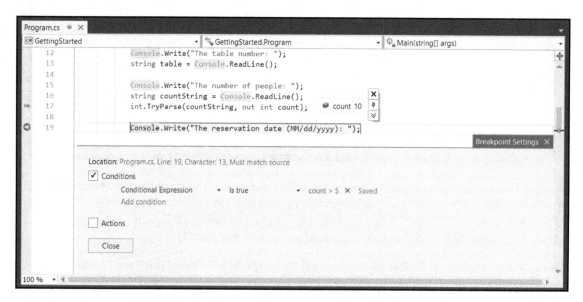

When the execution is stopped, you can use the step-by-step debugging technique. To move execution of the program to the next line (without incorporating another breakpoint), you can click on the **Step Over** icon in the main toolbar or press *F10*. If you want to step into the method, which is called in the line where the execution has stopped, just click on the **Step Into** button or press *F11*. Of course, you can also go to the next breakpoint by clicking on the **Continue** button or by pressing *F5*.

The next interesting feature, available in the IDE, is called **Immediate Window**. It allows developers to execute various expressions when the program execution is stopped using the current values of the variables. You just need to enter an expression in the **Immediate Window** and press the *Enter* key. The example is shown in the following screenshot:

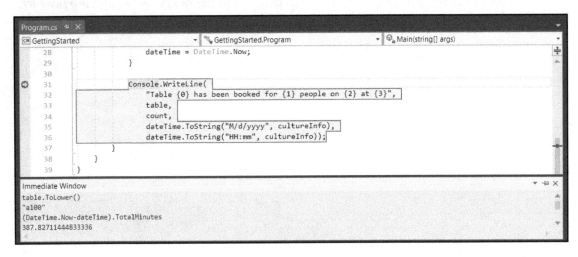

Here, the lower-case version of the table number is returned by executing `table.ToLower()`. Then, the total number of minutes between the current date and the `dateTime` variable is calculated and shown in the window.

Summary

This was only the first chapter of the book, but it contained quite a lot of information that will be useful while reading the remaining ones. At the beginning, you saw that using proper data structures and algorithms is not an easy task, but could have a significant impact on the performance of the developed solution. Then, the C# programming language was briefly presented with a focus on showing various data types, both value and reference ones. Classes, interfaces, and delegates were also described.

In the following part of the chapter, the process of installation and configuration of the IDE was presented. Then, you learned how to create a new project, and its structure has been described in details. Next, you saw how to read data from the standard input stream, as well as how to write data to the standard output stream. The read- and write-related operations were also mixed into one example.

At the end of the chapter, you saw how to run the example program, as well as how to debug it using breakpoints and step-by-step debugging to find the source of the problem. What's more, you learned the possibilities of the **Immediate Window** feature.

After this introduction, you should be ready to proceed to the next chapter and see how to use arrays and lists, as well as accompanying algorithms. Let's go!

2
Arrays and Lists

As a developer, you have certainly stored various collections within your applications, such as user data, books, and logs. One of the natural ways of storing such data is by using arrays and lists. However, have you ever thought about their variants? Have you heard about jagged arrays or circular-linked lists? In this chapter you will see such data structures in action, together with examples and detailed descriptions. That is not all, because the chapter is related to many topics regarding arrays and lists, suitable for developers with various levels of programming skills.

At the start of the chapter, the arrays will be presented and divided into single-dimensional, multi-dimensional, and jagged arrays. You will also get to know four sorting algorithms, namely selection, insertion, bubble sort, and quicksort. For each of them, you will see an illustration-based example, the implementation code, and a step-by-step explanation.

The arrays have a lot of possibilities. However, generic lists available while developing in the C# language are even more powerful. In the remaining part of the chapter, you will see how to use a few variants of lists, such as simple, sorted, double-linked, and circular-linked. For each of them, the C# code of an example will be shown with a detailed description.

You will cover the following topics in this chapter:

- Arrays
- Sorting algorithms
- Simple lists
- Sorted lists
- Linked lists
- Circular-linked lists

Arrays

Let's start with the array data structure. You can use it to store many variables of the same type, such as int, string, or a user-defined class. As mentioned in the introduction, while developing applications in the C# language, you can benefit from a few variants of arrays, as presented in the following diagram. You have access not only to single-dimensional arrays (indicated as **a**), but also multi-dimensional (**b**), and jagged (**c**). Examples of all of them are shown in the following diagram:

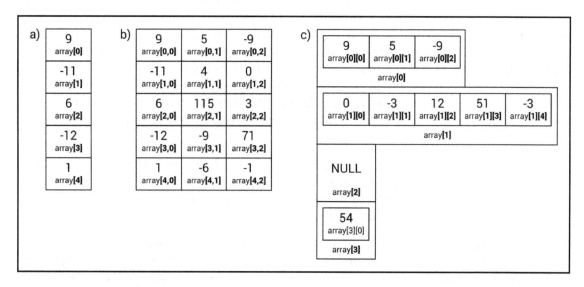

What is important is that the number of elements in an array cannot be changed after initialization. For this reason, you will not be able to easily add a new item at the end of the array or insert it in a given position within the array. If you need such features, you can use other data structures described in this chapter, such as generic lists.

You can find more information about arrays at https://docs.microsoft.com/en-us/dotnet/csharp/programming-gui de/arrays/.

After this short description, you should be ready to learn more about particular variants of arrays and to take a look at some C# code. Thus, let's proceed to the simplest variant of arrays, namely single-dimensional ones.

Single-dimensional arrays

A single-dimensional array stores a collection of items of the same type, which are accessible by an index. It is important to remember that indices of arrays in C# are zero-based. This means that the first element has an index equal to **0**, while the last one—length of the array minus one.

The example array is shown in the preceding diagram (on the left, indicated by **a**). It contains five elements with the following values: **9**, **-11**, **6**, **-12**, and **1**. The first element has an index equal to **0**, while the last one has an index equal to **4**.

To use a single-dimensional array, you need to declare and initialize it. The declaration is very simple, because you just need to specify a type of element and a name, as follows:

```
type[] name;
```

The declaration of an array with integer values is shown in the following line:

```
int[] numbers;
```

Now you know how to declare an array, but what about the initialization? To initialize the array elements to default values, you can use the new operator, as shown here:

```
numbers = new int[5];
```

Of course, you can combine a declaration and initialization in the same line, as follows:

```
int[] numbers = new int[5];
```

Unfortunately, all the elements currently have default values, that is, zeros in the case of integer values. Thus, you need to set the values of particular elements. You can do this using the [] operator and an index of an element, as shown in the following code snippet:

```
numbers[0] = 9;
numbers[1] = -11; (...)
numbers[4] = 1;
```

Moreover, you can combine a declaration and initialization of array elements to specific values using one of the following variants:

```
int[] numbers = new int[] { 9, -11, 6, -12, 1 };
int[] numbers = { 9, -11, 6, -12, 1 };
```

When you have the proper values of elements within an array, you can get values using the [] operator and by specifying the index, as shown in the following line of code:

```
int middle = numbers[2];
```

Here, you get a value of the third element (the index equal to 2) from the array named `numbers` and store it as a value of the `middle` variable.

 More information about single-dimensional arrays is available at https://docs.microsoft.com/en-us/dotnet/csharp/programming-gui de/arrays/single-dimensional-arrays.

Example – month names

To summarize the information you have learned about single-dimensional arrays, let's take a look at a simple example, where the array is used to store names of months in English. Such names should be obtained automatically, not by hardcoding them in the code.

The implementation is shown here:

```
string[] months = new string[12];

for (int month = 1; month <= 12; month++)
{
    DateTime firstDay = new DateTime(DateTime.Now.Year, month, 1);
    string name = firstDay.ToString("MMMM",
        CultureInfo.CreateSpecificCulture("en"));
    months[month - 1] = name;
}

foreach (string month in months)
{
    Console.WriteLine($"-> {month}");
}
```

At the start, a new single-dimensional array is declared and initialized with default values. It contains 12 elements to store names of months in a year. Then, the `for` loop is used to iterate through the numbers of all months, that is, from 1 to 12. For each of them, the `DateTime` instance representing the first day in a particular month is created.

The name of the month is obtained by calling the `ToString` method on the `DateTime` instance, passing the proper format of the date (MMMM), as well as specifying the culture (en in the example). Then, the name is stored in the array using the `[]` operator and an index of the element. It is worth noting that the index is equal to the current value of the `month` variable minus one. Such subtraction is necessary, because the first element in the array has an index equal to zero, not one.

The next interesting part of the code is the `foreach` loop, which iterates through all elements of the array. For each of them, one line is shown in the console, namely the name of the month after `->`. The result is as follows:

```
-> January
-> February (...)
-> November
-> December
```

As mentioned earlier, single-dimensional arrays are not the only available variant. You will learn more about multi-dimensional arrays in the following section.

Multi-dimensional arrays

The arrays in the C# language do not need to have only one dimension. It is also possible to create two-dimensional or even three-dimensional arrays. To start with, let's take a look at an example regarding the declaration and initialization of a two-dimensional array with 5 rows and 2 columns:

```
int[,] numbers = new int[5, 2];
```

If you want to create a three-dimensional array, the following code can be used:

```
int[, ,] numbers = new int[5, 4, 3];
```

Of course, you can also combine a declaration with an initialization, as shown in the following example:

```
int[,] numbers = new int[,] =
{
    { 9, 5, -9 },
    { -11, 4, 0 },
    { 6, 115, 3 },
    { -12, -9, 71 },
    { 1, -6, -1 }
};
```

Some small explanation is necessary for the way you access particular elements from a multi-dimensional array. Let's take a look at the following example:

```
int number = numbers[2][1];
numbers[1][0] = 11;
```

In the first line of code, the value from the third row (index equal to 2) and second column (index equal to 1) is obtained (that is, 115) and set as a value of the `number` variable. The other line replaces -11 with 11 in the second row and first column.

 More information about multi-dimensional arrays is available at https://docs.microsoft.com/en-us/dotnet/csharp/programming-guide/arrays/multidimensional-arrays.

Example – multiplication table

The first example shows basic operations on a two-dimensional array with the purpose of presenting a multiplication table. It writes the results of the multiplication of all integer values in the range from 1 to 10, as shown in the following output:

```
 1   2   3   4   5   6   7   8   9  10
 2   4   6   8  10  12  14  16  18  20
 3   6   9  12  15  18  21  24  27  30
 4   8  12  16  20  24  28  32  36  40
 5  10  15  20  25  30  35  40  45  50
 6  12  18  24  30  36  42  48  54  60
 7  14  21  28  35  42  49  56  63  70
 8  16  24  32  40  48  56  64  72  80
 9  18  27  36  45  54  63  72  81  90
10  20  30  40  50  60  70  80  90 100
```

Let's take a look at the method of declaration and initialization of the array:

```
int[,] results = new int[10, 10];
```

Here, a two-dimensional array with 10 rows and 10 columns is created and its elements are initialized to default values, that is, to zeros.

When the array is ready, you should fill it with the results of the multiplication. Such a task can be performed using two `for` loops:

```
for (int i = 0; i < results.GetLength(0); i++)
{
    for (int j = 0; j < results.GetLength(1); j++)
    {
        results[i, j] = (i + 1) * (j + 1);
    }
}
```

In the preceding code, you can find the `GetLength` method, which is called on an array object. The method returns the number of elements in a particular dimension, that is, the first (when passing `0` as the parameter) and the second (`1` as the parameter). In both cases, a value of `10` is returned, according to the values specified during the array initialization.

Another important part of the code is the way of setting a value of an element in a two-dimensional array. To do so, you need to provide two indices, such as `results[i, j]`.

At the end, you just need to present the results. You can do so using two `for` loops, as in the case of filling the array. This part of the code is shown here:

```
for (int i = 0; i < results.GetLength(0); i++)
{
    for (int j = 0; j < results.GetLength(1); j++)
    {
        Console.Write("{0,4}", results[i, j]);
    }
    Console.WriteLine();
}
```

The multiplication results, after conversion to `string` values, have different lengths, from one character (as in the case of `4` as a result of `2*2`) to three (`100` from `10*10`). To improve the presentation, you need to write each result always on `4` chars. Therefore, if the integer value takes less space, the leading spaces should be added. As an example, the result 1 will be shown with three leading spaces (___1, where _ is a space), while `100` with only one (_100). You can achieve this goal by using the proper composite format string (namely `{0,4}`) while calling the `Write` method from the `Console` class.

Example – game map

Another example of the application of a two-dimensional array is a program that presents a map of a game. The map is a rectangle with 11 rows and 10 columns. Each element of the array specifies a type of terrain as grass, sand, water, or wall. Each place on the map should be shown in a particular color (such as green for grass), as well as using a custom character that depicts the terrain type (such as ≈ for water), as shown in the screenshot:

At the start, let's declare the enumeration value, named `TerrainEnum`, with four constants, namely GRASS, SAND, WATER, and WALL, as follows:

```
public enum TerrainEnum
{
    GRASS,
    SAND,
    WATER,
    WALL
}
```

> **TIP**
>
> To improve the readability of the whole project, it is recommended to declare the `TerrainEnum` type in a separate file, named `TerrainEnum.cs`. This rule should also be applied to all user-defined types, including classes.

Then, you create two extension methods that make it possible to get a particular color and character depending on the terrain type (`GetColor` and `GetChar`, respectively). Such extension methods are declared within the `TerrainEnumExtensions` class, as follows:

```
public static class TerrainEnumExtensions
{
    public static ConsoleColor GetColor(this TerrainEnum terrain)
    {
        switch (terrain)
        {
            case TerrainEnum.GRASS: return ConsoleColor.Green;
            case TerrainEnum.SAND: return ConsoleColor.Yellow;
            case TerrainEnum.WATER: return ConsoleColor.Blue;
            default: return ConsoleColor.DarkGray;
        }
    }

    public static char GetChar(this TerrainEnum terrain)
    {
        switch (terrain)
        {
            case TerrainEnum.GRASS: return '\u201c';
            case TerrainEnum.SAND: return '\u25cb';
            case TerrainEnum.WATER: return '\u2248';
            default: return '\u25cf';
        }
    }
}
```

It is worth mentioning that the `GetChar` method returns a proper Unicode character depending on the `TerrainEnum` value. For example, in the case of the `WATER` constant, the `'\u2248'` value is returned, which is a representation of the ≈ character.

Have you heard about the **extension methods**? If not, think of them as methods that are "added" to a particular existing type (both built-in or user-defined), which can be called in the same way as when they are defined directly as instance methods. The declaration of an extension method requires you to specify it within a static class as a static method with the first parameter indicating the type, to which you want to "add" this method, with the `this` keyword. You can find more information at `https://docs.microsoft.com/en-us/dotnet/csharp/programming-gui de/classes-and-structs/extension-methods`.

Let's take a look at the body of the `Main` method in the `Program` class. Here, you configure the map, as well as present it in the console. The code is as follows:

```
TerrainEnum[,] map =
{
    { TerrainEnum.SAND, TerrainEnum.SAND, TerrainEnum.SAND,
      TerrainEnum.SAND, TerrainEnum.GRASS, TerrainEnum.GRASS,
      TerrainEnum.GRASS, TerrainEnum.GRASS, TerrainEnum.GRASS,
      TerrainEnum.GRASS }, (...)
    { TerrainEnum.WATER, TerrainEnum.WATER, TerrainEnum.WATER,
      TerrainEnum.WATER, TerrainEnum.WATER, TerrainEnum.WATER,
      TerrainEnum.WATER, TerrainEnum.WALL, TerrainEnum.WATER,
      TerrainEnum.WATER }
};
Console.OutputEncoding = UTF8Encoding.UTF8;
for (int row = 0; row < map.GetLength(0); row++)
{
    for (int column = 0; column < map.GetLength(1); column++)
    {
        Console.ForegroundColor = map[row, column].GetColor();
        Console.Write(map[row, column].GetChar() + " ");
    }
    Console.WriteLine();
}
Console.ForegroundColor = ConsoleColor.Gray;
```

Some comment can be useful regarding the way of getting a color and obtaining a character for a particular map place. Both these operations are performed using the extension methods "added" to the `TerrainEnum` user-defined type. For this reason, you first obtain the `TerrainEnum` value for a particular map place (using the `[]` operator and two indices) and then you call a suitable extension method, either `GetChar` or `GetColor`. To use Unicode values, you should not forget to choose the UTF-8 encoding by setting the `UTF8Encoding.UTF8` value for the `OutputEncoding` property.

So far, you have learned about both single- and multi-dimensional arrays, but one more variant remains to be presented in this book. Let's continue reading to get to know more about it.

Jagged arrays

The last variant of arrays described in this book is a jagged array, which is also referred to as an **array of arrays**. It sounds complicated, but fortunately, it is very simple. A jagged array could be understood as a single-dimensional array, where each element is another array. Of course, such inner arrays can have different lengths or they can even be not initialized.

If you take a look at the following diagram, you will see an example of a jagged array with four elements. The first element has an array with three elements (9, 5, -9), the second element has an array with five elements (0, -3, 12, 51, -3), the third is not initialized (NULL), while the last one is an array with only one element (54):

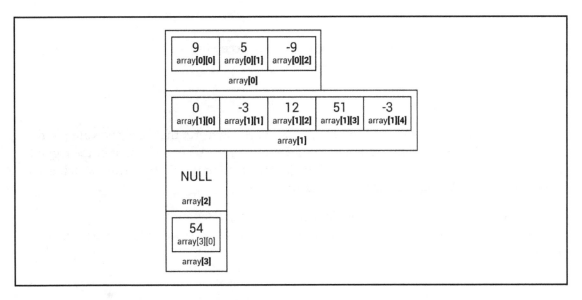

Before proceeding to the example, it is worth mentioning the way of declaring and initializing a jagged array, because it is a bit different to the arrays already described. Let's take a look at the following code snippet:

```
int[][] numbers = new int[4][];
numbers[0] = new int[] { 9, 5, -9 };
numbers[1] = new int[] { 0, -3, 12, 51, -3 };
numbers[3] = new int[] { 54 };
```

In the first line, you can see the declaration of a single-dimensional array with four elements. Each element is another single-dimensional array of integer values. When the first line is executed, the `numbers` array is initialized with default values, namely `NULL`. For this reason, you need to manually initialize particular elements, as shown in the following three lines of codes. It is worth noting that the third element is not initialized.

You can also write the preceding code in a different way, as shown here:

```
int[][] numbers =
{
    new int[] { 9, 5, -9 },
    new int[] { 0, -3, 12, 51, -3 },
    NULL,
    new int[] { 54 }
};
```

A small comment is also necessary for the method of accessing a particular element from a jagged array. You can do this in the following way:

```
int number = numbers[1][2];
number[1][3] = 50;
```

The first line of code sets the value of the `number` variable to `12`, that is, to the value of the third element (index equal to `2`) from the array, which is the second element of the jagged array. The other line changes the value of the fourth element within the array, which is the second element of the jagged array, from `51` to `50`.

 More information about jagged arrays is available at `https://docs.microsoft.com/en-us/dotnet/csharp/programming-gui de/arrays/jagged-arrays`.

Example – yearly transport plan

After the introduction of jagged arrays, let's proceed with an example. You will see how to develop a program that creates a plan of transportation for the whole year. For each day of each month, the application draws one of the available means of transport. At the end, the program presents the generated plan, as shown in the following screenshot:

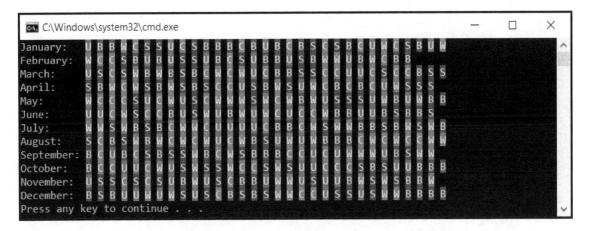

To start with, let's declare the enumeration type with constants representing available types of transport, namely a car, a bus, a subway, a bike, or on foot, as follows:

```
public enum TransportEnum
{
    CAR,
    BUS,
    SUBWAY,
    BIKE,
    WALK
}
```

In the next step, you create two extension methods that return a character and a color for the representation of a given mean of transport in the console. The code is shown here:

```
public static class TransportEnumExtensions
{
    public static char GetChar(this TransportEnum transport)
    {
        switch (transport)
        {
            case TransportEnum.BIKE: return 'B';
            case TransportEnum.BUS: return 'U';
            case TransportEnum.CAR: return 'C';
            case TransportEnum.SUBWAY: return 'S';
            case TransportEnum.WALK: return 'W';
            default: throw new Exception("Unknown transport");
        }
    }

    public static ConsoleColor GetColor(
        this TransportEnum transport)
```

```
    {
        switch (transport)
        {
            case TransportEnum.BIKE: return ConsoleColor.Blue;
            case TransportEnum.BUS: return ConsoleColor.DarkGreen;
            case TransportEnum.CAR: return ConsoleColor.Red;
            case TransportEnum.SUBWAY:
                return ConsoleColor.DarkMagenta;
            case TransportEnum.WALK:
                return ConsoleColor.DarkYellow;
            default: throw new Exception("Unknown transport");
        }
    }
}
```

The preceding code should not require additional clarification, because it is very similar to the one already presented in this chapter. Now let's proceed to the code from the `Main` method from the `Program` class, which will be shown and described in parts.

In the first part, a jagged array is created and filled with proper values. It is assumed that the jagged array has 12 elements, representing months from the current year. Each element is a single-dimensional array with `TransportEnum` values. The length of such an inner array depends on the number of days in a given month. For instance, it is set to 31 elements for January and 30 elements for April. The code is shown here:

```
Random random = new Random();
int transportTypesCount =
    Enum.GetNames(typeof(TransportEnum)).Length;
TransportEnum[][] transport = new TransportEnum[12][];
for (int month = 1; month <= 12; month++)
{
    int daysCount = DateTime.DaysInMonth(
        DateTime.Now.Year, month);
    transport[month - 1] = new TransportEnum[daysCount];
    for (int day = 1; day <= daysCount; day++)
    {
        int randomType = random.Next(transportTypesCount);
        transport[month - 1][day - 1] = (TransportEnum)randomType;
    }
}
```

Let's analyze the preceding code. At the beginning, a new instance of the `Random` class is created. It will be later used for drawing a suitable mean of transport from the available ones. In the next line, you get the number of constants from the `TransportEnum` enumeration type, that is, the number of available transport types. Then, the jagged array is created and the `for` loop is used to iterate through all months within the year. In each iteration, the number of days is obtained (using the `DaysInMonth` static method of `DateTime`) and an array (as an element from the jagged array) is initialized with zeros. In the following line of code, you can see the next `for` loop that iterates through all days of the month. Within this loop, you draw a transport type, and set it as a value of a suitable element within an array that is an element of the jagged array.

The next part of the code is related to the process of presenting the plan in the console:

```
string[] monthNames = GetMonthNames();
int monthNamesPart = monthNames.Max(n => n.Length) + 2;
for (int month = 1; month <= transport.Length; month++)
{
    Console.Write(
        $"{monthNames[month - 1]}:".PadRight(monthNamesPart));
    for (int day = 1; day <= transport[month - 1].Length; day++)
    {
        Console.ForegroundColor = ConsoleColor.White;
        Console.BackgroundColor =
            transport[month - 1][day - 1].GetColor();
        Console.Write(transport[month - 1][day - 1].GetChar());
        Console.BackgroundColor = ConsoleColor.Black;
        Console.ForegroundColor = ConsoleColor.Gray;
        Console.Write(" ");
    }
    Console.WriteLine();
}
```

At the beginning, a single-dimensional array with month names is created using the `GetMonthNames` method, which will be described later. Then, a value of the `monthNamesPart` variable is set to the maximum necessary length of text for storing the month name. To do so, the LINQ expression is used to find the maximum length of text from the collection with names of months. The obtained result is increased by 2 for reserving the place for a colon and a space.

One of the great features of the C# language is its ability to use LINQ. Such a mechanism makes it possible to get data not only from various collections, but also from **Structured Query Language (SQL)** databases and **Extensible Markup Language (XML)** documents in a consistent way. You can read more at `https://docs.microsoft.com/dotnet/csharp/linq/index`.

Then, the `for` loop is used to iterate through all elements of the jagged array, that is, through all months. In each iteration, the name of the month is presented in the console. Later, the next `for` loop is used to iterate through all the elements of the current element of the jagged array, that is, through all days of the month. For each of them, proper colors are set (for background and foreground), and a suitable character is presented.

At the end, let's take a look at the implementation of the `GetMonthNames` method:

```
private static string[] GetMonthNames()
{
    string[] names = new string[12];
    for (int month = 1; month <= 12; month++)
    {
        DateTime firstDay = new DateTime(
            DateTime.Now.Year, month, 1);
        string name = firstDay.ToString("MMMM",
            CultureInfo.CreateSpecificCulture("en"));
        names[month - 1] = name;
    }
    return names;
}
```

This code does not require additional explanation, because it is based on the code already described in the example for single-dimensional arrays.

Sorting algorithms

There are many algorithms that perform various operations on arrays. However, one of the most common tasks is sorting an array to arrange its elements in the correct order, either ascending or descending. The topic of sorting algorithms involves many approaches, including selection sort, insertion sort, bubble sort, and quicksort, which will be explained in detail in this part of the chapter.

Selection sort

Let's start with the **selection sort**, which is one of the simplest sorting algorithms. The algorithm divides the array into two parts, namely sorted and unsorted. In the following iterations, the algorithm finds the smallest element in the unsorted part and exchanges it with the first element in the unsorted part. It sounds very simple, doesn't it?

To better understand the algorithm, let's take a look at the following iterations for an array with nine elements (**-11, 12, -42, 0, 1, 90, 68, 6, -9**), as shown in the following diagram:

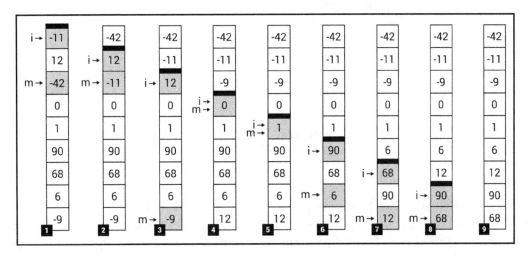

To simplify the analysis, the bold line is used to present the border between the sorted and unsorted parts of the array. At the beginning (*Step 1*), the border is located just at the top of the array, which means that the sorted part is empty. Thus, the algorithm finds the smallest value in the unsorted part (**-42**) and swaps it with the first element in this part (**-11**). The result is shown in *Step 2*, where the sorted part contains one element (**-42**), while the unsorted part consists of eight elements. The afore mentioned steps are performed a few times until only one element is left in the unsorted part. The final result is shown in *Step 9*.

Now you know how the selection sort algorithm works, but what role is performed by the i and m indicators shown on the left of the following steps in the preceding diagram? They are related to the variables used in the implementation of this algorithm. Thus, it is time to see the code in the C# language.

The algorithm implementation is created as the `SelectionSort` static class with the `Sort` generic static method, which is shown in the following code snippet:

```
public static class SelectionSort
{
    public static void Sort<T>(T[] array) where T : IComparable
    {
        for (int i = 0; i < array.Length - 1; i++)
        {
            int minIndex = i;
            T minValue = array[i];
            for (int j = i + 1; j < array.Length; j++)
            {
                if (array[j].CompareTo(minValue) < 0)
                {
                    minIndex = j;
                    minValue = array[j];
                }
            }
            Swap(array, i, minIndex);
        }
    } (...)
}
```

The `Sort` method takes one parameter, namely the array that should be sorted (`array`). Within the method, the `for` loop is used to iterate through the elements until only one item is left in the unsorted part. Thus, the number of iterations of the loop is equal to the length of the array minus one (`array.Length-1`). In each iteration, another `for` loop is used to find the smallest value in the unsorted part (`minValue`, from the `i+1` index until the end of array), as well as to store an index of the smallest value (`minIndex`, referred to as the `m` indicator in the preceding diagram). Then, the smallest element in the unsorted part (with an index equal to `minIndex`) is swapped with the first element in the unsorted part (`i` index), using the `Swap` auxiliary method, the implementation of which is as follows:

```
private static void Swap<T>(T[] array, int first, int second)
{
    T temp = array[first];
    array[first] = array[second];
    array[second] = temp;
}
```

If you want to test the implementation of the selection sort algorithm, you can place the following code in the `Main` method of the `Program` class:

```
int[] integerValues = { -11, 12, -42, 0, 1, 90, 68, 6, -9 };
SelectionSort.Sort(integerValues);
Console.WriteLine(string.Join(" | ", integerValues));
```

In the preceding code, a new array is declared and initialized. Then, the `Sort` static method is called, passing the array as a parameter. At the end, the `string` value is created by joining elements of the array (separated by the | character) and is shown in the console, as follows:

```
-42 | -11 | -9 | 0 | 1 | 6 | 12 | 68 | 90
```

By using the generic method, you can easily use the created class for sorting various arrays, such as with floating point numbers or strings. The example code is as follows:

```
string[] stringValues = { "Mary", "Marcin", "Ann", "James",
    "George", "Nicole" };
SelectionSort.Sort(stringValues);
Console.WriteLine(string.Join(" | ", stringValues));
```

As a result, you will receive the following output:

```
Ann | George | James | Marcin | Mary | Nicole
```

While talking about various algorithms, one of the most important topics is **computational complexity**, especially **time complexity**. There are a few of its variants, such as for the worst or average case. The complexity can be interpreted as the number of basic operations that need to be performed by the algorithm, depending on the input size (n). The time complexity can be specified using the **Big O notation**, for example, as $O(n)$, $O(n^2)$ or $O(n \log(n))$. However, what does this mean? The $O(n)$ notation indicates that the number of operations increases linearly with the input size (n). The $O(n^2)$ variant is named **quadratic**, while $O(n \log(n))$ is named **linearithmic**. There are other variants as well, such as $O(1)$, which is **constant**.

In the case of the selection sort, both the worst and average time complexity is $O(n^2)$. Why? Let's take a look at the code to answer this question. There are two loops (one within the other), each iterating through many elements of the array. For this reason, the complexity is indicated as $O(n^2)$.

More information about the selection sort and its implementations can be found at:

- https://en.wikipedia.org/wiki/Selection_sort
- https://en.wikibooks.org/wiki/Algorithm_Implementation/Sorting/Selection_sort

You have just learned about the first sorting algorithm! If you are interested in the next approach to sorting, let's proceed to the next section, where the insertion sort is presented.

Insertion sort

The **insertion sort** is another algorithm that makes it possible to sort a single-dimensional array in a simple way, as shown in the following diagram. Similarly, as in the case of the selection sort, the array is divided into two parts, namely sorted and unsorted. However, at the beginning, the first element is included in the sorted part. In each iteration, the algorithm takes the first element from the unsorted part and places it in a suitable location within the sorted part, to leave the sorted part in the correct order. Such operations are repeated until the unsorted part is empty.

Let's take a look at an example of sorting an array with nine elements (**-11, 12, -42, 0, 1, 90, 68, 6, -9**) using the insertion sort, which is presented in the following diagram:

Step 1	Step 2	Step 3	Step 4	Step 5	Step 6	Step 7	Step 8	Step 9	Step 10	Step 11
-11	-11	-11	-42	-42	-42	-42	-42	-42	-42	-42
12	12	-42	-11	-11	-11	-11	-11	-11	-11	-11
-42	-42	12	12	0	0	0	0	0	0	0
0	0	0	0	12	12	1	1	1	1	1
1	1	1	1	1	1	12	12	12	12	12
90	90	90	90	90	90	90	90	90	68	68
68	68	68	68	68	68	68	68	68	90	90
6	6	6	6	6	6	6	6	6	6	6
-9	-9	-9	-9	-9	-9	-9	-9	-9	-9	-9

Step 12	Step 13	Step 14	Step 15	Step 16	Step 17	Step 18	Step 19	Step 20	Step 21	Step 22
-42	-42	-42	-42	-42	-42	-42	-42	-42	-42	-42
-11	-11	-11	-11	-11	-11	-11	-11	-11	-11	-11
0	0	0	0	0	0	0	0	0	-9	-9
1	1	1	1	1	1	1	1	-9	0	0
12	12	6	6	6	6	6	-9	1	1	1
68	6	12	12	12	12	-9	6	6	6	6
6	68	68	68	68	-9	12	12	12	12	12
90	90	90	90	-9	68	68	68	68	68	68
-9	-9	-9	-9	90	90	90	90	90	90	90

At the beginning, only one element (**-11**) is located in the sorted part (*Step 1*). Then, the smallest element is found in the unsorted part (**-42**) and is moved to the correct location in the sorted part, that is, to the beginning of the array, performing a set of swap operations (*Steps 2* and *3*). Thus, the length of the sorted part is increased to two elements, namely **-42** and **-11**. Such operations are repeated until the unsorted part is empty (*Step 22*).

The implementation code for the insertion sort is very simple:

```
public static class InsertionSort
{
    public static void Sort<T>(T[] array) where T : IComparable
    {
        for (int i = 1; i < array.Length; i++)
        {
            int j = i;
            while (j > 0 && array[j].CompareTo(array[j - 1]) < 0)
            {
```

```
                    Swap(array, j, j - 1);
                    j--;
                }
            }
        } (...)
    }
```

Similarly, as in the case of the selection sort, the implementation is provided in a new class, namely `InsertionSort`. The static generic `Sort` method performs operations regarding sorting and takes an array as the parameter. Within this method, the `for` loop is used to iterate through all elements in the unsorted part. Thus, the initial value of the `i` variable is set to `1`, instead of `0`. In each iteration of the `for` loop, the `while` loop is executed to move the first element from the unsorted part of the array (with the index equal to a value of the `i` variable) to the correct location within the sorted part, using the `Swap` auxiliary method with the same implementation as shown in the case of the selection sort. The way of testing the insertion sort is also very similar, but another class name should be used, that is, `InsertionSort` instead of `SelectionSort`.

> More information about the insertion sort and its implementations can be found at:
>
> - https://en.wikipedia.org/wiki/Insertion_sort
> - https://en.wikibooks.org/wiki/Algorithm_Implementation/ Sorting/Insertion_sort

At the end, it is worth mentioning the time complexity of the insertion sort. Similarly, as in the case of the selection sort, both worst and average time complexity is $O(n^2)$. If you take a look at the code, you will also see two loops (`for` and `while`) placed one within the other, which could iterate multiple times, depending on the input size.

Bubble sort

The third sorting algorithm presented in the book is **bubble sort**. Its way of operation is very simple, because the algorithm just iterates through the array and compares adjacent elements. If they are located in an incorrect order, they are swapped. It sounds very easy, but the algorithm is not very efficient and its usage with large collections could cause performance-related problems.

To better understand how the algorithm works, let's take a look at the following diagram that shows how the algorithm operates in the case of sorting a single-dimensional array with nine elements (**-11**, **12**, **-42**, **0**, **1**, **90**, **68**, **6**, **-9**):

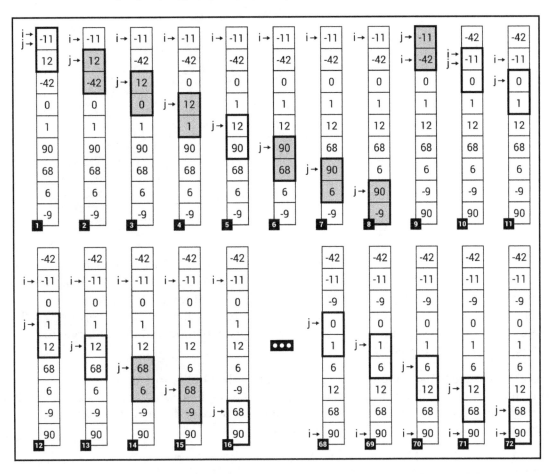

As you can see, in each step the algorithm compares two adjacent elements in the array and swaps them, if necessary. For example, in *Step 1*, **-11** and **12** are compared, but they are placed in the correct order, so it is not necessary to swap such elements. In *Step 2*, the next adjacent elements are compared (namely **12** and **-42**). This time, such elements are not placed in the correct order, thus they are swapped. The afore mentioned operations are performed several times. At the end, the array will be sorted, as shown in *Step 72*.

The algorithm seems to be very easy, but what about the implementation? Is it also so simple? Fortunately, yes! You just need to use two loops, compare adjacent elements, and swap them if necessary. That's all! Let's take a look at the following code snippet:

```
public static class BubbleSort
{
    public static void Sort<T>(T[] array) where T : IComparable
    {
        for (int i = 0; i < array.Length; i++)
        {
            for (int j = 0; j < array.Length - 1; j++)
            {
                if (array[j].CompareTo(array[j + 1]) > 0)
                {
                    Swap(array, j, j + 1);
                }
            }
        }
    } (...)
}
```

The `Sort` static generic method, declared in the `BubbleSort` class, contains the implementation of the bubble sort algorithm. As already mentioned, two `for` loops are used, together with a comparison and a call of the `Swap` method (with the same implementation as shown in the case of the previously described sorting algorithms). What is more, you can use similar code for testing the implementation, but do not forget to replace the name of the class to `BubbleSort`.

It is also possible to use a more optimized version of the bubble sort algorithm by introducing a simple modification in the implementation. It is based on the assumption that comparisons should be stopped when no changes are discovered during one iteration through the array. The modified code is as follows:

```
public static T[] Sort<T>(T[] array) where T : IComparable
{
    for (int i = 0; i < array.Length; i++)
    {
        bool isAnyChange = false;
        for (int j = 0; j < array.Length - 1; j++)
        {
            if (array[j].CompareTo(array[j + 1]) > 0)
            {
                isAnyChange = true;
                Swap(array, j, j + 1);
            }
        }
    }
```

```
        if (!isAnyChange)
        {
            break;
        }
    }
    return array;
}
```

By introducing such a simple modification, the number of comparisons could decrease significantly. In the preceding example, it decreases from 72 steps to 56 steps.

More information about the bubble sort and its implementations can be found at:

- https://en.wikipedia.org/wiki/Bubble_sort
- https://en.wikibooks.org/wiki/Algorithm_Implementation/ Sorting/Bubble_sort

Before moving to the next sorting algorithm, it is worth mentioning the time complexity of the bubble sort. As you may have already guessed, both worst and average cases are the same as in the case of the selection and insertion sort, that is, $O(n^2)$.

Quicksort

The last sorting algorithm described in this book is named **quicksort**. It is one of the popular **divide and conquer algorithms**, which divide a problem into a set of smaller ones. Moreover, such an algorithm provides developers with an efficient way of sorting. Does this mean that its idea and implementation are very complicated? Fortunately, no! You will learn how the algorithm works, as well as what its implementation code can look like in this section. Let's start!

How does the algorithm work? At the beginning, it picks some value (such as from the first or the middle element of the array) as a **pivot**. Then, it reorders the array in such a way that values lower than or equal to the pivot are placed before it (forming the lower subarray), while values greater than the pivot are placed after it (the higher subarray). Such a process is called **partitioning**. In this book, the **Hoare partition scheme** is used. Next, the algorithm recursively sorts each of the afore mentioned subarrays. Of course, each subarray is further divided into the next two subarrays, and so on. The recursive calls stop when there are one or zero elements in a subarray, because in such a case there is nothing to sort.

The preceding description may sound a bit complicated, so let's take a look at an example:

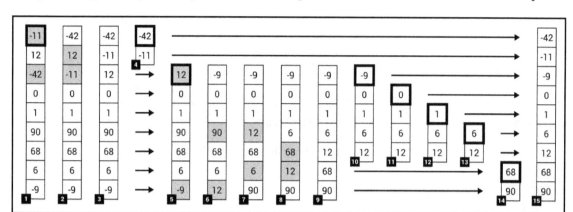

The example shows how the quicksort algorithm sorts a single-dimensional array with nine elements (**-11, 12, -42, 0, 1, 90, 68, 6, -9**). In this scenario, it is assumed that the pivot is chosen as a value of the first element of the subarray that is currently being sorted. In *Step 1*, value **-11** is chosen as the pivot. Then, it is necessary to reorder the array. Therefore, **-11** is swapped with **-42**, as well as **12** with **-11**, to ensure that only values lower than or equal to the pivot (**-42, -11**) are in the lower subarray and only values greater than the pivot (**12, 0, 1, 90, 68, 6, -9**) are placed in the higher subarray. Then, the algorithm is called recursively for both afore mentioned subarrays, namely (**-42, 11**) and (**12, 0, 1, 90, 68, 6, -9**), so they are analyzed in the same way as the input array.

As an example, *Step 5* shows that value **12** is chosen as the pivot. After partitioning, the subarray is divided into two other subarrays, namely (**-9, 0, 1, 6, 12**) and (**68, 90**). For both, other pivot elements are chosen, namely **-9** and **68**. After performing such operations for all remaining parts of the array, you will receive the final result, as shown on the right-hand side of the diagram (*Step 15*).

It is worth mentioning that the pivot can be selected variously in other implementations of this algorithm. As an example, let's take a look at how the following steps will change in the case when a value of the middle element of the array is chosen:

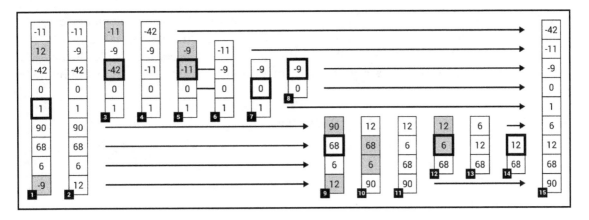

If you understand how the algorithm works, let's proceed to the implementation. It is more complicated than the examples shown earlier, and it uses **recursion** to call the sorting method for subarrays. The code is placed in the QuickSort class:

```
public static class QuickSort
{
    public static void Sort<T>(T[] array) where T : IComparable
    {
        Sort(array, 0, array.Length - 1);
    } (...)
}
```

The QuickSort class contains two variants of the Sort method. The first takes only one parameter, namely the array that should be sorted, and is shown in the preceding code snippet. It just calls another variant of the Sort method, which makes it possible to specify the lower and upper indices that indicate which part of the array should be sorted. The other version of the Sort method is shown here:

```
private static T[] Sort<T>(T[] array, int lower, int upper)
    where T : IComparable
{
    if (lower < upper)
    {
        int p = Partition(array, lower, upper);
        Sort(array, lower, p);
        Sort(array, p + 1, upper);
    }
    return array;
}
```

The Sort method checks whether the array (or subarray) has at least two elements, by comparing the values of the lower and upper variables. In such a case, it calls the Partition method, which is responsible for the partitioning phase, and then calls the Sort method recursively for two subarrays, namely lower (indices from lower to p) and higher (from p+1 to upper).

The code regarding the partitioning is shown here:

```
private static int Partition<T>(T[] array, int lower, int upper)
    where T : IComparable
{
    int i = lower;
    int j = upper;
    T pivot = array[lower];
    // or: T pivot = array[(lower + upper) / 2];
    do
    {
        while (array[i].CompareTo(pivot) < 0) { i++; }
        while (array[j].CompareTo(pivot) > 0) { j--; }
        if (i >= j) { break; }
        Swap(array, i, j);
    }
    while (i <= j);
    return j;
}
```

At the beginning, the pivot value is chosen and stored as a value of the pivot variable. As already mentioned, it can be chosen in various ways, such as by taking a value of the first element (shown in the preceding code snippet), a value of the middle element (as shown in the preceding code as the comment), or even as a random value. Then, the do-while loop is used to rearrange the array according to the Hoare partition scheme, using comparisons and by swapping elements. At the end, the current value of the j variable is returned.

The presented implementation is based on the Hoare partition scheme, the pseudocode and explanation of which are presented at https://en.wikipedia.org/wiki/Quicksort. There are various possible ways in which to implement quicksort. You can find more information at https://en.wikibooks.org/wiki/Algorithm_Implementation/Sorting/Quicksort.

What about the time complexity? Do you think that it differs in comparison with the selection, insertion, and bubble sort? If so, you are right! It has $O(n \log(n))$ average time complexity, despite having $O(n^2)$ worst time complexity.

Simple lists

Arrays are really useful data structures and they are applied in many algorithms. However, in some cases their application could be complicated due to their nature, which does not allow to increase or decrease the length of the already-created array. What should you do if you do not know the total number of elements to store in the collection? Do you need to create a very big array and just not use unnecessary elements? Such a solution does not sound good, does it? A much better approach is to use a data structure that makes it possible to dynamically increase the size of the collection if it is necessary.

Array list

The first data structure that meets this requirement is the **array list**, which is represented by the `ArrayList` class from the `System.Collections` namespace. You can use this class to store big collections of data, to which you can easily add new elements when necessary. Of course, you can also remove them, count items, and find an index of a particular value stored within the array list.

How can you do this? Let's take a look at the following code:

```
ArrayList arrayList = new ArrayList();
arrayList.Add(5);
arrayList.AddRange(new int[] { 6, -7, 8 });
arrayList.AddRange(new object[] { "Marcin", "Mary" });
arrayList.Insert(5, 7.8);
```

In the first line, a new instance of the `ArrayList` class is created. Then, you use the Add, AddRange, and Insert methods to add new elements to the array list. The first (namely, Add) allows you to add a new item at the end of the list. The AddRange method adds a collection of elements at the end of the array list, while Insert can be used to place an element in a specified location within the collection. When the preceding code is executed, the array list will contain the following elements: 5, 6, -7, 8, "Marcin", 7.8, and "Mary". As you can see, all items stored within the array list are of the type object. Thus, you can place in the same collection data of various types at the same time.

If you want to specify a type of each element stored within the list, you can use the generic `List` class, described just after `ArrayList`.

It is worth mentioning that you can easily access a particular element within the array list using the index, as shown in the following two lines of code:

```
object first = arrayList[0];
int third  = (int)arrayList[2];
```

Let's take a look at casting to `int` in the second line. Such casting is necessary, because the array list stores `object` values. As in the case of arrays, the zero-based indices are used while accessing particular elements within the collection.

Of course, you can use the `foreach` loop to iterate through all items, as follows:

```
foreach (object element in arrayList)
{
    Console.WriteLine(element);
}
```

That is not all! The `ArrayList` class has a set of properties and methods which you can use while developing applications utilizing the afore mentioned data structure. To start with, let's take a look at the `Count` and `Capacity` properties:

```
int count = arrayList.Count;
int capacity = arrayList.Capacity;
```

The first (`Count`) returns the number of elements stored in the array list, while the other (`Capacity`) indicates how many elements can be stored within it. If you check a value of the `Capacity` property after adding new elements to the array list, you will see that this value is automatically increased to prepare a place for new items. This is shown in the following diagram, presenting the difference between `Count` (as **A**) and `Capacity` (**B**):

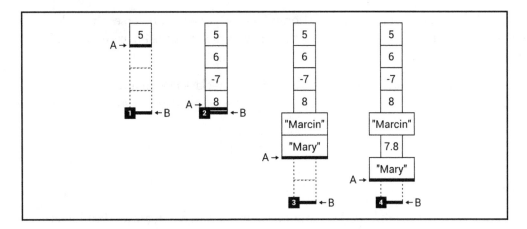

The next common and important task is checking whether the array list contains an element with a particular value. You can perform this operation by calling the `Contains` method, as shown in the following line of code:

```
bool containsMary = arrayList.Contains("Mary");
```

If the specified value is found in the array list, the `true` value is returned.
Otherwise, `false` is returned. Using this method, you can check whether the element exists in the collection. However, how can you find an index of this element? To do so, you can use the `IndexOf` or `LastIndexOf` method, as shown in the following line of code:

```
int minusIndex = arrayList.IndexOf(-7);
```

The `IndexOf` method returns an index of the first occurrence of the element in the array list, while `LastIndexOf` returns an index of the last occurrence. If a value is not found, `-1` is returned by the method.

Apart from adding some items to the array list, you can also easily remove added elements, as shown in the following code:

```
arrayList.Remove(5);
```

For removing items from the array list, you can use more than one method, namely `Remove`, `RemoveAt`, and `RemoveRange`. The first (`Remove`) removes the first occurrence of the value provided as the parameter. The `RemoveAt` method removes an item with the index equal to the value passed as the parameter, while the other (`RemoveRange`) makes it possible to remove the specified number of elements starting from the provided index. What is more, if you want to remove all elements, you can use the `Clear` method.

Among other methods, it is worth mentioning `Reverse`, which reverses the order of the elements within the array list, as well as `ToArray`, which returns an array with all items stored in the `ArrayList` instance.

 More information about the `ArrayList` class is available at https://msdn.microsoft.com/library/system.collections.arraylist.aspx.

Generic list

As you can see, the `ArrayList` class contains a broad range of features, but it has a significant drawback—it is not a strongly typed list. If you want to benefit from a strongly typed list, you can use the generic `List` class representing the collection, whose size can be increased or decreased, whenever necessary.

The generic `List` class contains many properties and methods that are very useful while developing applications that store data. You will see that many members are named exactly the same as in the `ArrayList` class, such as `Count` and `Capacity` properties, as well as the `Add`, `AddRange`, `Clear`, `Contains`, `IndexOf`, `Insert`, `InsertRange`, `LastIndexOf`, `Remove`, `RemoveAt`, `RemoveRange`, `Reverse`, and `ToArray` methods. You can also get a particular element from the list using the index and the `[]` operator.

Apart from the already-described features, you can also use the comprehensive set of extension methods from the `System.Linq` namespace, such as for finding the minimum or maximum value (`Min` or `Max`), calculating the average (`Average`), ordering in an ascending or descending order (`OrderBy` or `OrderByDescending`), as well as checking whether all the elements in the list satisfy a condition (`All`). Of course, these are not the only features available for developers while creating applications using generic lists in the C# language.

 More information about the generic `List` class is available at https://msdn.microsoft.com/library/6sh2ey19.aspx.

Let's take a look at two examples that show how to use the generic list in practice.

Example – average value

The first example utilizes the generic `List` class for storing floating point values (of the `double` type) entered by the user. After typing a number, the average value is calculated and presented in the console. The program stops the operation when an incorrect value is entered by the user.

The code from the `Main` method in the `Program` class is as follows:

```
List<double> numbers = new List<double>();
do
{
    Console.Write("Enter the number: ");
    string numberString = Console.ReadLine();
    if (!double.TryParse(numberString, NumberStyles.Float,
        new NumberFormatInfo(), out double number))
    {
        break;
    }

    numbers.Add(number);
    Console.WriteLine($"The average value: {numbers.Average()}");
}
while (true);
```

At the beginning, an instance of the `List` class is created. Then, within the infinite loop (do-while), the program waits until the user enters the number. If it is correct, the entered value is added to the list (by calling the `Add` method), and the average value from elements of the list is calculated (by calling the `Average` method) and shown in the console.

As a result, you could receive output similar to the following:

```
Enter the number: 10.5
The average value: 10.5 (...)
Enter the number: 1.5
The average value: 4.875
```

In the current example, you have seen how to use the list that stores `double` values. However, can it also store instances of user-defined classes? Of course! You will see how to achieve this goal in the next example.

Example – list of people

The second example regarding the `List` class shows how to use this data structure to create a very simple database of people. For each of them, a name, a country, and an age are stored. When the program is launched, some data of people are added to the list. Then, the data is sorted (using the LINQ expression) and presented in the console.

Let's start with declaration of the `Person` class, as shown in the following code:

```
public class Person
{
    public string Name { get; set; }
    public int Age { get; set; }
    public CountryEnum Country { get; set; }
}
```

The class contains three public properties, namely `Name`, `Age`, and `Country`. It is worth noting that the `Country` property is of the `CountryEnum` type, which defines three constants, that is, `PL` (Poland), `UK` (United Kingdom), and `DE` (Germany), as shown in the following code:

```
public enum CountryEnum
{
    PL,
    UK,
    DE
}
```

The following part of the code should be added in the `Main` method within the `Program` class. It creates a new instance of the `List` class, and adds data of a few people with different names, countries, and ages, as shown here:

```
List<Person> people = new List<Person>();
people.Add(new Person() { Name = "Marcin",
    Country = CountryEnum.PL, Age = 29 });
people.Add(new Person() { Name = "Sabine",
    Country = CountryEnum.DE, Age = 25 }); (...)
people.Add(new Person() { Name = "Ann",
    Country = CountryEnum.PL, Age = 31 });
```

In the next line, the LINQ expression is used to sort the list by names of people in ascending order, and convert the results into the list:

```
List<Person> results = people.OrderBy(p => p.Name).ToList();
```

Then, you can easily iterate through all the results using the `foreach` loop:

```
foreach (Person person in results)
{
    Console.WriteLine($"{person.Name} ({person.Age} years)
        from {person.Country}.");
}
```

After running the program, the following result is presented:

Marcin (29 years) from PL. (...)
Sabine (25 years) from DE.

That's all! Let's now talk a bit more about the LINQ expressions, which can be used not only to order elements, but also to perform the filtering of items based on the provided criteria, and even more.

As an example, let's take a look at the following query using the **method syntax**:

```
List<string> names = people.Where(p => p.Age <= 30)
    .OrderBy(p => p.Name)
    .Select(p => p.Name)
    .ToList();
```

It selects the names (the `Select` clause) of all people whose age is lower than or equal to 30 years (the `Where` clause), ordered by names (the `OrderBy` clause). The query is then executed and the results are returned as a list.

The same task could be accomplished using the **query syntax**, as shown in the following example, combined with calling the `ToList` method:

```
List<string> names = (from p in people
                      where p.Age <= 30
                      orderby p.Name
                      select p.Name).ToList();
```

In this part of the chapter, you have seen how to use the `ArrayList` class and the generic `List` class for storing data in collections, the size of which could be dynamically adjusted. However, this is not the end of list-related topics within this chapter. Are you ready to get to know another data structure, which maintains the elements in the sorted order? If so, let's proceed to the next section, which is focused on sorted lists.

Sorted lists

In this chapter, you have already learned how to store data using arrays and lists. However, do you know that you can even use a data structure that ensures that the elements are sorted? If not, let's get to know the SortedList generic class (from the System.Collections.Generic namespace), which is a collection of **key-value pairs**, sorted by keys, without the necessity of sorting them on your own. It is worth mentioning that all keys must be unique and cannot be equal to null.

You can easily add an element to the collection using the Add method, and remove a specified item using the Remove method. Among other methods, it is worth noting ContainsKey and ContainsValue for checking whether the collection contains an item with a given key or value, as well as IndexOfKey and IndexOfValue for returning an index of a given key or value within the collection. As the sorted list stores the key-value pairs, you have also access to the Keys and Values properties. Particular keys and values can be easily obtained using the index and the [] operator.

 More information about the SortedList generic class is available at https://msdn.microsoft.com/library/ms132319.aspx.

After this short introduction, let's take a look at an example that will show you how to use this data structure, and will also indicate some significant differences in the code compared with the previously-described List class.

Example – address book

This example uses the SortedList class to create a very simple address book, which is sorted by names of people. For each person, the following data is stored: Name, Age, and Country. The declaration of the Person class is shown in the following code:

```
public class Person
{
    public string Name { get; set; }
    public int Age { get; set; }
    public CountryEnum Country { get; set; }
}
```

A value of the Country property can be set to one of the constants from CountryEnum:

```
public enum CountryEnum
{
    PL,
    UK,
    DE
}
```

The most interesting part of code is placed in the Main method within the Program class. Here, a new instance of the SortedList generic class is created, specifying types for keys and values, namely string and Person, as presented in the following code:

```
SortedList<string, Person> people =
    new SortedList<string, Person>();
```

Then, you can easily add data to the sorted list by calling the Add method, passing two parameters, namely a key (that is, a name), and a value (that is, an instance of the Person class), as shown in the following code snippet:

```
people.Add("Marcin", new Person() { Name = "Marcin",
    Country = CountryEnum.PL, Age = 29 });
people.Add("Sabine", new Person() { Name = "Sabine",
    Country = CountryEnum.DE, Age = 25 }); (...)
people.Add("Ann", new Person() { Name = "Ann",
    Country = CountryEnum.PL, Age = 31 });
```

When all the data are stored within the collection, you can easily iterate through its elements (key-value pairs) using the foreach loop. It is worth mentioning that a type of the variable used in the loop is KeyValuePair<string, Person>. Thus, you need to use the Key and Value properties to get access to a key and a value, respectively, as follows:

```
foreach (KeyValuePair<string, Person> person in people)
{
    Console.WriteLine($"{person.Value.Name} ({person.Value.Age}
        years) from {person.Value.Country}.");
}
```

When the program is launched, you will receive the following results in the console:

```
Ann (31 years) from PL. (...)
Marcin (29 years) from PL. (...)
Sabine (25 years) from DE.
```

As you can see, the collection is automatically sorted by names, which are used as keys for the sorted list. However, you need to remember that keys must be unique, so you cannot add more than one person with the same name in this example.

Linked lists

While using the `List` generic class, you can easily get access to particular elements of the collection using indices. However, when you get a single element, how can you move to the next element of the collection? Is it possible? To do so, you may consider the `IndexOf` method to get an index of the element. Unfortunately, it returns an index of the first occurrence of a given value in the collection, so it will not always work as expected in this scenario.

It would be great to have some kind of *pointer* to the next element, as shown in the following diagram:

With this approach, you can easily navigate from one element to the next one using the `Next` property. Such a structure is named the **single-linked list**. However, can it be further expanded by adding the `Previous` property to allow navigating in forward and backward directions? Of course! Such a data structure is named the **double-linked list** and is presented in the following diagram:

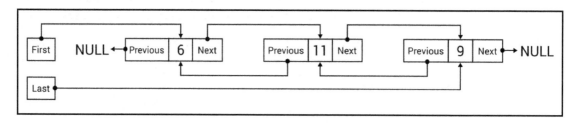

As you can see, the double-linked list contains the `First` property that indicates the first element in the list. Each item has two properties that point to the previous and next element (`Previous` and `Next`, respectively). If there is no previous element, the `Previous` property is equal to `null`. Similarly, when there is no next element, the `Next` property is set to `null`. Moreover, the double-linked list contains the `Last` property that indicates the last element. When there are no items in the list, both the `First` and `Last` properties are set to `null`.

However, do you need to implement such a data structure on your own if you want to use it in your C#-based applications? Fortunately, no, because it is available as the `LinkedList` generic class in the `System.Collections.Generic` namespace.

While creating an instance of the class, you need to specify the type parameter that indicates a type of a single element within the list, such as `int` or `string`. However, a type of a single node is not just `int` or `string`, because in such a case you will not have access to any additional properties related to the double-linked list, such as `Previous` or `Next`. To solve this problem, each node is an instance of the `LinkedListNode` generic class, such as `LinkedListNode<int>` or `LinkedListNode<string>`.

Some additional explanation is necessary for the methods of adding new nodes to the double-linked list. For this purpose, you can use a set of methods, namely:

- `AddFirst`: For adding an element at the beginning of the list
- `AddLast`: For adding an element at the end of the list
- `AddBefore`: For adding an element before the specified node in the list
- `AddAfter`: For adding an element after the specified node in the list

All these methods return an instance of the `LinkedListNode` class. Moreover, there are also other methods, such as `Contains` for checking whether the specified value exists in the list, `Clear` for removing all elements from the list, and `Remove` for removing a node from the list.

More information about the `LinkedList` generic class is available at `https://msdn.microsoft.com/library/he2s3bh7.aspx`.

After this short introduction, you should be ready to take a look at an example that shows how to apply the double-linked list, implemented as the `LinkedList` class, in practice.

Example – book reader

As an example, you will prepare a simple application that allows a user to read a book by changing the pages. One should be able to move to the next page (if it exists) after pressing the *N* key, and go back to the previous page (if it exists) after pressing the *P* key. The content of the current page, together with the page number, should be shown in the console, as presented in the following screenshot:

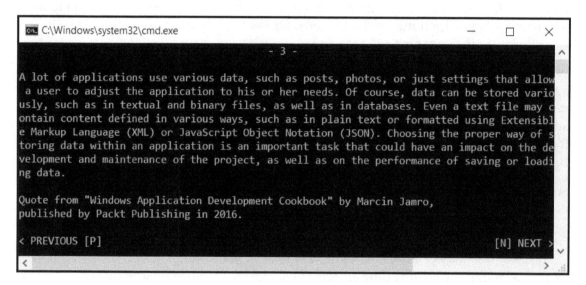

Let's start with the declaration of the Page class, as shown in the following code:

```
public class Page
{
    public string Content { get; set; }
}
```

This class represents a single page and contains the Content property. You should create a few instances of the Page class, representing six pages of the book, in the Main method in the Program class, as presented in the following code snippet:

```
Page pageFirst = new Page() { Content = "Nowadays (...)" };
Page pageSecond = new Page() { Content = "Application (...)" };
Page pageThird = new Page() { Content = "A lot of (...)" };
Page pageFourth = new Page() { Content = "Do you know (...)" };
Page pageFifth = new Page() { Content = "While (...)" };
Page pageSixth = new Page() { Content = "Could you (...)" };
```

When the instances are created, let's proceed to constructing the linked list, using a few addition-related methods, as shown in the following lines of code:

```
LinkedList<Page> pages = new LinkedList<Page>();
pages.AddLast(pageSecond);
LinkedListNode<Page> nodePageFourth = pages.AddLast(pageFourth);
pages.AddLast(pageSixth);
pages.AddFirst(pageFirst);
pages.AddBefore(nodePageFourth, pageThird);
pages.AddAfter(nodePageFourth, pageFifth);
```

In the first line, a new list is created. Then, the following operations are performed:

- Adding the data of the second page at the end of the list ([2])
- Adding the data of the fourth page at the end of the list ([2, 4])
- Adding the data of the sixth page at the end of the list ([2, 4, 6])
- Adding the data of the first page at the beginning of the list ([1, 2, 4, 6])
- Adding the data of the third page before the node of the fourth page ([1, 2, 3, 4, 6])
- Adding the data of the fifth page after the node of the fourth page ([1, 2, 3, 4, 5, 6])

The next part of the code is responsible for presenting the page in the console, as well as for navigating between pages after pressing the appropriate keys. The code is as follows:

```
LinkedListNode<Page> current = pages.First;
int number = 1;
while (current != null)
{
    Console.Clear();
    string numberString = $"- {number} -";
    int leadingSpaces = (90 - numberString.Length) / 2;
    Console.WriteLine(numberString.PadLeft(leadingSpaces
        + numberString.Length));
    Console.WriteLine();

    string content = current.Value.Content;
    for (int i = 0; i < content.Length; i += 90)
    {
        string line = content.Substring(i);
        line = line.Length > 90 ? line.Substring(0, 90) : line;
        Console.WriteLine(line);
    }

    Console.WriteLine();
```

```
Console.WriteLine($"Quote from "Windows Application
    Development Cookbook" by Marcin
    Jamro,{Environment.NewLine}published by Packt Publishing
    in 2016.");

Console.WriteLine();
Console.Write(current.Previous != null
    ? "< PREVIOUS [P]" : GetSpaces(14));
Console.Write(current.Next != null
    ? "[N] NEXT >".PadLeft(76) : string.Empty);
Console.WriteLine();

switch (Console.ReadKey(true).Key)
{
    case ConsoleKey.N:
        if (current.Next != null)
        {
            current = current.Next;
            number++;
        }
        break;
    case ConsoleKey.P:
        if (current.Previous != null)
        {
            current = current.Previous;
            number--;
        }
        break;
    default:
        return;
}
}
}
```

Some explanation may be useful for this part of the code. In the first line, a value of the current variable is set to the first node in the linked list. Generally speaking, the current variable represents the page which is currently presented in the console. Then, the initial value for the page number is set to 1 (the number variable). However, the most interesting and complicated part of the code is shown in the while loop.

Within the loop, the current content of the console is cleared and the string for presenting the page number is properly formatted to display. Before and after it, the – characters are added. Moreover, leading spaces are inserted (using the PadLeft method) to prepare the string that is centered horizontally.

Then, the content of the page is divided into lines of no more than 90 characters and written in the console. For dividing the string, the Substring method and the Length properties are used. In a similar way, additional information (about quotations from another book) is presented in the console. It is worth mentioning the Environment.NewLine property that inserts the line break in a specified place of the string. Then, the PREVIOUS and NEXT captions are shown, if the previous or the next page is available.

In the following part of the code, the program waits until the user presses any key and does not present it in the console (by passing the true value as the parameter). When the user presses the N key, the current variable is set to the next node, using the Next property. Of course, the operation should not be performed when the next page is unavailable. In a similar way, the P key is handled, which causes the user to be navigated to the previous page. It is worth mentioning that the number of the page (the number variable) is modified together with changing a value of the current variable.

At the end, the code of the auxiliary GetSpaces method is shown:

```
private static string GetSpaces(int number)
{
    string result = string.Empty;
    for (int i = 0; i < number; i++)
    {
        result += " ";
    }
    return result;
}
```

This just prepares and returns the string variable with the specified number of spaces.

Circular-linked lists

In the previous section, you have learned about the double-linked list. As you can see, the implementation of such a data structure allows for navigating between the nodes using the Previous and Next properties. However, the Previous property of the first node is set to null, as is the Next property of the last node. Do you know that you can easily expand this approach to create the **circular-linked list**?

Such a data structure is presented in the following diagram:

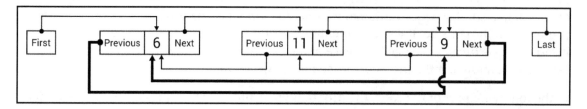

Here, the `Previous` property of the first node navigates to the last one, while the `Next` property of the last node navigates to the first. This data structure can be useful in some specific cases, as you will see while developing a real-world example.

 It is worth mentioning that the way of navigating between nodes does not need to be implemented as properties. It can also be replaced with methods, as you will see in the example within the following section.

Implementation

After the short introduction to the topic of circular-linked lists, it is time to take a look at the implementation code. Let's start with the following code snippet:

```
public class CircularLinkedList<T> : LinkedList<T>
{
    public new IEnumerator GetEnumerator()
    {
        return new CircularLinkedListEnumerator<T>(this);
    }
}
```

The implementation of the circular-linked list can be created as a generic class that extends `LinkedList`, as shown in the preceding code. It is worth mentioning the implementation of the `GetEnumerator` method, which uses the `CircularLinkedListEnumerator` class. By creating it, you will be able to indefinitely iterate through all the elements of the circular-linked list, using the `foreach` loop.

The code of the `CircularLinkedListEnumerator` class is as follows:

```
public class CircularLinkedListEnumerator<T> : IEnumerator<T>
{
    private LinkedListNode<T> _current;
    public T Current => _current.Value;
    object IEnumerator.Current => Current;

    public CircularLinkedListEnumerator(LinkedList<T> list)
    {
        _current = list.First;
    }

    public bool MoveNext()
    {
        if (_current == null)
        {
            return false;
        }

        _current = _current.Next ?? _current.List.First;
        return true;
    }

    public void Reset()
    {
        _current = _current.List.First;
    }

    public void Dispose() { }
}
```

The `CircularLinkedListEnumerator` class implements the `IEnumerator` interface. The class declares the `private` field representing the current node (`_current`) in the iteration over the list. It also contains two properties, namely `Current` and `IEnumerator.Current`, which are required by the `IEnumerator` interface. The constructor just sets a value of the `_current` variable, based on an instance of the `LinkedList` class, passed as the parameter.

One of the most important parts of code is the `MoveNext` method. It stops iterating when the `_current` variable is set to `null`, that is, if there are no items in the list. Otherwise, it changes the current element to the next one or to the first node in the list, if the next node is unavailable. In the `Reset` method, you just set a value of the `_current` field to the first node in the list.

At the end, you need to create two extension methods that make it possible to navigate to the first element while trying to get the next element from the last item in the list, as well as to navigate to the last element while trying to get the previous element from the first item in the list. To simplify the implementation, such features will be available as `Next` and `Previous` methods, instead of `Next` and `Previous` properties, as shown in the preceding diagram. The code is shown here:

```
public static class CircularLinkedListExtensions
{
    public static LinkedListNode<T> Next<T>(
        this LinkedListNode<T> node)
    {
        if (node != null && node.List != null)
        {
            return node.Next ?? node.List.First;
        }
        return null;
    }
    public static LinkedListNode<T> Previous<T>(
        this LinkedListNode<T> node)
    {
        if (node != null && node.List != null)
        {
            return node.Previous ?? node.List.Last;
        }
        return null;
    }
}
```

The first extension method, namely `Next`, checks whether the node exists and whether the list is available. In such a case, it returns a value of the `Next` property of the node (if such a value is not equal to `null`) or returns a reference to the first element in the list, using the `First` property. The `Previous` method operates in a similar way.

That's all! You have just completed the C#-based implementation of the circular-linked list, which can be used later in various applications. But how? Let's take a look at the following example that uses this data structure.

Example – spin the wheel

This example simulates a game in which the user spins a wheel with random speed. The wheel rotates slower and slower until it stops. Then the user can spin it again, from the previous stop position, as shown in the following diagram:

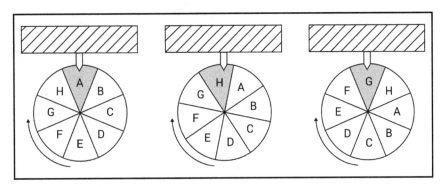

Let's proceed to the first part of code of the `Main` method in the `Program` class:

```
CircularLinkedList<string> categories =
    new CircularLinkedList<string>();
categories.AddLast("Sport");
categories.AddLast("Culture");
categories.AddLast("History");
categories.AddLast("Geography");
categories.AddLast("People");
categories.AddLast("Technology");
categories.AddLast("Nature");
categories.AddLast("Science");
```

At the beginning, a new instance of the `CircularLinkedList` class is created, which represents the circular-linked list with `string` elements. Then, eight values are added, namely `Sport`, `Culture`, `History`, `Geography`, `People`, `Technology`, `Nature`, and `Science`.

The following part of the code performs the most important operations:

```
Random random = new Random();
int totalTime = 0;
int remainingTime = 0;
foreach (string category in categories)
{
    if (remainingTime <= 0)
    {
```

```
Console.WriteLine("Press [Enter] to start
    or any other to exit.");
switch (Console.ReadKey().Key)
{
    case ConsoleKey.Enter:
        totalTime = random.Next(1000, 5000);
        remainingTime = totalTime;
        break;
    default:
        return;
}
}

int categoryTime = (-450 * remainingTime) / (totalTime - 50)
    + 500 + (22500 / (totalTime - 50));
remainingTime -= categoryTime;
Thread.Sleep(categoryTime);

Console.ForegroundColor = remainingTime <= 0
    ? ConsoleColor.Red : ConsoleColor.Gray;
Console.WriteLine(category);
Console.ForegroundColor = ConsoleColor.Gray;
}
```

First, three variables are declared, namely for drawing random values (`random`), the total drawn time of spinning of the wheel in milliseconds (`totalTime`), as well as the remaining time of spinning of the wheel in milliseconds (`remainingTime`).

Then, the `foreach` loop is used to iterate through all the elements within the circular-linked list. If there are no `break` or `return` instructions within such a loop, it will execute indefinitely due to the nature of the circular-linked list. If the last item is reached, the first element in the list is taken automatically in the next iteration.

In the loop, the remaining time is checked. If it is less than or equal to zero, that is, the wheel has stopped or has not been started yet, the message is presented to the user and the program waits until the *Enter* key is pressed. In such a situation, the new spinning operation is configured by drawing the total time of spinning and setting the remaining time. When the user presses any other key, the program stops the execution.

In the next step, the time for one iteration of the loop is calculated. The formula makes it possible to provide smaller times at the beginning (the wheel spins faster) and bigger times at the end (the wheel spins slower). Then, the remaining time decreases and the program waits for the specified number of milliseconds, using the `Sleep` method.

At the end, the foreground color is changed to red, if the final result is shown, and the currently-chosen category on the spinning wheel is presented in the console.

When you run the application, you can get the following result:

```
Press [Enter] to start or any other to exit.
Culture
History
Geography (...)
Culture
History
Press [Enter] to start or any other to exit.
Geography (...)
Nature
Science (...)
People
Technology
Press [Enter] to start or any other to exit.
```

You have already completed the example that uses the circular-linked list. It is one of the data structures that have been described in this chapter. If you want to briefly summarize the information you have learned, let's proceed to the short summary of this topic.

Summary

Arrays and lists are among the most common data structures used while developing various kinds of applications. However, this topic is not as easy as it seems to be, because even arrays can be divided into a few variants, namely single-dimensional, multi-dimensional, and jagged arrays, also referred to as arrays of arrays.

In the case of lists, the differences are even more visible, as you could see in the case of simple, generic, sorted, single-linked, double-linked, and circular-linked lists. Fortunately, the built-in implementation is available for the array list, as well as the generic, sorted, and double-linked lists. Furthermore, you can quite easily extend the double-linked list to behave as the circular-linked list. Therefore, you can benefit from the features of suitable structures without the significant development effort.

The available types of data structures can sound quite complicated, but in this chapter you have seen detailed descriptions of particular data structures, together with the implementation code of C#-based examples. They should simplify things for you and could be used as the base for your future projects.

Are you ready to learn other data structures? If so, let's proceed to the next chapter and read about stacks and queues!

3
Stacks and Queues

So far, you have learned a lot about arrays and lists. However, these structures are not the only ones available. Among others, there is also a group of more specialized data structures, which are called **limited access data structures**.

What does this mean? To explain the name, let's return to the topic of arrays for the moment, which belong to the group of **random access data structures**. The difference between them is only one word, that is, limited or random. As you already know, arrays allow you to store data and get access to various elements using indices. Thus, you can easily get the first, the middle, the nth, or the last element from the array. For this reason, it can be named as the random access data structure.

However, what does *limited* mean? The answer is very simple—with a limited access data structure, you cannot access every element from the structure. Thus, the way of getting elements is strictly specified. For example, you can get only the first or the last element, but you cannot get the nth element from the data structure. The popular representatives of limited access data structures are stacks and queues.

In this chapter, the following topics will be covered:

- Stacks
- Queues
- Priority queues

Stacks

To begin, let's talk about a **stack**. It is an easy-to-understand data structure and can be represented using the example of a pile of many plates, each placed on top of the other. You can only add a new plate to the top of the pile, and you can only get a plate from the top of the pile. You cannot remove the seventh plate without taking the previous six from the top, and you cannot add a plate to the middle of the pile.

The stack operates in exactly the same way! It allows you to add a new element at the top (the **push** operation) and get an element by removing it from the top (the **pop** operation). For this reason, a stack is consistent with the **LIFO** principle, which stands for **Last-In First-Out**. According to our example of the pile of plates, the last added plate (last-in) will be removed from the pile first (first-out).

The diagram of a stack with push and pop operations is shown as follows:

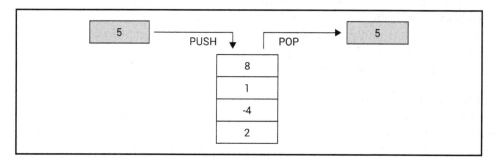

It seems to be very easy, doesn't it? It really is, and you can benefit from the features of stacks using the built-in generic `Stack` class from the `System.Collections.Generic` namespace. It is worth mentioning three methods from this class, namely:

- `Push`, to insert an element at the top of the stack
- `Pop`, to remove an element from the top of the stack and return it
- `Peek`, to return an element from the top of the stack without removing it

Of course, you also have access to other methods, such as for removing all elements from the stack (`Clear`) or for checking whether a given element is available in the stack (`Contains`). You can get the number of elements in the stack using the `Count` property.

It is worth noting that the `Push` method is an *O(1)* operation, if the capacity does not need to increase, or *O(n)* otherwise, where *n* is the number of elements in the stack. Both `Pop` and `Peek` are *O(1)* operations.

You can find more information about the `Stack` generic class at https://msdn.microsoft.com/library/3278tedw.aspx.

It is high time to take a look at some examples. Let's go!

Example – reversing words

For the first example, let's try to reverse a word using a stack. You can do this by iterating through characters that form a string, adding each at the top of the stack, and then removing all elements from the stack. At the end, you receive the reversed word, as shown in the following diagram, which presents the process of reversing the **MARCIN** word:

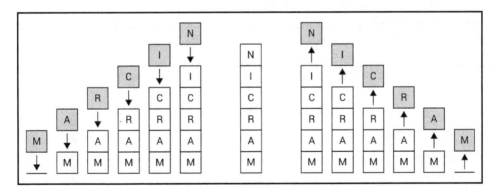

The implementation code, which should be added to the `Main` method within the `Program` class, is shown in the following code snippet:

```
Stack<char> chars = new Stack<char>();
foreach (char c in "LET'S REVERSE!")
{
    chars.Push(c);
}
```

```
while (chars.Count > 0)
{
    Console.Write(chars.Pop());
}
Console.WriteLine();
```

In the first line, a new instance of the `Stack` class is created. It is worth mentioning that in this scenario, the stack can contain only `char` elements. Then, you iterate through all characters using the `foreach` loop and insert each character at the top of the stack by calling the `Push` method on the `Stack` instance. The remaining part of the code consists of the `while` loop, which is executed until the stack is empty. This condition is checked using the `Count` property. In each iteration, the top element is removed from the stack (by calling `Pop`) and written in the console (using the `Write` static method of the `Console` class).

After running the code, you will receive the following result:

```
!ESREVER S'TEL
```

Example – Tower of Hanoi

The next example is a significantly more complex application of stacks. It is related to the mathematical game **Tower of Hanoi**. Let's start with the rules. The game requires three rods, onto which you can put discs. Each disc has a different size. At the beginning, all discs are placed on the first rod, forming the stack, ordered from the smallest (at the top) to the biggest (at the bottom), as follows:

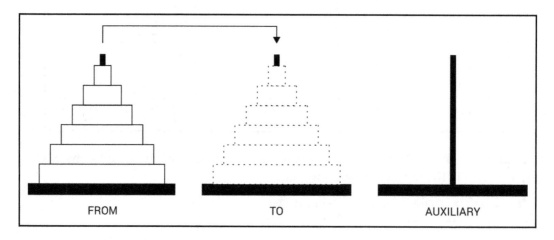

The aim of the game is to move all the discs from the first rod (**FROM**) to the second one (**TO**). However, during the whole game, you cannot place a bigger disc on a smaller one. Moreover, you can only move one disc at a time and, of course, you can only take a disc from the top of any rod. How could you move discs between the rods to comply with the afore mentioned rules? The problem can be divided into sub problems.

Let's start with the example of moving only one disc. Such a case is trivial and you just need to move a disc from the **FROM** rod to the **TO** one, without using the **AUXILIARY** rod.

A bit more complex scenario is moving two discs. In such a case, you should move one disc from the **FROM** rod to the **AUXILIARY** one. Then, you move the remaining disc from **FROM** to **TO**. At the end, you only need to move a disc from **AUXILIARY** to **TO**.

If you want to move three discs, you should start by moving two discs from **FROM** to **AUXILIARY**, using the mechanism described earlier. The operation will involve the **TO** rod as the auxiliary one. Then, you move the remaining disc from **FROM** to **TO**, and then move two discs from **AUXILIARY** to the **TO** rod, using **FROM** as the auxiliary rod.

As you can see, you can solve the problem of moving *n* discs by moving *n-1* discs from **FROM** to **AUXILIARY**, using **TO** as the auxiliary rod. Then, you should move the remaining disc from **FROM** to **TO**. At the end, you just need to move *n-1* discs from **AUXILIARY** to the **TO** rod, using **FROM** as the auxiliary rod.

That's all! Now that you know the basic rules, let's proceed to the code.

First, let's focus on the `HanoiTower` class, which contains the logic related to the game. A part of the code is shown as follows:

```
public class HanoiTower
{
    public int DiscsCount { get; private set; }
    public int MovesCount { get; private set; }
    public Stack<int> From { get; private set; }
    public Stack<int> To { get; private set; }
    public Stack<int> Auxiliary { get; private set; }
    public event EventHandler<EventArgs> MoveCompleted; (...)
}
```

The class contains five properties, storing the overall number of discs (`DiscsCount`), the number of performed moves (`MovesCount`), and the representations for the three rods (`From`, `To`, `Auxiliary`). The `MoveCompleted` event is declared as well. It will be fired after each move to inform that the user interface should be refreshed. Therefore, you can show the proper content, illustrating the current state of the rods.

Apart from the properties and the event, the class also has the following constructor:

```
public HanoiTower(int discs)
{
    DiscsCount = discs;
    From = new Stack<int>();
    To = new Stack<int>();
    Auxiliary = new Stack<int>();
    for (int i = 1; i <= discs; i++)
    {
        int size = discs - i + 1;
        From.Push(size);
    }
}
```

The constructor takes only one parameter, namely the number of discs (`discs`), and sets it as a value of the `DiscsCount` property. Then, new instances of the `Stack` class are created and references to them are stored in the `From`, `To`, and `Auxiliary` properties. At the end, the `for` loop is used to create the necessary number of discs and to add elements to the first stack (`From`). It is worth noting that `From`, `To`, and `Auxiliary` stacks only store integer values (`Stack<int>`). Each integer value represents a size of a particular disc. Such data is crucial due to the rules of moving discs between rods.

The operation of the algorithm is started by calling the `Start` method, whose code is shown in the following lines:

```
public void Start()
{
    Move(DiscsCount, From, To, Auxiliary);
}
```

The method just calls the `Move` recursive method, passing the overall number of discs and references to three stacks as parameters. However, what happens in the `Move` method? Let's look inside:

```
public void Move(int discs, Stack<int> from, Stack<int> to,
    Stack<int> auxiliary)
{
    if (discs > 0)
    {
        Move(discs - 1, from, auxiliary, to);

        to.Push(from.Pop());
        MovesCount++;
        MoveCompleted?.Invoke(this, EventArgs.Empty);
```

```
        Move(discs - 1, auxiliary, to, from);
    }
}
```

As you already know, this method is called recursively. For this reason, it is necessary to specify some exit conditions to prevent the method being called infinitely. In this case, the method will not call itself when the value of the discs parameter is equal to or lower than zero. If such a value is greater than zero, then the Move method is called, but the order of stacks is changed. Then, the element is removed from the stack represented by the second parameter (from) and inserted at the top of the stack represented by the third parameter (to). In the following lines, the number of moves (MovesCount) is incremented and the MoveCompleted event is fired. At the end, the Move method is called again, with another configuration of rod order. By calling this method several times, the discs will be moved from the first (From) to the second (To) rod. The operations performed in the Move method are consistent with the description of the problem of moving *n* discs between rods, as explained in the introduction to this example.

After the class with the logic regarding the Tower of Hanoi game is created, let's see how to create the user interface that allows you to present the following moves of the algorithm. The necessary changes in the Program class are as follows:

```
private const int DISCS_COUNT = 10;
private const int DELAY_MS = 250;
private static int _columnSize = 30;
```

First, two constants are declared, namely with the overall number of discs (DISCS_COUNT, set to 10) and the delay (in milliseconds) between two following moves of the algorithm (DELAY_MS, set to 250). Moreover, the private static field is declared, which represents the number of characters used to present a single rod (_columnSize, set to 30).

The Main method in the Program class is shown in the following code snippet:

```
static void Main(string[] args)
{
    _columnSize = Math.Max(6, GetDiscWidth(DISCS_COUNT) + 2);
    HanoiTower algorithm = new HanoiTower(DISCS_COUNT);
    algorithm.MoveCompleted += Algorithm_Visualize;
    Algorithm_Visualize(algorithm, EventArgs.Empty);
    algorithm.Start();
}
```

First, the width of a single column (representing a rod) is calculated with the use of the auxiliary GetDiscWidth method, whose code will be shown later. Then, a new instance of the HanoiTower class is created and it is indicated that the Algorithm_Visualize method will be called when the MoveCompleted event is fired. Next, the afore mentioned Algorithm_Visualize method is called to present the initial state of the game. Finally, the Start method is called to start moving discs between rods.

The code of the Algorithm_Visualize method is as follows:

```
private static void Algorithm_Visualize(
    object sender, EventArgs e)
{
    Console.Clear();

    HanoiTowers algorithm = (HanoiTowers)sender;
    if (algorithm.DiscsCount <= 0)
    {
        return;
    }

    char[][] visualization = InitializeVisualization(algorithm);
    PrepareColumn(visualization, 1, algorithm.DiscsCount,
        algorithm.From);
    PrepareColumn(visualization, 2, algorithm.DiscsCount,
        algorithm.To);
    PrepareColumn(visualization, 3, algorithm.DiscsCount,
        algorithm.Auxiliary);

    Console.WriteLine(Center("FROM") + Center("TO") +
        Center("AUXILIARY"));
    DrawVisualization(visualization);
    Console.WriteLine();
    Console.WriteLine($"Number of moves: {algorithm.MovesCount}");
    Console.WriteLine($"Number of discs: {algorithm.DiscsCount}");

    Thread.Sleep(DELAY_MS);
}
```

The visualization of the algorithm should present the current state of the game in the console. Thus, whenever a refresh is necessary, the `Algorithm_Visualize` method clears the current content of the console (by calling the `Clear` method). Then, it calls the `InitializeVisualization` method to prepare the jagged array with content that should be written in the console. Such content consists of three columns, which are prepared by calling the `PrepareColumn` method. After calling it, the `visualization` array contains data that should just be presented in the console, without any additional transformations. To do so, the `DrawVisualization` method is called. Of course, the header and additional explanations are written to the console using the `WriteLine` method of the `Console` class.

The important role is performed by the last line of code, where the `Sleep` method of the `Thread` class (from the `System.Threading` namespace) is called. It suspends the current thread for `DELAY_MS` milliseconds. Such a line is added to present the following steps of the algorithm in a convenient way for the user.

Let's take a look at the code for the `InitializeVisualization` method:

```
private static char[][] InitializeVisualization(
    HanoiTowers algorithm)
{
    char[][] visualization = new char[algorithm.DiscsCount][];

    for (int y = 0; y < visualization.Length; y++)
    {
        visualization[y] = new char[_columnSize * 3];
        for (int x = 0; x < _columnSize * 3; x++)
        {
            visualization[y][x] = ' ';
        }
    }

    return visualization;
}
```

The method declares the jagged array, with the number of rows equal to the overall number of discs (the `DiscsCount` property). The number of columns is equal to the value of the `_columnSize` field multiplied by 3 (to present three rods). Within the method, two `for` loops are used to iterate through the following rows (the first `for` loop) and through all columns (the second `for` loop). By default, all elements in the array are initialized with single spaces. Finally, the initialized array is returned.

To fill the afore mentioned jagged array with the illustration of the current state of the rod, you need to call the `PrepareColumn` method, whose code is as follows:

```
private static void PrepareColumn(char[][] visualization,
    int column, int discsCount, Stack<int> stack)
{
    int margin = _columnSize * (column - 1);
    for (int y = 0; y < stack.Count; y++)
    {
        int size = stack.ElementAt(y);
        int row = discsCount - (stack.Count - y);
        int columnStart = margin + discsCount - size;
        int columnEnd = columnStart + GetDiscWidth(size);
        for (int x = columnStart; x <= columnEnd; x++)
        {
            visualization[row][x] = '=';
        }
    }
}
```

First, the left margin is calculated to add data in the correct section within the overall array, that is, within the correct range of columns. However, the main part of the method is the `for` loop, where the number of iterations is equal to the number of discs located in the given stack. In each iteration, the size of the current disc is read using the `ElementAt` extension method (from the `System.Linq` namespace). Next, you calculate an index of a row, where the disc should be shown, as well as the start and end indices for the columns. Finally, the `for` loop is used to insert the equals sign (=) in proper locations in the jagged array, passed as the `visualization` parameter.

The next visualization-related method is `DrawVisualization`, which is as follows:

```
private static void DrawVisualization(char[][] visualization)
{
    for (int y = 0; y < visualization.Length; y++)
    {
        Console.WriteLine(visualization[y]);
    }
}
```

The method just iterates through all elements of the jagged array passed as the `visualization` parameter and calls the `WriteLine` method for each array located within the jagged array. As a result, data located in the whole array are written to the console.

One of the auxiliary methods is `Center`. Its aim is to add additional spaces before and after the text, passed as the parameter, to center the text in the column. The code of this method is as follows:

```
private static string Center(string text)
{
    int margin = (_columnSize - text.Length) / 2;
    return text.PadLeft(margin + text.Length)
        .PadRight(_columnSize);
}
```

Another method is `GetDiscWidth`, which just returns the number of characters necessary to present the disc with the size specified by the parameter. Its code is as follows:

```
private static int GetDiscWidth(int size)
{
    return 2 * size - 1;
}
```

You have already added the necessary code to run the application, which will present the following moves in the Tower of Hanoi mathematical game. Let's launch the application and see it in action!

Just after starting the program, you will see a result similar to the following, where all discs are located in the first rod (FROM):

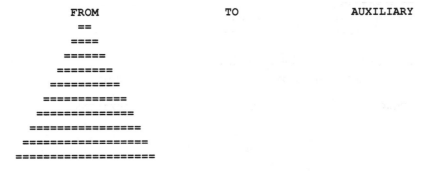

In the next step, the smallest disc is moved from the top of the first rod (FROM) to the top of the third rod (AUXILIARY), as shown in the following illustration:

While making many other moves, you can see how discs are moved between all three rods. One of the intermediate states is as follows:

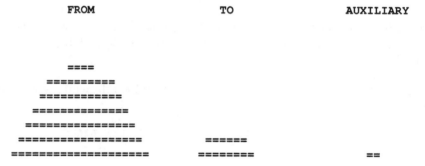

When the necessary moves are completed, all discs are moved from the first disc (FROM) to the second one (TO). The final result is presented in the following illustration:

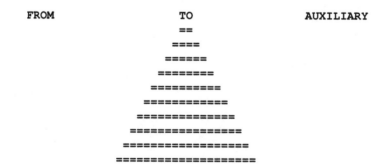

Finally, it is worth mentioning the number of moves necessary to complete the Tower of Hanoi game. In the case of 10 discs, the number of moves is 1,023. If you use only three discs, the number of moves is only seven. Generally speaking, the number of moves can be calculated with the formula 2^n-1, where n is the number of discs.

That's all! In this section, you have learned the first limited access data structure, namely a stack. Now, it is high time that you get to know more about queues. Let's start!

Queues

A **queue** is a data structure that can be presented using the example of a line of people waiting in a shop at the checkout. New people stand at the end of the line, and the next person is taken to the checkout from the beginning of the line. You are not allowed to choose a person from the middle and serve him or her in a different order.

The queue data structure operates in exactly the same way. You can only add new elements at the end of the queue (the **enqueue** operation) and remove an element from the queue only from the beginning of the queue (the **dequeue** operation). For this reason, this data structure is consistent with the **FIFO** principle, which stands for **First-In First-Out**. In the example regarding a line of people waiting in a shop at the checkout, people who come first (first-in) will be served before those who come later (first-out).

The operation of a queue is presented in the following diagram:

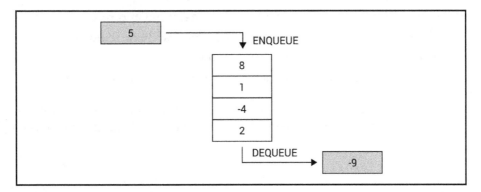

It is worth mentioning that a queue is a **recursive data structure**, similarly as a stack. This means that a queue can be either empty or consists of the first element and the rest of the queue, which also forms a queue, as shown in the following diagram (the beginning of the queue is marked in gray):

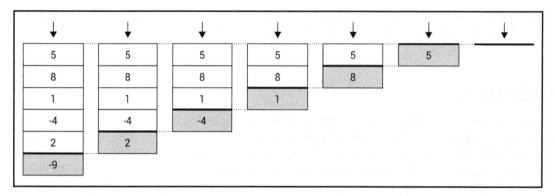

The queue data structure seems to be very easy to understand, as well as similar to a stack, apart from the way of removing an element. Does this mean that you can also use a built-in class to use a queue in your programs? Fortunately, yes! The available generic class is named Queue and is defined in the System.Collections.Generic namespace.

The Queue class contains a set of methods, such as:

- Enqueue, to add an element at the end of the queue
- Dequeue, to remove an element from the beginning and return it
- Peek, to return an element from the beginning without removing it
- Clear, to remove all elements from the queue
- Contains, to check whether the queue contains the given element

The Queue class also contains the Count property, which returns the total number of elements located in the queue. It can be used to easily check whether the queue is empty.

It is worth mentioning that the `Enqueue` method is an *O(1)* operation, if the internal array does not need to be reallocated, or *O(n)* otherwise, where *n* is the number of elements in the queue. Both `Dequeue` and `Peek` are *O(1)* operations.

 You can find more information about the `Queue` class at `https://msdn.microsoft.com/library/7977ey2c.aspx`.

The additional comment is necessary for the scenarios where you want to use a queue concurrently from many threads. In such a case, it is necessary to choose the thread-safe variant of the queue, which is represented by the `ConcurrentQueue` generic class from the `System.Collections.Concurrent` namespace. This class contains a set of built-in methods to perform various operations of the thread-safe queue, such as:

- `Enqueue`, to add an element at the end of the queue
- `TryDequeue`, to try to remove an element from the beginning and return it
- `TryPeek`, to try to return an element from the beginning without removing it

It is worth mentioning that both `TryDequeue` and `TryPeek` have a parameter with the `out` keyword. If the operation is successful, such methods return `true` and the result is returned as a value of the `out` parameter. Moreover, the `ConcurrentQueue` class also contains two properties, namely `Count` to get the number of elements stored in the collection, and `IsEmpty` to return a value indicating whether the queue is empty.

 You can find more information about the `ConcurrentQueue` class at `https://msdn.microsoft.com/library/dd267265.aspx`.

After this short introduction, you should be ready to proceed to two examples representing a queue in the context of a call center, with many callers and one or many consultants.

Example – call center with a single consultant

This first example represents the simple approach to the call center solution, where there are many callers (with different client identifiers), and only one consultant, who answers waiting calls in the same order in which they appear. This scenario is presented in the following diagram:

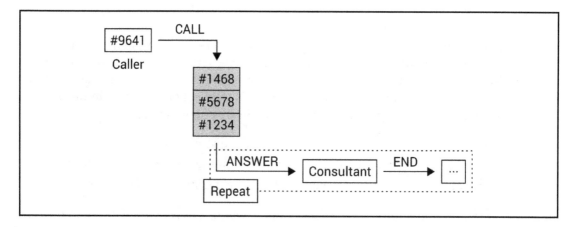

As you can see in the preceding diagram, four calls are performed by callers. They are added to the queue with waiting phone calls, namely from clients **#1234**, **#5678**, **#1468**, and **#9641**. When the consultant is available, he or she answers the phone. When the call ends, the consultant can answer the next waiting call. According to this rule, the consultant will talk with clients in the following order: **#1234**, **#5678**, **#1468**, and **#9641**.

Let's take a look at the code of the first class, named `IncomingCall`, which represents a single incoming call performed by a caller. Its code is as follows:

```
public class IncomingCall
{
    public int Id { get; set; }
    public int ClientId { get; set; }
    public DateTime CallTime { get; set; }
    public DateTime StartTime { get; set; }
    public DateTime EndTime { get; set; }
    public string Consultant { get; set; }
}
```

The class contains six properties representing an identifier of a call (`Id`), a client identifier (`ClientId`), the date and time when the call was started (`CallTime`), when it was answered (`StartTime`), and when it was ended (`EndTime`), as well as the name of the consultant (`Consultant`).

The most important part of this implementation is related to the `CallCenter` class, which represents call-related operations. Its fragment is as follows:

```
public class CallCenter
{
    private int _counter = 0;
    public Queue<IncomingCall> Calls { get; private set; }

    public CallCenter()
    {
        Calls = new Queue<IncomingCall>();
    }
}
```

The `CallCenter` class contains the `_counter` field with the identifier of the last call, as well as the `Calls` queue (with `IncomingCall` instances), where data of waiting calls are stored. In the constructor, a new instance of the `Queue` generic class is created, and its reference is assigned to the `Calls` property.

Of course, the class also contains some methods, such as `Call`, with the following code:

```
public void Call(int clientId)
{
    IncomingCall call = new IncomingCall()
    {
        Id = ++_counter,
        ClientId = clientId,
        CallTime = DateTime.Now
    };
    Calls.Enqueue(call);
}
```

Here, you create a new instance of the `IncomingCall` class and set values of its properties, namely its identifier (together with pre-incrementing the `_counter` field), the client identifier (using the `clientId` parameter), and the call time. The created instance is added to the queue by calling the `Enqueue` method.

The next method is `Answer`, which represents the operation of answering the call, from the person waiting in the queue for the longest time, that is, which is located at the beginning of the queue. The `Answer` method is shown in the following code snippet:

```
public IncomingCall Answer(string consultant)
{
    if (Calls.Count > 0)
    {
        IncomingCall call = Calls.Dequeue();
        call.Consultant = consultant;
        call.StartTime = DateTime.Now;
        return call;
    }
    return null;
}
```

Within this method, you check whether the queue is empty. If so, the method returns `null`, which means that there are no phone calls that can be answered by the consultant. Otherwise, the call is removed from the queue (using the `Dequeue` method), and its properties are updated by setting the consultant name (using the `consultant` parameter) and start time (to the current date and time). At the end, the data of the call is returned.

Apart from the `Call` and `Answer` methods, you should also implement the `End` method, which is called whenever the consultant ends a call with a particular client. In such a case, you just set the end time, as shown in the following piece of code:

```
public void End(IncomingCall call)
{
    call.EndTime = DateTime.Now;
}
```

The last method in the `CallCenter` class is named `AreWaitingCalls`. It returns a value indicating whether there are any waiting calls in the queue, using the `Count` property of the `Queue` class. Its code is as follows:

```
public bool AreWaitingCalls()
{
    return Calls.Count > 0;
}
```

Let's proceed to the `Program` class and its `Main` method:

```
static void Main(string[] args)
{
    Random random = new Random();

    CallCenter center = new CallCenter();
    center.Call(1234);
    center.Call(5678);
    center.Call(1468);
    center.Call(9641);

    while (center.AreWaitingCalls())
    {
        IncomingCall call = center.Answer("Marcin");
        Log($"Call #{call.Id} from {call.ClientId}
            is answered by {call.Consultant}.");
        Thread.Sleep(random.Next(1000, 10000));
        center.End(call);
        Log($"Call #{call.Id} from {call.ClientId}
            is ended by {call.Consultant}.");
    }
}
```

Here, you create a new instance of the `Random` class (for getting random numbers), as well as an instance of the `CallCenter` class. Then, you simulate making a few calls by callers, namely with the following client identifiers: `1234`, `5678`, `1468`, and `9641`. The most interesting part of the code is located in the `while` loop, which is executed until there are no waiting calls in the queue. Within the loop, the consultant answers the call (using the `Answer` method) and the log is generated (using the `Log` auxiliary method). Then, the thread is suspended for a random number of milliseconds (between 1,000 and 10,000) to simulate the various length of a call. When this has elapsed, the call ends (by calling the `End` method) and the proper log is generated.

The last part of code necessary for this example is the `Log` method:

```
private static void Log(string text)
{
    Console.WriteLine($"[{DateTime.Now.ToString("HH:mm:ss")}]
        {text}");
}
```

When you run the example, you will receive a result similar to the following:

```
[15:24:36] Call #1 from 1234 is answered by Marcin.
[15:24:40] Call #1 from 1234 is ended by Marcin.
[15:24:40] Call #2 from 5678 is answered by Marcin.
[15:24:48] Call #2 from 5678 is ended by Marcin.
[15:24:48] Call #3 from 1468 is answered by Marcin.
[15:24:53] Call #3 from 1468 is ended by Marcin.
[15:24:53] Call #4 from 9641 is answered by Marcin.
[15:24:57] Call #4 from 9641 is ended by Marcin.
```

That's all! You have just completed the first example regarding the queue data structure. If you want to learn more about the thread-safe version of the queue, let's proceed to the next section and take a look at the next example.

Example – call center with many consultants

The example shown in the preceding section has been intentionally simplified to make understanding a queue much simpler. However, it is high time you make it more related to real-world problems. In this section, you will see how to expand it to support many consultants, as shown in the following diagram:

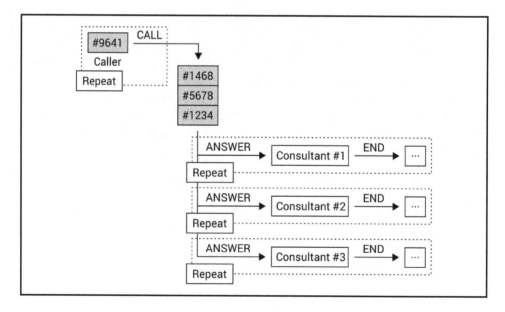

What is important is that both callers and consultants will work at the same time. If there are more incoming calls than available consultants, a new call will be added to the queue and will wait until there is a consultant who can answer the call. If there are too many consultants and few calls, the consultants will wait for a call. To perform this task, you will create a few threads, which will access the queue. Therefore, you need to use the thread-safe version of the queue using the `ConcurrentQueue` class.

Let's take a look at the code! First, you need to declare the `IncomingCall` class, of which the code is exactly the same as in the previous example:

```
public class IncomingCall
{
    public int Id { get; set; }
    public int ClientId { get; set; }
    public DateTime CallTime { get; set; }
    public DateTime StartTime { get; set; }
    public DateTime EndTime { get; set; }
    public string Consultant { get; set; }
}
```

There are various modifications necessary in the `CallCenter` class, such as replacing an instance of the `Queue` class with an instance of the `ConcurrentQueue` generic class. The suitable fragment is shown in the following code snippet:

```
public class CallCenter
{
    private int _counter = 0;
    public ConcurrentQueue<IncomingCall> Calls
        { get; private set; }

    public CallCenter()
    {
        Calls = new ConcurrentQueue<IncomingCall>();
    }
}
```

As the `Enqueue` method is available in both the `Queue` and `ConcurrentQueue` classes, no changes are necessary in the most important part of the `Call` method. However, the small modification is introduced to return the number of waiting calls after adding a new call to the queue. The modified code is follows:

```
public int Call(int clientId)
{
    IncomingCall call = new IncomingCall()
    {
        Id = ++_counter,
        ClientId = clientId,
        CallTime = DateTime.Now
    };
    Calls.Enqueue(call);
    return Calls.Count;
}
```

The `Dequeue` method does not exist in the `ConcurrentQueue` class. For this reason, you need to slightly modify the `Answer` method to use the `TryDequeue` method, which returns a value indicating whether the element is removed from the queue. The removed element is returned using the `out` parameter. The suitable part of code is as follows:

```
public IncomingCall Answer(string consultant)
{
    if (Calls.Count > 0
        && Calls.TryDequeue(out IncomingCall call))
    {
        call.Consultant = consultant;
        call.StartTime = DateTime.Now;
        return call;
    }
    return null;
}
```

No further modifications are necessary in the remaining methods declared in the `CallCenter` class, namely `End` and `AreWaitingCalls`. Their code is as follows:

```
public void End(IncomingCall call)
{
    call.EndTime = DateTime.Now;
}

public bool AreWaitingCalls()
{
    return Calls.Count > 0;
}
```

Significantly more changes are required in the `Program` class. Here, you need to start four threads. The first represents callers, while the other three represent consultants. First, let's take a look at the code of the `Main` method:

```
static void Main(string[] args)
{
    CallCenter center = new CallCenter();
    Parallel.Invoke(
        () => CallersAction(center),
        () => ConsultantAction(center, "Marcin",
            ConsoleColor.Red),
        () => ConsultantAction(center, "James",
            ConsoleColor.Yellow),
        () => ConsultantAction(center, "Olivia",
            ConsoleColor.Green));
}
```

Here, just after the creation of the `CallCenter` instance, you start the execution of four actions, namely representing callers and three consultants, using the `Invoke` static method of the `Parallel` class from the `System.Threading.Tasks` namespace. The lambda expressions are used to specify methods that will be called, namely `CallersAction` for callers-related operations and `ConsultantAction` for consultant-related tasks. You can also specify additional parameters, such as a name and color for a given consultant.

The `CallersAction` method represents operations performed in a cyclical way by many callers. Its code is shown in the following block:

```
private static void CallersAction(CallCenter center)
{
    Random random = new Random();
    while (true)
    {
        int clientId = random.Next(1, 10000);
        int waitingCount = center.Call(clientId);
        Log($"Incoming call from {clientId},
            waiting in the queue: {waitingCount}");
        Thread.Sleep(random.Next(1000, 5000));
    }
}
```

The most important part of the code is the `while` loop, which is executed infinitely. Within it, you get a random number as an identifier of a client (`clientId`) and the `Call` method is called. The number of waiting calls is logged, together with the client identifier. At the end, the callers-related thread is suspended for a random number of milliseconds in the range between 1,000 ms and 5,000 ms, that is, between 1 and 5 seconds, to simulate the delay between another call made by a caller.

The next method is named `ConsultantAction` and is executed on a separate thread for each consultant. The method takes three parameters, namely an instance of the `CallCenter` class, as well as a name and color for the consultant. The code is as follows:

```
private static void ConsultantAction(CallCenter center,
    string name, ConsoleColor color)
{
    Random random = new Random();
    while (true)
    {
        IncomingCall call = center.Answer(name);
        if (call != null)
        {
            Console.ForegroundColor = color;
            Log($"Call #{call.Id} from {call.ClientId} is answered
                by {call.Consultant}.");
            Console.ForegroundColor = ConsoleColor.Gray;

            Thread.Sleep(random.Next(1000, 10000));
            center.End(call);

            Console.ForegroundColor = color;
            Log($"Call #{call.Id} from {call.ClientId}
                is ended by {call.Consultant}.");
            Console.ForegroundColor = ConsoleColor.Gray;

            Thread.Sleep(random.Next(500, 1000));
        }
        else
        {
            Thread.Sleep(100);
        }
    }
}
```

Similar to the `CallersAction` method, the most important and interesting operations are performed in the infinite `while` loop. Within it, the consultant tries to answer the first waiting call using the `Answer` method. If there are no waiting calls, the thread is suspended for 100 ms. Otherwise, the log is presented in the proper color, depending on the current consultant. Then, the thread is suspended for a random period of time between 1 and 10 seconds. After this time, the consultant ends the call, which is indicated by calling the `End` method, and generates the log. At the end, the thread is suspended for the random time between 500 ms and 1,000 ms, which represents the delay between the end of a call and the start of another one.

The last auxiliary method is named `Log` and is exactly the same as in the previous example. Its code is as follows:

```
private static void Log(string text)
{
    Console.WriteLine($"[{DateTime.Now.ToString("HH:mm:ss")}]
        {text}");
}
```

When you run the program and wait for some time, you will receive a result similar to the one shown in the following screenshot:

Congratulations! You have just completed two examples representing the application of a queue in the case of a call center scenario.

It is a good idea to modify various parameters of the program, such as the number of consultants, as well as delay times, especially the delay between the following calls performed by the callers. Then, you will see how the algorithm works in the case when there are too many callers or consultants.

However, how can you handle clients with priority support? In the current solution, they will wait in the same queue as clients with the standard support plan. Do you need to create two queues and first take clients from the prioritized queue? If so, what should happen if you introduce another support plan? Do you need to add another queue and introduce such modifications in the code? Fortunately, no! You can use another data structure, namely a priority queue, to support such a scenario, as explained in detail in the following section.

Priority queues

A **priority queue** makes it possible to extend the concept of a queue by setting **priority** for each element in the queue. It is worth mentioning that the priority can be specified simply as an integer value. However, it depends on the implementation whether smaller or greater values indicate higher priority. Within this chapter, it is assumed that the highest priority is equal to 0, while lower priority is specified by 1, 2, 3, and so on. Thus, the **dequeue** operation will return the element with the highest priority, which has been added first to the queue, as shown in the following diagram:

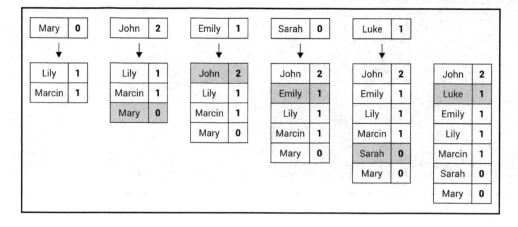

Let's analyze the diagram. First, the priority queue contains two elements with the same priority (equal to **1**), namely **Marcin** and **Lily**. Then, the **Mary** element is added with higher priority (**0**), which means that this element is placed at the beginning of the queue, that is, before **Marcin**. In the next step, the **John** element is added with the lowest priority (**2**), so it is added at the end of the priority queue. The third column presents the addition of the **Emily** element with a priority equal to **1**, that is, the same as **Marcin** and **Lily**. For this reason, the **Emily** element is added just after **Lily**. According to the afore mentioned rules, you add the following elements, namely **Sarah** with a priority set to **0** and **Luke** with a priority equal to **1**. The final order is shown on the right-hand side of the preceding diagram.

Of course, it is possible to implement the priority queue on your own. However, you can simplify this task by using one of the available NuGet packages, namely `OptimizedPriorityQueue`. More information about this package is available at `https://www.nuget.org/packages/OptimizedPriorityQueue`.

Do you know how you can add this package to your project? If not, you should follow these steps:

1. Select **Manage NuGet Packages** from the context menu of the project node in the **Solution Explorer** window.
2. Choose the **Browse** tab in the opened window.
3. Type `OptimizedPriorityQueue` in the search box.
4. Click on the **OptimizedPriorityQueue** item.
5. Press the **Install** button on the right.
6. Click on **OK** in the **Preview Changes** window.
7. Wait until the **Finished** message is shown in the **Output** window.

The `OptimizedPriorityQueue` library significantly simplifies the application of a priority queue in various applications. Within it, the `SimplePriorityQueue` generic class is available, which contains a few useful methods, such as:

- `Enqueue`, to add an element to the priority queue
- `Dequeue`, to remove an element from the beginning and return it
- `GetPriority`, to return the priority of an element
- `UpdatePriority`, to update the priority of an element
- `Contains`, to check whether an element exists in the priority queue
- `Clear`, to remove all elements from the priority queue

You can get the number of elements in the queue using the `Count` property. If you want to get an element from the beginning of the priority queue without removing it, you can use the `First` property. Moreover, the class contains a set of methods, which can be useful in multithreading scenarios, such as `TryDequeue` and `TryRemove`. It is worth mentioning that both the `Enqueue` and `Dequeue` methods are *O(log n)* operations.

After this short introduction to the topic of priority queues, let's proceed to the example of a call center with priority support, which is described in the following section.

Example – call center with priority support

As an example of a priority queue, let's present a simple approach to the call center example, where there are many callers (with different client identifiers), and only one consultant, who answers waiting calls, first from the priority queue and then from the clients with the standard support plan.

The afore mentioned scenario is presented in the following diagram. Calls with the standard priority are marked with **-**, while calls with priority support are indicated by *****, as shown as follows:

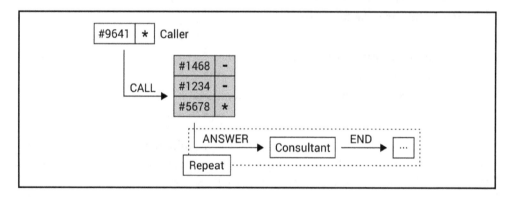

Let's take a look at the order of elements in the priority queue. Currently, it contains only three elements, which will be served in the following order: **#5678** (who has priority support), **#1234**, and **#1468**. However, the call from the client with the identifier **#9641** causes the order to change to **#5678**, **#9641** (due to the priority support), **#1234**, and **#1468**.

It is high time to write some code! First, do not forget to add the
`OptimizedPriorityQueue` package to the project, as explained earlier. When the library is
configured properly, you can proceed to the implementation of the `IncomingCall` class:

```
public class IncomingCall
{
    public int Id { get; set; }
    public int ClientId { get; set; }
    public DateTime CallTime { get; set; }
    public DateTime StartTime { get; set; }
    public DateTime EndTime { get; set; }
    public string Consultant { get; set; }
    public bool IsPriority { get; set; }
}
```

Here, there is only one change in comparison to the previously presented scenario of the
simple call center application, namely the `IsPriority` property is added. It indicates
whether the current call has priority support (`true`) or standard support (`false`).

Some modifications are also necessary in the `CallCenter` class, whose fragment is shown
in the following code snippet:

```
public class CallCenter
{
    private int _counter = 0;
    public SimplePriorityQueue<IncomingCall> Calls
        { get; private set; }

    public CallCenter()
    {
        Calls = new SimplePriorityQueue<IncomingCall>();
    }
}
```

As you can see, the type of the `Calls` property has been changed from `Queue` to the
`SimplePriorityQueue` generic class. The following changes are necessary in the `Call`
method, with the code being presented as follows:

```
public void Call(int clientId, bool isPriority = false)
{
    IncomingCall call = new IncomingCall()
    {
        Id = ++_counter,
        ClientId = clientId,
        CallTime = DateTime.Now,
        IsPriority = isPriority
```

```
    };
    Calls.Enqueue(call, isPriority ? 0 : 1);
}
```

Within this method, a value of the `IsPriority` property (mentioned earlier) is set using the parameter. Moreover, while calling the `Enqueue` method, two parameters are used, not only the value of the element (an instance of the `IncomingCall` class), but also an integer value of the priority, namely 0 in the case of priority support, or 1 otherwise.

No more changes are necessary in the methods of the `CallCenter` class, namely in `Answer`, `End`, and `AreWaitingCalls`. The relevant code is as follows:

```
public IncomingCall Answer(string consultant)
{
    if (Calls.Count > 0)
    {
        IncomingCall call = Calls.Dequeue();
        call.Consultant = consultant;
        call.StartTime = DateTime.Now;
        return call;
    }
    return null;
}

public void End(IncomingCall call)
{
    call.EndTime = DateTime.Now;
}

public bool AreWaitingCalls()
{
    return Calls.Count > 0;
}
```

Finally, let's take a look at the code of the `Main` and `Log` methods in the `Program` class:

```
static void Main(string[] args)
{
    Random random = new Random();

    CallCenter center = new CallCenter();
    center.Call(1234);
    center.Call(5678, true);
    center.Call(1468);
    center.Call(9641, true);

    while (center.AreWaitingCalls())
```

```
        {
            IncomingCall call = center.Answer("Marcin");
            Log($"Call #{call.Id} from {call.ClientId}
                is answered by {call.Consultant} /
                Mode: {(call.IsPriority ? "priority" : "normal")}.");
            Thread.Sleep(random.Next(1000, 10000));
            center.End(call);
            Log($"Call #{call.Id} from {call.ClientId}
                is ended by {call.Consultant}.");
        }
    }
    private static void Log(string text)
    {
        Console.WriteLine($"[{DateTime.Now.ToString("HH:mm:ss")}]
            {text}");
    }
}
```

You may be surprised to learn that only two changes are necessary in this part of the code! The reason for this is that the logic regarding the used data structure is hidden in the CallCenter class. Within the Program class, you call some methods and use properties exposed by the CallCenter class. You just need to modify how you add calls to the queue, as well as adjust the log presented when the call is answered by the consultant to also present the call's priority. That's all!

When you run the application, you will receive a result similar to the following:

```
[15:40:26] Call #2 from 5678 is answered by Marcin / Mode:
priority.
[15:40:35] Call #2 from 5678 is ended by Marcin.
[15:40:35] Call #4 from 9641 is answered by Marcin / Mode:
priority.
[15:40:39] Call #4 from 9641 is ended by Marcin.
[15:40:39] Call #1 from 1234 is answered by Marcin / Mode: normal.
[15:40:48] Call #1 from 1234 is ended by Marcin.
[15:40:48] Call #3 from 1468 is answered by Marcin / Mode: normal.
[15:40:57] Call #3 from 1468 is ended by Marcin.
```

As you can see, the calls are served in the correct order. This means that the calls from clients with priority support are served earlier than calls from clients with the standard support plan, despite the fact that such calls need to wait much longer to be answered.

Summary

In this chapter, you have learned about three limited access data structures, namely stacks, queues, and priority queues. It is worth remembering that such data structures have strictly specified ways of accessing elements. All of them also have various real-world applications, and some have been mentioned and described in this book.

First, you saw how the stack operates according to the LIFO principle. In this case, you can only add an element at the top of the stack (the push operation), and only remove an element from the top (the pop operation). The stack has been shown in two examples, namely for reversing a word and for solving the Tower of Hanoi mathematical game.

In the following part of the chapter, you got to know the queue as a data structure, which operates according to the FIFO principle. In this case, enqueue and dequeue operations were presented. The queue has been explained using two examples, both regarding the application simulating a call center. Furthermore, you have learned how to run a few threads, as well as how to use the thread-safe variant of the queue, which is available while developing applications in the C# language.

The third data structure shown in this chapter is named the priority queue and is an extension of the queue that supports priorities of particular elements. To make using this data structure easier, you have been shown how to use the external NuGet package. As an example, the call center scenario has been extended to handle two support plans.

This is just the third chapter of this book and you have already learned a lot about various data structures and algorithms which are useful while developing applications in C#! Are you interested in increasing your knowledge by learning about dictionaries and sets? If so, let's proceed to the next chapter and learn more about such data structures!

4
Dictionaries and Sets

The current chapter will focus on data structures related to dictionaries and sets. A proper application of these data structures makes it possible to map keys to values and perform fast lookup, as well as make various operations on sets. To simplify the understanding of dictionaries and sets, this chapter will contain illustrations and code snippets.

In the first parts of this chapter, you will learn both non-generic and generic versions of a dictionary, that is, a collection of pairs, each consisting of a key and a value. Then, a sorted variant of a dictionary will be presented, as well. You will also see some similarities between dictionaries and lists.

The remaining part of the chapter will show you how to use hash sets, together with the variant, which is named a "sorted" set. Is it possible to have a "sorted" set? You will get to know how to understand this topic while reading the last section.

In this chapter, the following topics will be covered:

- Hash tables
- Dictionaries
- Sorted dictionaries
- Hash sets
- "Sorted" sets

Hash tables

Let's start with the first data structure, which is a **hash table**, also known as a **hash map**. It allows **mapping** keys to particular values, as shown in the following diagram:

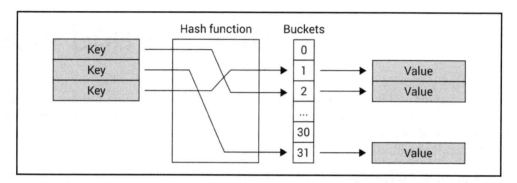

One of the most important assumptions of the hash table is the possibility of very fast lookup for a **Value** based on the **Key**, which should be the *O(1)* operation. To achieve this goal, the **Hash function** is used. It takes the **Key** to generate an index of a bucket, where the **Value** can be found.

For this reason, if you need to find a value of the key, you do not need to iterate through all items in the collection, because you can just use the hash function to easily locate a proper bucket and get the value. Due to the great performance of the hash table, such a data structure is frequently used in many real-world applications, such as for associative arrays, database indices, or cache systems.

As you can see, the role of the hash function is critical and ideally it should generate a unique result for all keys. However, it is possible that the same result is generated for different keys. Such a situation is called a **hash collision** and should be dealt with.

The topic of hash table implementation from scratch seems to be quite difficult, especially when it comes to using the hash function, handling hash collisions, as well as assigning particular keys to buckets. Fortunately, a suitable implementation is available while developing applications in the C# language, and its usage is very simple.

 There are two variants of the hash table-related classes, namely non-generic (`Hashtable`) and generic (`Dictionary`). The first is described in this section, while the other is described in the following section. If you can use the strongly-typed generic version, I strongly recommend using it.

Let's take a look at the `Hashtable` class from the `System.Collections` namespace. As already mentioned, it stores a collection of pairs, where each contains a key and a value. A pair is represented by the `DictionaryEntry` instance.

You can easily get access to a particular element using the indexer. As the `Hashtable` class is a non-generic variant of hash table-related classes, you need to cast the returned result to the proper type (for example, `string`), as shown here:

```
string value = (string)hashtable["key"];
```

In a similar way, you can set the value:

```
hashtable["key"] = "value";
```

It is worth mentioning that the `null` value is incorrect for a `key` of an element, but it is acceptable for `value` of an element.

Apart from the indexer, the class is equipped with a few properties, which makes it possible to get the number of stored elements (`Count`), as well as return the collection of keys or values (`Keys` and `Values`, respectively). Moreover, you can use some available methods, such as to add a new element (`Add`), to remove an element (`Remove`), to remove all elements (`Clear`), as well as to check whether the collection contains a particular key (`Contains` and `ContainsKey`) or a given value (`ContainsValue`).

If you want to get all entries from the hash table, you can use the `foreach` loop to iterate through all pairs stored in the collection, as presented here:

```
foreach (DictionaryEntry entry in hashtable)
{
    Console.WriteLine($"{entry.Key} - {entry.Value}");
}
```

The variable used in the loop has the `DictionaryEntry` type. Therefore, you need to use its `Key` and `Value` properties to access the key and the value, respectively.

 You can find more information about the `Hashtable` class at `https://msdn.microsoft.com/library/system.collections.hashtable.aspx`.

After this short introduction, it is now time to take a look at an example.

Example – phone book

As an example, you will create an application for a phone book. The `Hashtable` class will be used to store entries where the person name is a key and the phone number is a value, as shown in the following diagram:

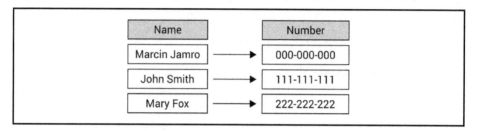

The program will demonstrate how to add elements to the collection, check the number of stored items, iterate through all of them, check whether an element with a given key exists, as well as how to get a value based on the key.

The whole code presented here should be placed in the body of the `Main` method in the `Program` class. At the beginning, let's create a new instance of the `Hashtable` class, as well as initialize it with some entries, as shown in the following code:

```
Hashtable phoneBook = new Hashtable()
{
    { "Marcin Jamro", "000-000-000" },
    { "John Smith", "111-111-111" }
};
phoneBook["Lily Smith"] = "333-333-333";
```

You can add elements to the collection in various ways, such as while creating a new instance of the class (phone numbers for `Marcin Jamro` and `John Smith` in the preceding example), by using the indexer (`Lily Smith`), and using the `Add` method (`Mary Fox`), as shown in the following part of the code:

```
try
{
    phoneBook.Add("Mary Fox", "222-222-222");
}
catch (ArgumentException)
{
    Console.WriteLine("The entry already exists.");
}
```

As you can see, the call of the `Add` method is placed within the `try-catch` statement. Why? The answer is very simple—you cannot add more than one element with the same key, and in such a scenario, `ArgumentException` is thrown. To prevent the application from crashing, the `try-catch` statement is used and a proper message is shown in the console to inform the user about the situation.

> When you use the indexer to set a value for a particular key, it will not throw any exception when there is already an item with the given key. In such a situation, a value of this element will be updated.

In the following part of the code, you iterate through all pairs from the collection and present the results in the console. When there are no items, the additional information will be presented to the user, as shown in the following code snippet:

```
Console.WriteLine("Phone numbers:");
if (phoneBook.Count == 0)
{
    Console.WriteLine("Empty");
}
else
{
    foreach (DictionaryEntry entry in phoneBook)
    {
        Console.WriteLine($" - {entry.Key}: {entry.Value}");
    }
}
```

You can check whether there are no elements in the collection using the `Count` property and comparing its value with `0`. The way of iterating through all pairs is simplified by the availability of the `foreach` loop. However, you need to remember that a single pair from the `Hashtable` class is represented by the `DictionaryEntry` instance and you can access its key and value using the `Key` and `Value` properties.

At the end, let's see how to check whether a specific key exists in the collection, as well as how to get its value. The first task can be accomplished just by calling the `Contains` method, which returns a value indicating whether a suitable element exists (`true`) or not (`false`). The other job (getting a value), uses the indexer and is required to cast the returned value to a suitable type (`string` in this example). This requirement is caused by the non-generic version of the hash table-related class. The code is as follows:

```
Console.WriteLine();
Console.Write("Search by name: ");
string name = Console.ReadLine();
if (phoneBook.Contains(name))
{
    string number = (string)phoneBook[name];
    Console.WriteLine($"Found phone number: {number}");
}
else
{
    Console.WriteLine("The entry does not exist.");
}
```

Your first program using the hash table is ready! After launching it, you will receive a result similar to the following:

```
Phone numbers:
 - John Smith: 111-111-111
 - Mary Fox: 222-222-222
 - Lily Smith: 333-333-333
 - Marcin Jamro: 000-000-000
Search by name: Mary Fox
Found phone number: 222-222-222
```

It is worth noting that the order of pairs stored using the `Hashtable` class is not consistent with the order of their addition or keys. For this reason, if you need to present the sorted results, you need to sort the elements on your own or use another data structure, namely `SortedDictionary`, which is described later in the book.

However, for now, let's take a look at one of the most common classes used while developing in C#, namely `Dictionary`, which is a generic version of hash table-related classes.

Dictionaries

In the previous section, you got to know the `Hashtable` class as a non-generic variant of the hash table-related classes. However, it has a significant limitation, because it does not allow you to specify a type of a key and a value. Both the `Key` and `Value` properties of the `DictionaryEntry` class are of the `object` type. Therefore, you need to perform boxing and unboxing operations, even if all keys and values have the same type.

If you want to benefit from the strongly typed variant, you can use the `Dictionary` generic class, which is the main subject of this section of the chapter.

First of all, you should specify two types namely, a type of a key and a value, while creating an instance of the `Dictionary` class. Moreover, it is possible to define initial content of the dictionary using the following code:

```
Dictionary<string, string> dictionary =
    new Dictionary<string, string>
{
    { "Key 1", "Value 1" },
    { "Key 2", "Value 2" }
};
```

In the preceding code, a new instance of the `Dictionary` class is created. It stores `string`-based keys and values. By default, two entries exist in the dictionary, namely the keys `Key 1` and `Key 2`. Their values are `Value 1` and `Value 2`.

Similar to the `Hashtable` class, here you can also use the indexer to get access to a particular element within the collection, as shown in the following line of code:

```
string value = dictionary["key"];
```

It is worth noting that casting to the `string` type is unnecessary, because `Dictionary` is the strongly typed version of the hash table-related classes. Therefore, the returned value already has the proper type.

If an element with the given key does not exist in the collection, `KeyNotFoundException` is thrown. To avoid problems, you can do one of the following:

- Place the line of code in the `try-catch` block
- Check whether the element exists (by calling `ContainsKey`)
- Use the `TryGetValue` method

You can add a new element or update a value of the existing one using the indexer, as shown in the following line of code:

```
dictionary["key"] = "value";
```

Similar to the non-generic variant, the key cannot be equal to null, but a value can be, of course, if it is allowed by the type of values stored in the collection. Moreover, the performance of getting a value of an element, adding a new element, or updating an existing one, is approaching the *O(1)* operation.

The Dictionary class is equipped with a few properties, which makes it possible to get the number of stored elements (Count), as well as return the collection of keys or values (Keys and Values, respectively). Moreover, you can use the available methods, such as for adding a new element (Add), removing an item (Remove), removing all elements (Clear), as well as checking whether the collection contains a particular key (ContainsKey) or a given value (ContainsValue). You can also use the TryGetValue method to try to get a value for a given key and return it (if the element exists) or return null (otherwise).

 While scenarios of returning a value by a given key (using an indexer or TryGetValue) and checking whether the given key exists (ContainsKey) are approaching the *O(1)* operation, the process of checking whether the collection contains a given value (ContainsValue) is the *O(n)* operation and requires you to search the entire collection for the particular value.

If you want to iterate through all pairs stored in the collection, you can use the foreach loop. However, the variable used in the loop is an instance of the KeyValuePair generic class with Key and Value properties, allowing you to access the key and the value. The foreach loop is shown in the following code snippet:

```
foreach (KeyValuePair<string, string> pair in dictionary)
{
    Console.WriteLine($"{pair.Key} - {pair.Value}");
}
```

Do you remember the thread-safe versions of some classes from the previous chapter? If so, the situation looks quite similar in the case of the Dictionary class, because the ConcurrentDictionary class (from the System.Collections.Concurrent namespace) is available. It is equipped with a set of methods, such as TryAdd, TryUpdate, AddOrUpdate, and GetOrAdd.

You can find more information about the `Dictionary` generic class at https://msdn.microsoft.com/library/xfhwa508.aspx, while details of the thread-safe alternative, namely `ConcurrentDictionary`, are shown at https://msdn.microsoft.com/library/dd287191.aspx.

Let's start coding! In the following sections, you will find two examples presenting dictionaries.

Example – product location

The first example is the application that helps employees of a shop to find the location of where a product should be placed. Let's imagine that each employee has a phone with your application, which is used to scan the code of the product and the application tells them that the product should be located in area **A1** or **C9**. Sounds interesting, doesn't it?

As the number of products in the shop is often very high, it is necessary to find results quickly. For this reason, the data of products together with their locations will be stored in the hash table, using the generic `Dictionary` class. The key will be the barcode, while the value will be the area code, as shown in the following diagram:

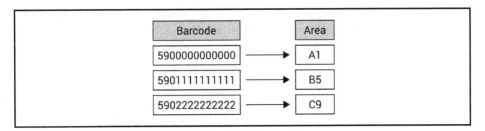

Let's take a look at the code, which should be added to the `Main` method in the `Program` class. At the beginning, you need to create a new collection, as well as add some data:

```
Dictionary<string, string> products =
    new Dictionary<string, string>
{
    { "5900000000000", "A1" },
    { "5901111111111", "B5" },
    { "5902222222222", "C9" }
};
products["5903333333333"] = "D7";
```

The code shows two ways of adding elements to the collection, namely by passing their data while creating a new instance of the class and by using the indexer. A third solution also exists and uses the Add method, as shown in the following part of the code:

```
try
{
    products.Add("5904444444444", "A3");
}
catch (ArgumentException)
{
    Console.WriteLine("The entry already exists.");
}
```

As mentioned in the case of the Hashtable class, ArgumentException is thrown if you want to add the element with the same key as the one already existing in the collection. You can prevent the application from crashing by using the try-catch block.

In the following part of the code, you present the data of all products available in the system. To do so, you use the foreach loop, but before that you check whether there are any elements in the dictionary. If not, the proper message is presented to the user. Otherwise, keys and values from all pairs are presented in the console. It is worth mentioning that a type of the variable within the foreach loop is KeyValuePair<string, string>, thus its Key and Value properties are of the string type, not object, as in the case of the non-generic variant. The code is shown here:

```
Console.WriteLine("All products:");
if (products.Count == 0)
{
    Console.WriteLine("Empty");
}
else
{
    foreach (KeyValuePair<string, string> product in products)
    {
        Console.WriteLine($" - {product.Key}: {product.Value}");
    }
}
```

At the end, let's take a look at the part of the code that makes it possible to find a location for the product by its barcode. To do so, you use `TryGetValue` to check whether the element exists. If so, a message with the target location is presented in the console. Otherwise, other information is shown. What is important is that the `TryGetValue` method uses the `out` parameter to return the found value of the element. The code is as follows:

```
Console.WriteLine();
Console.Write("Search by barcode: ");
string barcode = Console.ReadLine();
if (products.TryGetValue(barcode, out string location))
{
    Console.WriteLine($"The product is in the area {location}.");
}
else
{
    Console.WriteLine("The product does not exist.");
}
```

When you run the program, you will see the list of all products in the shop and the program will ask you to enter the barcode. After typing it, you will receive the message with the area code. The result shown in the console will be similar to the following one:

```
All products:
  - 5900000000000: A1
  - 5901111111111: B5
  - 5902222222222: C9
  - 5903333333333: D7
  - 5904444444444: A3
Search by barcode: 5902222222222
The product is in the area C9.
```

You have just completed the first example! Let's proceed to the next one.

Example – user details

The second example will show you how to store more complex data in the dictionary. In this scenario, you will create an application that shows details of a user based on him or her identifier, as shown in the following diagram:

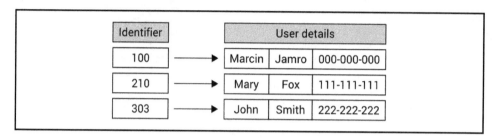

The program should start with the data of three users. You should be able to enter the identifier and see details of the found user. Of course, the situation of non-existence of a given user should be handled by presenting the proper information in the console.

At the beginning, let's add the `Employee` class that just stores the data of an employee, namely first name, last name, and phone number. The code is as follows:

```
public class Employee
{
    public string FirstName { get; set; }
    public string LastName { get; set; }
    public string PhoneNumber { get; set; }
}
```

The next modifications will be performed in the `Main` method in the `Program` class. Here, you create a new instance of the `Dictionary` class and add the data of three employees, using the `Add` method, as shown in the following code snippet:

```
Dictionary<int, Employee> employees =
    new Dictionary<int, Employee>();
employees.Add(100, new Employee() { FirstName = "Marcin",
    LastName = "Jamro", PhoneNumber = "000-000-000" });
employees.Add(210, new Employee() { FirstName = "Mary",
    LastName = "Fox", PhoneNumber = "111-111-111" });
employees.Add(303, new Employee() { FirstName = "John",
    LastName = "Smith", PhoneNumber = "222-222-222" });
```

The most interesting operations are performed in the following do-while loop:

```
bool isCorrect = true;
do
{
    Console.Write("Enter the employee identifier: ");
    string idString = Console.ReadLine();
    isCorrect = int.TryParse(idString, out int id);
    if (isCorrect)
    {
        Console.ForegroundColor = ConsoleColor.White;
        if (employees.TryGetValue(id, out Employee employee))
        {
            Console.WriteLine("First name: {1}{0}Last name: 
                {2}{0}Phone number: {3}",
                Environment.NewLine,
                employee.FirstName,
                employee.LastName,
                employee.PhoneNumber);
        }
        else
        {
            Console.WriteLine("The employee with the given 
                identifier does not exist.");
        }
        Console.ForegroundColor = ConsoleColor.Gray;
    }
}
while (isCorrect);
```

First, the user is asked to enter the identifier of the employee, which is then parsed to the integer value. If this operation is completed successfully, the TryGetValue method is used to try to get details of the user. If the user is found, that is, TryGetValue returns true, the details are presented in the console. Otherwise, "The employee with the given identifier does not exist." message is shown. The loop is executed until the provided identifier cannot be parsed to the integer value.

When you run the application and enter some data, you will receive the following result:

```
Enter the employee identifier: 100
First name: Marcin
Last name: Jamro
Phone number: 000-000-000
Enter the employee identifier: 500
The employee with the given identifier does not exist.
```

That's all! You have just completed two examples showing how to use dictionaries while developing applications in the C# language.

However, another kind of dictionary has been mentioned in the section regarding the `Hashtable` class, namely a sorted dictionary. Are you interested in finding out what it does and how you can use it in your programs? If so, let's proceed to the next section.

Sorted dictionaries

Both non-generic and generic variants of the hash table-related classes do not keep the order of the elements. For this reason, if you need to present data from the collection sorted by keys, you need to sort them prior to presentation. However, you can use another data structure, the **sorted dictionary,** to solve this problem and keep keys sorted all the time. Therefore, you can easily get the sorted collection whenever necessary.

The sorted dictionary is implemented as the `SortedDictionary` generic class, available in the `System.Collections.Generic` namespace. You can specify types for keys and values while creating a new instance of the `SortedDictionary` class. Moreover, the class contains similar properties and methods to `Dictionary`.

First of all, you can use the indexer to get access to a particular element within the collection, as shown in the following line of code:

```
string value = dictionary["key"];
```

You should ensure that the element exists in the collection. Otherwise, `KeyNotFoundException` is thrown.

You can add a new element or update a value of the existing one, as shown in the code:

```
dictionary["key"] = "value";
```

Similar to the `Dictionary` class, a key cannot be equal to `null`, but value can be, of course, if it is allowed by the type of values stored in the collection.

The class is equipped with a few properties, which makes it possible to get the number of stored elements (`Count`), as well as return the collection of keys and values (`Keys` and `Values`, respectively). Moreover, you can use the available methods, such as for adding a new element (`Add`), removing an item (`Remove`), removing all elements (`Clear`), as well as checking whether the collection contains a particular key (`ContainsKey`) or a given value (`ContainsValue`). You can use the `TryGetValue` method to try to get a value for a given key and return it (if the element exists) or return `null` (otherwise).

If you want to iterate through all pairs stored in the collection, you can use the `foreach` loop. The variable used in the loop is an instance of the `KeyValuePair` generic class with `Key` and `Value` properties, allowing you to access the key and the value.

Despite the automatic sorting advantages, the `SortedDictionary` class has some performance drawbacks in comparison with `Dictionary`, because retrieval, insertion, and removal are the *O(log n)* operations, where *n* is the number of elements in the collection, instead of *O(1)*. Moreover, `SortedDictionary` is quite similar to `SortedList`, described in Chapter 2, *Arrays and Lists*. However, it differs in memory-related and performance-related results. The retrieval for both these classes is the *O(log n)* operation, but insertion and removal for unsorted data is *O(log n)* for `SortedDictionary` and *O(n)* for `SortedList`. Of course, more memory is necessary for `SortedDictionary` than for `SortedList`. As you can see, choosing a proper data structure is not an easy task and you should think carefully about the scenarios in which particular data structures will be used and take into account the both pros and cons.

You can find more information about the `SortedDictionary` generic class at `https://msdn.microsoft.com/library/f7fta44c.aspx`.

Let's see the sorted dictionary in action by creating an example.

Example – definitions

As an example, you will create a simple encyclopedia, where you can add entries, as well as show its full content. The encyclopedia can contain millions of entries, so it is crucial to provide its users with the possibility of browsing entries in the correct order, alphabetically by keys, as well as finding entries quickly. For this reason, the sorted dictionary is a good choice in this example.

The idea of the encyclopedia is shown in the following diagram:

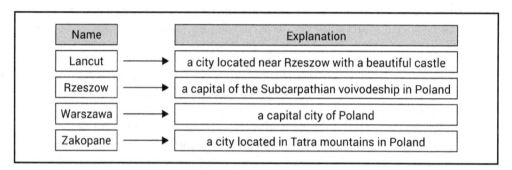

When the program is launched, it presents a simple menu with two options, namely [a] – add and [l] – list. After pressing the *A* key, the application asks you to enter the name and explanation for the entry. If the provided data are correct, a new entry is added to the encyclopedia. If the user presses the *L* key, the data of all entries, sorted by keys, are presented in the console. When any other key is pressed, the additional confirmation is shown and, if confirmed, the program exits.

Let's take a look at the code, which should be placed as the body of the `Main` method in the `Program` class:

```
SortedDictionary<string, string> definitions =
    new SortedDictionary<string, string>();
do
{
    Console.Write("Choose an option ([a] - add, [l] - list): ");
    ConsoleKeyInfo keyInfo = Console.ReadKey();
    Console.WriteLine();
    if (keyInfo.Key == ConsoleKey.A)
    {
        Console.ForegroundColor = ConsoleColor.White;
        Console.Write("Enter the name: ");
        string name = Console.ReadLine();
        Console.Write("Enter the explanation: ");
```

```
        string explanation = Console.ReadLine();
        definitions[name] = explanation;
        Console.ForegroundColor = ConsoleColor.Gray;
    }
    else if (keyInfo.Key == ConsoleKey.L)
    {
        Console.ForegroundColor = ConsoleColor.White;
        foreach (KeyValuePair<string, string> definition
            in definitions)
        {
            Console.WriteLine($"{definition.Key}:
                {definition.Value}");
        }
        Console.ForegroundColor = ConsoleColor.Gray;
    }
    else
    {
        Console.ForegroundColor = ConsoleColor.White;
        Console.WriteLine("Do you want to exit the program?
            Press [y] (yes) or [n] (no).");
        Console.ForegroundColor = ConsoleColor.Gray;
        if (Console.ReadKey().Key == ConsoleKey.Y)
        {
            break;
        }
    }
}
while (true);
```

At the beginning, a new instance of the `SortedDictionary` class is created, which represents a collection of pairs with `string`-based keys and `string`-based values. Then, the infinite `do-while` loop is used. Within it, the program waits until the user presses any key. If it is the *A* key, a name and explanation for the entry are obtained from the values entered by the user. Then, a new entry is added to the dictionary using the indexer. Thus, if the entry with the same key already exists, it will be updated. In the case of pressing the *L* key, the `foreach` loop is used to show all entered entries. When any other key is pressed, another question is presented to the user and the program waits for confirmation. If the user presses *Y*, you break out of the loop.

When you run the program, you can enter a few entries, as well as present them. The result from the console is shown in the following block:

```
Choose an option ([a] - add, [l] - list): a
Enter the name: Zakopane
Enter the explanation: a city located in Tatra mountains in Poland
Choose an option ([a] - add, [l] - list): a
Enter the name: Rzeszow
Enter the explanation: a capital of the Subcarpathian voivodeship
in Poland
Choose an option ([a] - add, [l] - list): a
Enter the name: Warszawa
Enter the explanation: a capital city of Poland
Choose an option ([a] - add, [l] - list): a
Enter the name: Lancut
Enter the explanation: a city located near Rzeszow with
a beautiful castle
Choose an option ([a] - add, [l] - list): l
Lancut: a city located near Rzeszow with a beautiful castle
Rzeszow: a capital of the Subcarpathian voivodeship in Poland
Warszawa: a capital city of Poland
Zakopane: a city located in Tatra mountains in Poland
Choose an option ([a] - add, [l] - list): q
Do you want to exit the program? Press [y] (yes) or [n] (no).
yPress any key to continue . . .
```

So far, you have learned three dictionary-related classes, namely `Hashtable`, `Dictionary`, and `SortedDictionary`. All of them have some specific advantages and they can be used in various scenarios. To make understanding them easier, a few examples have been presented, together with a detailed explanation.

However, do you know that there are also some other data structures that store just keys, without values? Do you want to learn more about them? If so, let's proceed to the next section.

Hash sets

In some algorithms, it is necessary to perform operations on sets with various data. However, what is a **set**? A set is a collection of distinct objects without duplicated elements and without a particular order. Therefore, you can only get to know whether a given element is in the set or not. The sets are strictly connected with the mathematical models and operations, such as union, intersection, subtraction, and symmetric difference.

A set can store various data, such as integer or string values, as shown in the following diagram. Of course, you can also create a set with instances of a user-defined class, as well as add and remove elements from the set at any time.

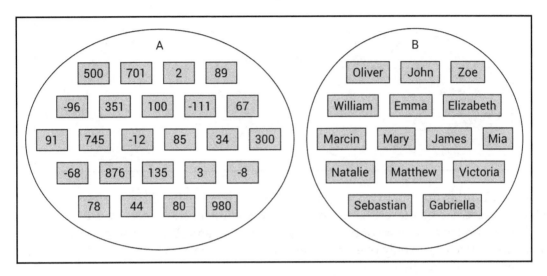

Before seeing sets in action, it is a good idea to remind you of some basic operations that can be performed on two sets, named **A** and **B**. Let's start with the union and intersection, as shown in the following illustration. As you can see, the **union** (shown on the left as **A∪B**) is a set with all elements that belong to **A** or **B**. The **intersection** (presented on the right as **A∩B**) contains only the elements that belong to both **A** and **B**:

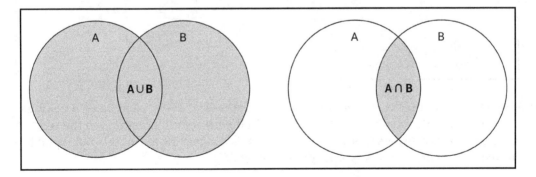

Another common operation is the **set subtraction**. The result set of **A** \ **B** contains elements which are the members of **A** and not the members of **B**. In the following illustration, two examples are presented, namely **A** \ **B** and **B** \ **A**:

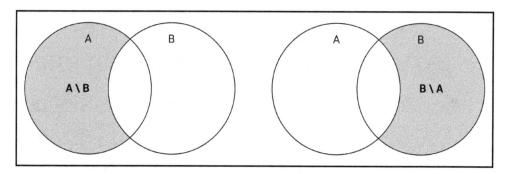

While performing operations on sets, it is also worth mentioning the **symmetric difference**, which is presented on the left-hand side of the following illustration, as **A Δ B**. The final set can be interpreted as a union of two sets, namely (**A** \ **B**) and (**B** \ **A**). Therefore, it contains elements that belong to only one set, either **A** or **B**. The elements that belong to both sets are excluded from the result:

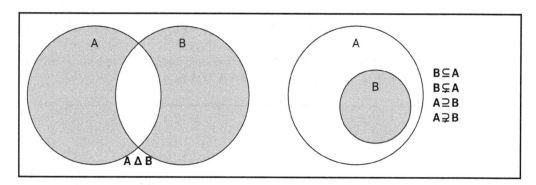

Another important topic is the **relationship** between sets. If every element of **B** belongs also to **A**, it means that **B** is a **subset** of **A**, as shown in the preceding diagram, on the right. At the same time, **A** is a **superset** of **B**. Moreover, if **B** is a subset of **A**, but **B** is not equal to **A**, **B** is a **proper subset** of **A**, and **A** is a **proper superset** of **B**.

While developing applications in the C# language, you can benefit from high-performance operations provided by the HashSet class from the System.Collections.Generic namespace. The class contains a few properties, including Count that returns the number of elements in the set. Moreover, you can use many methods to perform operations of sets, as explained next.

The first group of methods makes it possible to modify the current set (on which the method is called) to create the following, with the set passed as the parameter:

- The union (UnionWith)
- The intersection (IntersectWith)
- The subtraction (ExceptWith)
- The symmetric difference (SymmetricExceptWith)

You can also check the relationships between two sets, such as checking whether the current set (on which the method is called) is:

- A subset (IsSubsetOf) of the set passed as the parameter
- A superset (IsSupersetOf) of the set passed as the parameter
- A proper subset (IsProperSubsetOf) of the set passed as the parameter
- A proper superset (IsProperSupersetOf) of the set passed as the parameter

Furthermore, you can verify whether two sets contain the same elements (SetEquals) or whether two sets have at least one common element (Overlaps).

Apart from the mentioned operations, you can add a new element to the set (Add), remove a particular element (Remove), or remove all elements (Clear), as well as check whether the given element exists in the set (Contains).

 You can find more information about the HashSet generic class at https://msdn.microsoft.com/library/bb359438.aspx.

After this introduction, it is a good idea to try to put the learned information into practice. Thus, let's proceed to two examples that will show you how you can apply hash sets in your applications.

Example – coupons

The first example represents the system that checks whether a one-time coupon has already been used. If so, a suitable message should be presented to the user. Otherwise, the system should inform the user that the coupon is valid and it should be marked as used and cannot be used again. Due to the high number of coupons, it is necessary to choose a data structure that allows for quickly checking whether an element exists in some collection. For this reason, the hash set is chosen as a data structure for storing identifiers of the used coupons. Therefore, you just need to check whether an entered identifier exists in the set.

Let's take a look at the code, which should be added to the `Main` method in the `Program` class. The first part is shown here:

```
HashSet<int> usedCoupons = new HashSet<int>();
do
{
    Console.Write("Enter the coupon number: ");
    string couponString = Console.ReadLine();
    if (int.TryParse(couponString, out int coupon))
    {
        if (usedCoupons.Contains(coupon))
        {
            Console.ForegroundColor = ConsoleColor.Red;
            Console.WriteLine("It has been already used :-(");
            Console.ForegroundColor = ConsoleColor.Gray;
        }
        else
        {
            usedCoupons.Add(coupon);
            Console.ForegroundColor = ConsoleColor.Green;
            Console.WriteLine("Thank you! :-)");
            Console.ForegroundColor = ConsoleColor.Gray;
        }
    }
    else
    {
        break;
    }
}
while (true);
```

At the beginning, a new instance of the `HashSet` generic class, storing integer values, is created. Then, the majority of the operations are performed within the `do-while` loop. Here, the program waits until the user enters the coupon identifier. If it cannot be parsed to the integer value, you break out of the loop. Otherwise, it is checked whether the set already contains an element equal to the identifier of the coupon (using the `Contains` method). If so, the suitable warning information is presented. However, if it does not exist, you add it to the collection of used coupons (using the `Add` method) and inform the user.

When you break out of the loop, you just need to show the complete list of identifiers of the used coupons. You can achieve this goal using the `foreach` loop, iterating over the set, and writing its elements in the console, as shown in the following code:

```
Console.WriteLine();
Console.WriteLine("A list of used coupons:");
foreach (int coupon in usedCoupons)
{
    Console.WriteLine(coupon);
}
```

Now you can launch the application, enter some data, and see how it works. The result written in the console is presented here:

```
Enter the coupon number: 100
Thank you! :-)
Enter the coupon number: 101
Thank you! :-)
Enter the coupon number: 500
Thank you! :-)
Enter the coupon number: 345
Thank you! :-)
Enter the coupon number: 101
It has been already used :-(
Enter the coupon number: 1
A list of used coupons:
100
101
500
345
```

This is the end of the first example. Let's proceed to the next one, where you will see a more complex solution that uses the hash set.

Example – swimming pools

This example presents the system for a SPA center with four swimming pools, namely recreation, competition, thermal, and for kids. Each visitor receives a special wrist band that allows one to enter all the pools. However, it is necessary to scan the wrist band while entering any pool and your program can use such data for creating various statistics.

In this example, the hash set is chosen as a data structure for storing unique numbers of wrist bands that have been scanned in the entrance to each swimming pool. Four sets will be used, one per each pool, as shown in the following diagram. Moreover, they will be grouped in the dictionary to simplify and shorten the code, as well as make future modifications easier:

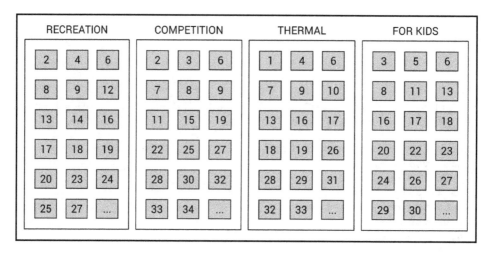

To simplify testing the application, the initial data will be set randomly. Thus, you just need to create statistics, namely the number of visitors by a pool type, the most popular pool, the number of people who visited at least one pool, and the number of people who visited all the pools. All the statistics will use sets.

Let's start with the `PoolTypeEnum` enumeration (declared in the `PoolTypeEnum.cs` file), which represents possible types of swimming pools, as shown in the following code:

```
public enum PoolTypeEnum
{
    RECREATION,
    COMPETITION,
    THERMAL,
    KIDS
};
```

Next, add the `random` private static field to the `Program` class. It will be used to fill the hash set with some random values. The code is as follows:

```
private static Random random = new Random();
```

Then, declare the `GetRandomBoolean` static method in the `Program` class to return the `true` or `false` value, according to the random value. The code is shown here:

```
private static bool GetRandomBoolean()
{
    return random.Next(2) == 1;
}
```

The next changes are necessary only in the `Main` method. The first part is as follows:

```
Dictionary<PoolTypeEnum, HashSet<int>> tickets =
    new Dictionary<PoolTypeEnum, HashSet<int>>()
{
    { PoolTypeEnum.RECREATION, new HashSet<int>() },
    { PoolTypeEnum.COMPETITION, new HashSet<int>() },
    { PoolTypeEnum.THERMAL, new HashSet<int>() },
    { PoolTypeEnum.KIDS, new HashSet<int>() }
};
```

Here, you create a new instance of `Dictionary`. It contains four entries. Each key is of the `PoolTypeEnum` type and each value of the `HashSet<int>` type, that is, a set with integer values.

In the next part, you fill the sets with random values, as shown here:

```
for (int i = 1; i < 100; i++)
{
    foreach (KeyValuePair<PoolTypeEnum, HashSet<int>> type
        in tickets)
    {
        if (GetRandomBoolean())
        {
            type.Value.Add(i);
        }
    }
}
```

To do so, you use two loops, namely `for` and `foreach`. The first iterates 100 times and simulates 100 wrist bands. Within it there is the `foreach` loop that iterates through all available pool types. For each of them, you randomly check whether a visitor entered a particular swimming pool. It is checked by getting a random Boolean value. If `true` is received, an identifier is added to the proper set. The `false` value indicates that the user with the given number of wrist band (`i`) has not entered the current swimming pool.

The remaining code is related to generating various statistics. First, let's present the number of visitors by a pool type. Such a task is very easy, because you just need to iterate through the dictionary, as well as write the pool type and the number of elements in the set (using the `Count` property), as shown in the following part of the code:

```
Console.WriteLine("Number of visitors by a pool type:");
foreach (KeyValuePair<PoolTypeEnum, HashSet<int>> type in tickets)
{
    Console.WriteLine($" - {type.Key.ToString().ToLower()}:
        {type.Value.Count}");
}
```

The next part finds the swimming pool with the maximum number of visitors. It is performed using LINQ and its methods, namely:

- `OrderByDescending` to order elements by the number of elements in the set, in descending order
- `Select` to choose only a pool type
- `FirstOrDefault` to take the first result

Then, you just present the result. The code for doing this is shown here:

```
PoolTypeEnum maxVisitors = tickets
    .OrderByDescending(t => t.Value.Count)
    .Select(t => t.Key)
    .FirstOrDefault();
Console.WriteLine($"Pool '{maxVisitors.ToString().ToLower()}'
    was the most popular.");
```

Then, you need to get the number of people who have visited at least one pool. You can perform this task by creating the union of all the sets and getting the count of the final set. At the beginning, you create a new set and fill it with identifiers regarding the recreation swimming pool. In the following lines of code, you call the `UnionWith` method to create a union with the following three sets. This part of the code is shown here:

```
HashSet<int> any =
    new HashSet<int>(tickets[PoolTypeEnum.RECREATION]);
any.UnionWith(tickets[PoolTypeEnum.COMPETITION]);
any.UnionWith(tickets[PoolTypeEnum.THERMAL]);
any.UnionWith(tickets[PoolTypeEnum.KIDS]);
Console.WriteLine($"{any.Count} people visited at least
    one pool.");
```

The last statistic is the number of people who have visited all the pools during one visit in the SPA center. To perform such a calculation, you just need to create the intersection of all the sets and get the count of the final set. To do so, let's create a new set and fill it with identifiers regarding the recreation swimming pool. Then, call the `IntersectWith` method to create an intersection with the following three sets. At the end, get the number of elements in the set using the `Count` property and present the results, as follows:

```
HashSet<int> all =
    new HashSet<int>(tickets[PoolTypeEnum.RECREATION]);
all.IntersectWith(tickets[PoolTypeEnum.COMPETITION]);
all.IntersectWith(tickets[PoolTypeEnum.THERMAL]);
all.IntersectWith(tickets[PoolTypeEnum.KIDS]);
Console.WriteLine($"{all.Count} people visited all pools.");
```

And that's all! When you run the application, you may receive a result similar to the following one:

```
Number of visitors by a pool type:
 - recreation: 54
 - competition: 44
 - thermal: 48
 - kids: 51

Pool 'recreation' was the most popular.
93 people visited at least one pool.
5 people visited all pools.
```

You have just completed two examples regarding the hash sets. It is a good idea to try to modify the code and add new features to learn more about such a data structure. When you are ready to learn the next data structure, let's continue reading.

"Sorted" sets

The previously described class, HashSet, can be understood as a dictionary that stores only keys, without values. So, if there is the SortedDictionary class, maybe there is also the SortedSet class? Indeed, there is! However, can a set be "sorted"? Why is the "sorted" word written with quotation marks? The answer is simple—by definition, a set stores a collection of distinct objects without duplicated elements and without a particular order. If a set does not support order, how can it be "sorted"? For this reason, a "sorted" set can be understood as a combination of HashSet and SortedList, not a set itself.

The "sorted" set can be used if you want to have a sorted collection of distinct objects without duplicated elements. The suitable class is named SortedSet and is available in the System.Collections.Generic namespace. It has a set of methods, similar to those already described in the case of the HashSet class, such as UnionWith, IntersectWith, ExceptWith, SymmetricExceptWith, Overlaps, IsSubsetOf, IsSupersetOf, IsProperSubsetOf, and IsProperSupersetOf. However, it contains additional properties for returning the minimum and maximum values (Min and Max, respectively). It is worth mentioning also the GetViewBetween method that returns a SortedSet instance with values from the given range.

 You can find more information about the SortedSet generic class at https://msdn.microsoft.com/library/dd412070.aspx.

Let's proceed to a simple example to see how to use the "sorted" set in the code.

Example – removing duplicates

As an example, you will create a simple application that removes duplicates from the list of names. Of course, the comparison of names should be case-insensitive, thus it is not allowed to have both "Marcin" and "marcin" in the same collection.

To see how to perform this goal, let's add the following code as the body of the Main method in the Program class:

```
List<string> names = new List<string>()
{
    "Marcin",
    "Mary",
    "James",
```

```
        "Albert",
        "Lily",
        "Emily",
        "marcin",
        "James",
        "Jane"
};
SortedSet<string> sorted = new SortedSet<string>(
        names,
        Comparer<string>.Create((a, b) =>
            a.ToLower().CompareTo(b.ToLower())));
foreach (string name in sorted)
{
        Console.WriteLine(name);
}
```

At the beginning, a list of names is created and initialized with nine elements, including "Marcin" and "marcin". Then, you create a new instance of the SortedSet class, passing two parameters, namely the list of names and the case-insensitive comparer. At the end, you just iterate through the collection to write names in the console.

When you run the application, you will see the following result:

```
Albert
Emily
James
Jane
Lily
Marcin
Mary
```

This is the last example shown in this chapter. Thus, let's proceed to the summary.

Summary

This fourth chapter of the book focused on hash tables, dictionaries, and sets. All of these collections are interesting data structures that can be used in various scenarios. By presenting such collections with detailed descriptions and examples, you have seen that choosing a proper data structure is not a trivial task and requires analysis of performance-related topics, because some of them operate better in retrieving values and some promote the addition and removal of data.

At the beginning, you have learned how to use two variants of a hash table, namely non-generic (the `Hashtable` class) and generic (`Dictionary`). The huge advantage of these is the very fast lookup for a value based on the key, which is the close *O(1)* operation. To achieve this goal, the hash function is used. Moreover, the sorted dictionary has been introduced as an interesting solution to solve the problem of unsorted items in the collection and to keep keys sorted all the time.

Afterwards, the high-performance solution to set operations was presented. It uses the `HashSet` class, which represents a collection of distinct objects without duplicated elements and without particular order. The class makes it possible to perform various operations on sets, such as union, intersection, subtraction, and symmetric difference. Then, the concept of the "sorted" set (the `SortedSet` class), has been introduced as a sorted collection of distinct objects without duplicated elements.

Do you want to dive deeper into the topic of data structures and algorithms, while developing applications in the C# language? If so, let's proceed to the next chapter where trees are presented.

Variants of Trees

5

In the previous chapters, you have learned about many data structures, starting with simple ones, such as arrays. Now, it is time for you to get to know a significantly more complex group of data structures, namely **trees**.

At the beginning of this chapter, the basic tree will be presented, together with its implementation in the C# language and some examples showing it in action. Then, the binary tree will be introduced with a detailed description of its implementation and an example of its application. The binary search tree is another tree variant, which is one of the most popular types of trees, used in many algorithms. The following two sections will cover self-balancing trees, namely AVL and red-black trees.

The remaining part of the chapter is dedicated to heaps as tree-based data structures. Three kinds of heaps will be presented: binary, binomial, and Fibonacci. Such types will be briefly introduced, and the application of these data structures will be shown, using the external package.

Arrays, lists, stacks, queues, dictionaries, sets, and now... trees. Are you ready to increase the level of difficulty and learn the next set of data structures? If so, let's start reading!

In this chapter, the following topics will be covered:

- Basic trees
- Binary trees
- Binary search trees
- AVL trees
- Red-black trees
- Binary heaps
- Binomial heaps
- Fibonacci heaps

Basic trees

Let's start with introducing trees. What are they? Do you have any ideas about how such a data structure should look? If not, let's take a look at the following diagram, which depicts a tree with captions regarding its particular elements:

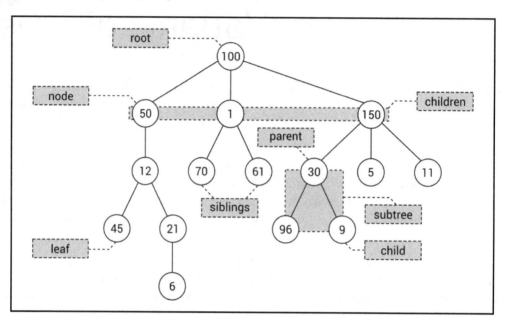

A tree consists of multiple **nodes**, including one **root** (**100** in the diagram). The root does not contain a **parent** node, while all other nodes do. For example, the parent element of node **1** is **100**, while node **96** has node **30** as the **parent**. Moreover, each node can have any number of **child** nodes, such as three **children** (that is, **50**, **1**, and **150**) in the case of the **root**. The child nodes of the same node can be named **siblings**, as in the case of nodes **70** and **61**. A node without children is named a **leaf**, such as **45** and **6** in the diagram. Take a look at the rectangle with three nodes (that is, **30**, **96**, and **9**). Such a part of the tree can be called a **subtree**. Of course, you can find many subtrees in the tree.

Let's briefly talk about the minimum and maximum numbers of children of a node. In general, such numbers are not limited and each node can contain zero, one, two, three, or even more children. However, in practical applications, the number of children is often limited to two, as you will see in the following section.

Implementation

The C#-based implementation of a basic tree seems to be quite obvious and not complicated. To do so, you can declare two classes, representing a single node and a whole tree, as described in the following section.

Node

The first class is named `TreeNode` and is declared as the generic class to provide a developer with the ability to specify the type of data stored in each node. Thus, you can create the strongly-typed solution, which eliminates the necessity of casting objects to target types. The code is as follows:

```
public class TreeNode<T>
{
    public T Data { get; set; }
    public TreeNode<T> Parent { get; set; }
    public List<TreeNode<T>> Children { get; set; }

    public int GetHeight()
    {
        int height = 1;
        TreeNode<T> current = this;
        while (current.Parent != null)
        {
            height++;
            current = current.Parent;
        }
        return height;
    }
}
```

The class contains three properties: the data stored in the node (`Data`) of the type (`T`) specified while creating an instance of the class, a reference to the parent node (`Parent`), and a collection of references to child nodes (`Children`).

Apart from the properties, the `TreeNode` class contains the `GetHeight` method, which returns a height of the node, that is, the distance to the root node. The implementation of this method is very simple, because it just uses the `while` loop to go up from the node until there is no parent element (when the root is reached).

Tree

The next necessary class is named `Tree`, and it represents the whole tree. Its code is even simpler than that presented in the preceding section, and is as follows:

```
public class Tree<T>
{
    public TreeNode<T> Root { get; set; }
}
```

The class contains only one property, `Root`. You can use this property to get access to the root node, and then you can use its `Children` property to obtain data of other nodes located in the tree.

It is worth noting that both `TreeNode` and `Tree` classes are generic and the same type is used in the case of these classes. For instance, if tree nodes should store `string` values, the `string` type should be used in the case of instances of `Tree` and `TreeNode` classes.

Example – hierarchy of identifiers

Do you want to see how to use a tree in a C#-based application? Let's take a look at the first example. The aim is to construct the tree with a few nodes, as shown in the following diagram. Only the group of nodes with darker backgrounds will be presented in the code. However, it is a good idea to adjust the code to extend this tree by yourself.

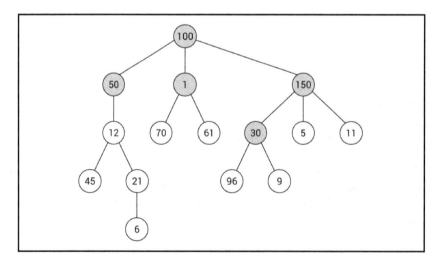

As you can see in the example, each node stores an integer value. Thus, int will be the type used for both Tree and TreeNode classes. The following part of code should be placed in the Main method in the Program class:

```
Tree<int> tree = new Tree<int>();
tree.Root = new TreeNode<int>() { Data = 100 };
tree.Root.Children = new List<TreeNode<int>>
{
    new TreeNode<int>() { Data = 50, Parent = tree.Root },
    new TreeNode<int>() { Data = 1, Parent = tree.Root },
    new TreeNode<int>() { Data = 150, Parent = tree.Root }
};
tree.Root.Children[2].Children = new List<TreeNode<int>>()
{
    new TreeNode<int>()
        { Data = 30, Parent = tree.Root.Children[2] }
};
```

The code looks quite simple, doesn't it?

At the beginning, a new instance of the Tree class is created. Then, the root node is configured by creating a new instance of the TreeNode class, setting a value of the Data property (to 100), and assigning a reference to the TreeNode instance to the Root property.

In the following lines, the child nodes of the root node are specified—nodes with values equal to 50, 1, and 150. For each of them, a value of the Parent property is set to a reference to the previously-added root node.

The remaining part of the code shows how to add a child node for a given node, namely for the third child of the root node, that is, the node with value equal to 150. Here, only one node is added, the one with the value set to 30. Of course, you need to specify a reference to the parent node as well.

That's all! You have created the first program that uses trees. Now you can run it, but you will not see any output in the console. If you want to see how data of nodes are organized, you can debug the program and see values of variables while debugging.

Example – company structure

In the previous example, you saw how to use integer values as data for each node in a tree. However, it is also possible to store instances of user-defined classes in nodes. In this example, you will see how to create a tree presenting the structure of a company, divided into three main departments: development, research, and sales.

Within each department there can be another structure, such as in the case of the development team. Here, **John Smith** is **Head of Development**. He is a boss for **Chris Morris**, who is a manager for two junior developers, **Eric Green** and **Ashley Lopez**. The latter is also a supervisor of **Emily Young**, who is a **Developer Intern**.

An example tree is shown in the following diagram:

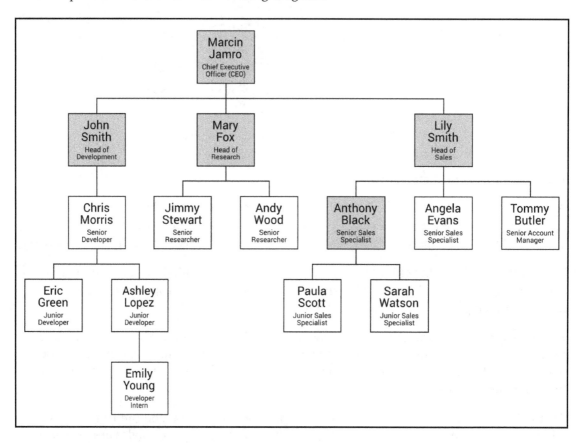

As you can see, each node should store more information than just an integer value. There should be an identifier, a name, and a role. Such data are stored as values of properties in an instance of the `Person` class, as shown in the following code snippet:

```csharp
public class Person
{
    public int Id { get; set; }
    public string Name { get; set; }
    public string Role { get; set; }
```

```
    public Person() { }

    public Person(int id, string name, string role)
    {
        Id = id;
        Name = name;
        Role = role;
    }
}
```

The class contains three properties (Id, Name, and Role), as well as two constructors. The first constructor does not take any parameters, while the other takes three and sets values of particular properties.

Apart from creating a new class, it is also necessary to add some code in the Main method in the Program class. The necessary lines are as follows:

```
Tree<Person> company = new Tree<Person>();
company.Root = new TreeNode<Person>()
{
    Data = new Person(100, "Marcin Jamro", "CEO"),
    Parent = null
};
company.Root.Children = new List<TreeNode<Person>>()
{
    new TreeNode<Person>()
    {
        Data = new Person(1, "John Smith", "Head of Development"),
        Parent = company.Root
    },
    new TreeNode<Person>()
    {
        Data = new Person(50, "Mary Fox", "Head of Research"),
        Parent = company.Root
    },
    new TreeNode<Person>()
    {
        Data = new Person(150, "Lily Smith", "Head of Sales"),
        Parent = company.Root
    }
};
company.Root.Children[2].Children = new List<TreeNode<Person>>()
{
    new TreeNode<Person>()
    {
```

```
        Data = new Person(30, "Anthony Black", "Sales Specialist"),
        Parent = company.Root.Children[2]
    }
};
```

In the first line, a new instance of the `Tree` class is created. It is worth mentioning that the `Person` class is used as a type specified while creating new instances of `Tree` and `TreeNode` classes. Thus, you can easily store more than one simple data for each node.

The remaining lines of code look similar to the first example for basic trees. Here, you also specify the root node (for the CEO role), then configure its child elements (John Smith, Mary Fox, and Lily Smith), and set a child node for one of the existing nodes, namely the node for the Head of Sales.

Does it look simple and straightforward? In the next section, you will see a more restricted, but very important and well-known, variant of trees: the binary tree.

Binary trees

Generally speaking, each node in a basic tree can contain any number of children. However, in the case of **binary trees**, a node cannot contain more than two children. It means that it can contain zero, one, or two child nodes. Such a requirement has an important impact on the shape of a binary tree, as shown in the following two diagrams presenting binary trees:

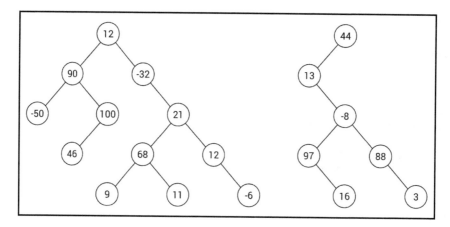

As already mentioned, a node in a binary tree can contain at most two children. For this reason, they are referred to as the **left child** and **right child**. In the case of the binary tree shown on the left-hand side of the preceding diagram, node **21** has two children, **68** as the left child and **12** as the right child, while node **100** has only a left child.

Have you thought about how you can iterate through all the nodes in a tree? How can you specify an order of nodes during **traversal** of a tree? There are three common approaches: pre-order, in-order, and post-order, as shown in the following diagram:

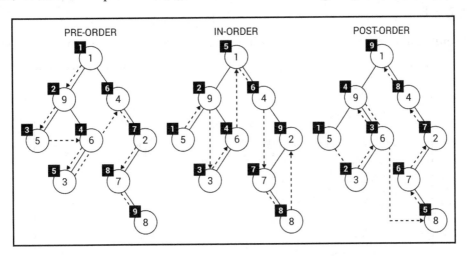

As you can see in the diagram, there are clearly visible differences between the approaches. However, do you have any idea how you can apply pre-order, in-order, or post-order traversals for binary trees? Let's explain all of these approaches in detail.

If you want to traverse a binary tree with the **pre-order** approach, you first need to visit the root node. Then, you visit the left child. Finally, the right child is visited. Of course, such a rule does not apply only to the root node, but to any node within a tree. For this reason, you can understand the order of pre-order traversal as first visiting the current node, then its left child (the whole left subtree using the pre-order approach recursively), and finally its right child (the right subtree in a similar way).

The explanation can sound a bit complicated, so let's take a look at the simple example regarding the tree shown on the left of the preceding diagram. First, the root node (that is, **1**) is visited. Then, you analyze its left child node. For this reason, the next visited node is the current node, **9**. The next step is the pre-order traversal of its left child. Thus, **5** is visited. As this node does not contain any children, you can return to the stage of traversing when **9** is the current node. It has already been visited, as has its left child node, so it is time to proceed to its right child. Here, you first visit the current node, **6**, and follow to its left child, **3**. You can apply the same rules to continue traversing the tree. The final order is **1, 9, 5, 6, 3, 4, 2, 7, 8**.

If it still sounds a bit confusing, the following diagram should remove any confusions:

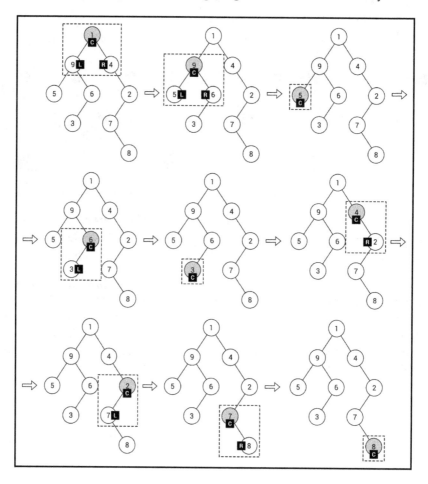

The diagram presents the following steps of the pre-order traversal with additional indicators: **C** for the **current node**, **L** for the **left child**, and **R** for the **right child**.

The second traversal mode is called **in-order**. It differs from the pre-order approach in the order that nodes are visited in: first the left child, then the current node, and then the right child. If you take a look at the example shown in the diagram with all three traversal modes, you can see that the first visited node is **5**. Why? At the beginning, the root node is analyzed, but it is not visited, because the in-order traversal starts with the left child node. Thus, it analyzes node **9**, but it also has a left child, **5**, so you proceed to this node. As this node does not have any children, the current node (**5**) is visited. Then, you return to the step when the current node is **9** and—as its left child has been already visited—you visit also the current node. Next, you follow to the right child, but it has a left child, **3**, which should be visited first. According to the same rules, you visit the remaining nodes in the binary tree. The final order is **5, 9, 3, 6, 1, 4, 7, 8, 2**.

The last traversal mode is named **post-order** and supports the following order of node traversal: the left child, the right child, then the current node. Let's analyze the post-order example shown on the right side of the diagram. At the beginning, the root node is analyzed, but it is not visited, because the post-order traversal starts with the left child node. Thus—as in the case of the in-order approach—you proceed to node **9**, then **5**. Then, you need to analyze the right child of node **9**. However, node **6** has the left child (**3**), which should be visited first. For this reason, after **5**, you visit **3**, and then **6**, followed by **9**. What is interesting is that the root node of the binary tree is visited at the end. The final order is **5, 3, 6, 9, 8, 7, 2, 4, 1**.

You can find more information about binary trees at `https://en.wikipedia.org/wiki/Binary_tree`.

After this short introduction, let's proceed to the C#-based implementation.

Implementation

The implementation of a binary tree is really simple, especially if you use the already-described code for the basic tree. For your convenience, the whole necessary code is placed in the following sections, but only its new parts are explained in detail.

Node

A node in a binary tree is represented by an instance of `BinaryTreeNode`, which inherits from the `TreeNode` generic class with the following code:

```
public class TreeNode<T>
{
    public T Data { get; set; }
    public TreeNode<T> Parent { get; set; }
    public List<TreeNode<T>> Children { get; set; }

    public int GetHeight()
    {
        int height = 1;
        TreeNode<T> current = this;
        while (current.Parent != null)
        {
            height++;
            current = current.Parent;
        }
        return height;
    }
}
```

In the `BinaryTreeNode` class, it is necessary to declare two properties, `Left` and `Right`, which represent both possible children of a node. The relevant part of code is as follows:

```
public class BinaryTreeNode<T> : TreeNode<T>
{
    public BinaryTreeNode() => Children =
        new List<TreeNode<T>>() { null, null };

    public BinaryTreeNode<T> Left
    {
        get { return (BinaryTreeNode<T>)Children[0]; }
        set { Children[0] = value; }
    }

    public BinaryTreeNode<T> Right
    {
        get { return (BinaryTreeNode<T>)Children[1]; }
        set { Children[1] = value; }
    }
}
```

Moreover, you need to ensure that the collection of child nodes contains exactly two items, initially set to `null`. You can achieve this goal by assigning a default value to the `Children` property in the constructor, as shown in the preceding code. Thus, if you want to add a child node, a reference to it should be placed as the first or the second element of the list (the `Children` property). Therefore, such a collection always has exactly two elements and you can access the first or the second element without any exception. If it is set to any node, a reference to it is returned, otherwise `null` is returned.

Tree

The next necessary class is named `BinaryTree`. It represents the whole binary tree. By using the generic class, you can easily specify a type of data stored in each node. The first part of the implementation of the `BinaryTree` class is as follows:

```
public class BinaryTree<T>
{
    public BinaryTreeNode<T> Root { get; set; }
    public int Count { get; set; }
}
```

The `BinaryTree` class contains two properties: `Root`, which indicates the root node (as an instance of the `BinaryTreeNode` class), as well as `Count`, which has the total number of nodes placed in the tree. Of course, these are not the only members of the class, because it can also be equipped with a set of methods regarding traversing the tree.

The first traversal method, described in this book, is pre-order. As a reminder, it first visits the current node, then its left child, followed by the right child. The code of the `TraversePreOrder` method is as follows:

```
private void TraversePreOrder(BinaryTreeNode<T> node,
    List<BinaryTreeNode<T>> result)
{
    if (node != null)
    {
        result.Add(node);
        TraversePreOrder(node.Left, result);
        TraversePreOrder(node.Right, result);
    }
}
```

The method takes two parameters: the current node (node) and the list of already-visited nodes (result). The recursive implementation is very simple. First, you check whether the node exists by ensuring that the parameter is not equal to null. Then, you add the current node to the collection of visited nodes, start the same traversal method for the left child, and—at the end—start it for the right child.

Similar implementation is possible for the in-order and post-order traversal modes. Let's start with the code of the TraverseInOrder method, as follows:

```
private void TraverseInOrder(BinaryTreeNode<T> node,
    List<BinaryTreeNode<T>> result)
{
    if (node != null)
    {
        TraverseInOrder(node.Left, result);
        result.Add(node);
        TraverseInOrder(node.Right, result);
    }
}
```

Here, you recursively call the TraverseInOrder method for the left child, add the current node to the list of visited nodes, and start the in-order traversal for the right child.

The next method is related to the post-order traversal mode, as follows:

```
private void TraversePostOrder(BinaryTreeNode<T> node,
    List<BinaryTreeNode<T>> result)
{
    if (node != null)
    {
        TraversePostOrder(node.Left, result);
        TraversePostOrder(node.Right, result);
        result.Add(node);
    }
}
```

The code is very similar to the already-described methods, but, of course, another order of visiting nodes is applied. Here, you start with the left child, then you visit the right child, followed by the current node.

Finally, let's add the public method for traversing the tree in various modes, which calls private methods presented earlier. The relevant code is as follows:

```
public List<BinaryTreeNode<T>> Traverse(TraversalEnum mode)
{
    List<BinaryTreeNode<T>> nodes = new List<BinaryTreeNode<T>>();
    switch (mode)
    {
        case TraversalEnum.PREORDER:
            TraversePreOrder(Root, nodes);
            break;
        case TraversalEnum.INORDER:
            TraverseInOrder(Root, nodes);
            break;
        case TraversalEnum.POSTORDER:
            TraversePostOrder(Root, nodes);
            break;
    }
    return nodes;
}
```

The method takes only one parameter, a value of the `TraversalEnum` enumeration, which chooses the proper mode from pre-order, in-order, and post-order. The `Traverse` method uses the `switch` statement to call a suitable private method, depending on a value of the parameter.

For using the `Traverse` method, it is also necessary to declare the `TraversalEnum` enumeration, as shown in the following code snippet:

```
public enum TraversalEnum
{
    PREORDER,
    INORDER,
    POSTORDER
}
```

The last method described in this section is `GetHeight`. It returns the height of the tree, which can be understood as the maximum number of steps to travel from any leaf node to the root. The implementation is as follows:

```
public int GetHeight()
{
    int height = 0;
    foreach (BinaryTreeNode<T> node
        in Traverse(TraversalEnum.PREORDER))
    {
```

```
        height = Math.Max(height, node.GetHeight());
    }
    return height;
}
```

The code just iterates through all nodes of the tree using the pre-order traversal, reads the height for the current node (using the GetHeight method from the TreeNode class, described earlier), and saves it as the maximum one, if it is larger than the current maximum value. At the end, the calculated height is returned.

After the introduction to the topic of binary trees, let's see an example where this data structure is used for storing questions and answers in a simple quiz.

Example – simple quiz

As an example of a binary tree, a simple quiz application will be used. The quiz consists of a few questions and answers, shown depending on the previously-taken decisions. The application presents the question, waits until the user presses *Y* (yes) or *N* (no), and proceeds to the next question or shows the answer.

The structure of the quiz is created in the form of a binary tree, as follows:

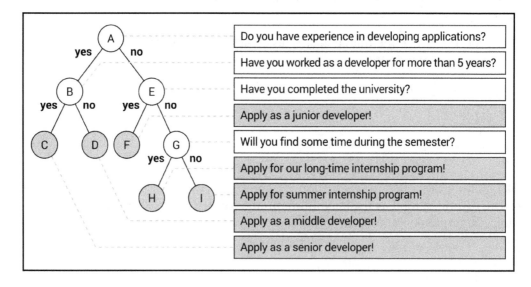

At the beginning, the user is asked whether he or she has any experience in application development. If so, the program asks whether he or she has worked as a developer for more than five years. In the case of a positive answer, the result regarding applying to work as a senior developer is presented. Of course, other answers and questions are shown in the case of different decisions taken by the user.

The implementation of the simple quiz requires the `BinaryTree` and `BinaryTreeNode` classes, which were presented and explained earlier. Apart from them, you should declare the `QuizItem` class to represent a single item, such as a question or an answer. Each item contains only the textual content, stored as a value of the `Text` property. The proper implementation is as follows:

```
public class QuizItem
{
    public string Text { get; set; }
    public QuizItem(string text) => Text = text;
}
```

Some modifications are necessary in the `Program` class. Let's take a look at the modified `Main` method:

```
static void Main(string[] args)
{
    BinaryTree<QuizItem> tree = GetTree();
    BinaryTreeNode<QuizItem> node = tree.Root;
    while (node != null)
    {
        if (node.Left != null || node.Right != null)
        {
            Console.Write(node.Data.Text);
            switch (Console.ReadKey(true).Key)
            {
                case ConsoleKey.Y:
                    WriteAnswer(" Yes");
                    node = node.Left;
                    break;
                case ConsoleKey.N:
                    WriteAnswer(" No");
                    node = node.Right;
                    break;
            }
        }
        else
        {
            WriteAnswer(node.Data.Text);
            node = null;
```

```
            }
        }
    }
```

In the first line within the method, the `GetTree` method (shown in the following code snippet) is called to construct the tree with questions and answers. Then, the root node is taken as the current node, for which the following operations are taken until the answer is reached.

At the beginning, you check whether the left or right child node exists, that is, whether it is a question (not an answer). Then, the textual content is written in the console and the program waits until the user presses a key. If it is equal to *Y*, the information about choosing the *yes* option is shown and the current node's left child is used as the current node. Similar operations are performed in the case of choosing *no*, but then the current node's right child is used instead.

When decisions taken by the user cause the answer to be shown, it is presented in the console and `null` is assigned to the `node` variable. Therefore, you break out of the `while` loop.

As mentioned, the `GetTree` method is used to construct the binary tree with questions and answers. Its code is presented as follows:

```
private static BinaryTree<QuizItem> GetTree()
{
    BinaryTree<QuizItem> tree = new BinaryTree<QuizItem>();
    tree.Root = new BinaryTreeNode<QuizItem>()
    {
        Data = new QuizItem("Do you have experience in developing
            applications?"),
        Children = new List<TreeNode<QuizItem>>()
        {
            new BinaryTreeNode<QuizItem>()
            {
                Data = new QuizItem("Have you worked as a
                    developer for more than 5 years?"),
                Children = new List<TreeNode<QuizItem>>()
                {
                    new BinaryTreeNode<QuizItem>()
                    {
                        Data = new QuizItem("Apply as a senior
                            developer!")
                    },
                    new BinaryTreeNode<QuizItem>()
                    {
                        Data = new QuizItem("Apply as a middle
```

```
                            developer!")
                    }
                }
            },
            new BinaryTreeNode<QuizItem>()
            {
                Data = new QuizItem("Have you completed
                    the university?"),
                Children = new List<TreeNode<QuizItem>>()
                {
                    new BinaryTreeNode<QuizItem>()
                    {
                        Data = new QuizItem("Apply for a junior
                            developer!")
                    },
                    new BinaryTreeNode<QuizItem>()
                    {
                        Data = new QuizItem("Will you find some
                            time during the semester?"),
                        Children = new List<TreeNode<QuizItem>>()
                        {
                            new BinaryTreeNode<QuizItem>()
                            {
                                Data = new QuizItem("Apply for our
                                    long-time internship program!")
                            },
                            new BinaryTreeNode<QuizItem>()
                            {
                                Data = new QuizItem("Apply for
                                    summer internship program!")
                            }
                        }
                    }
                }
            }
        }
    };
    tree.Count = 9;
    return tree;
}
```

At the beginning, a new instance of the BinaryTree generic class is created. It is also configured that each node contains data as an instance of the QuizItem class. Then, you assign a new instance of the BinaryTreeNode to the Root property.

What is interesting is that even while creating questions and answers programmatically, you create some kind of tree-like structure, because you use the `Children` property and specify items directly within such constructions. Therefore, you do not need to create many local variables for all questions and answers. It is worth noting that a question-related node is an instance of the `BinaryTreeNode` class with two child nodes (for *yes* and *no* decisions), while an answer-related node cannot contain any child nodes.

 In the presented solution, the values of the `Parent` property of the `BinaryTreeNode` instances are not set. If you want to use them or get the height of a node or a tree, you should set them on your own.

The last auxiliary method is `WriteAnswer`, with the code being as follows:

```
private static void WriteAnswer(string text)
{
    Console.ForegroundColor = ConsoleColor.White;
    Console.WriteLine(text);
    Console.ForegroundColor = ConsoleColor.Gray;
}
```

The method just presents the text, passed as the parameter, in the white color in the console. It is used to show decisions taken by the user and the textual content of the answer.

The simple quiz application is ready! You can build the project, launch it, and answer a few questions to see the results. Then, let's close the program and proceed to the next section, where a variant of the binary tree data structure is presented.

Binary search trees

A binary tree is an interesting data structure that allows creating a hierarchy of elements, with the restriction that each node can contain at most two children, but without any rules about relationships between the nodes. For this reason, if you want to check whether the binary tree contains a given value, you need to check each node, traversing the tree using one of three available modes: pre-order, in-order, or post-order. This means that the lookup time is linear, namely $O(n)$.

What about a situation where there are some precise rules regarding relations between nodes in the tree? Let's imagine a scenario where you know that the left subtree contains nodes with values smaller than the root's value, while the right subtree contains nodes with values greater than the root's value. Then, you can compare the searched value with the current node and decide whether you should continue searching in the left or right subtree. Such an approach can significantly limit the number of operations necessary to check whether the tree contains a given value. It seems quite interesting, doesn't it?

This approach is applied in the **binary search tree** data structure, which is also referred to as **BST**. It is a kind of a binary tree that introduces two strict rules regarding relations between nodes in the tree. The rules states that for any node:

- Values of all nodes in its left subtree must be smaller than its value
- Values of all nodes in its right subtree must be greater than its value

In general, a BST can contain two or more elements with the same value. However, within this book a simplified version is given, which does not accept more than one element with the same value.

How does it look in practice? Let's take a look at the following diagram of BSTs:

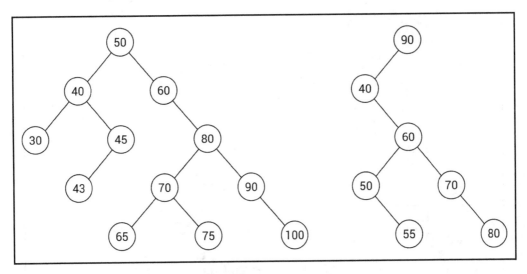

The tree shown on the left-hand side contains 12 nodes. Let's check whether it complies with the BST rule. You can do so by analyzing each node, except leaf nodes, in the tree.

Let's start with the root node (with value **50**) that contains four descendant nodes in the left subtree (**40, 30, 45, 43**), all smaller than **50**. The root node contains seven descendant nodes in the right subtree (**60, 80, 70, 65, 75, 90, 100**), all greater than **50**. That means that the BST rule is satisfied for the root node. If you want to check the BST rule for the node **80**, you will see that the values of all descendant nodes in the left subtree (**70, 65, 75**) are smaller than **80**, while the values in the right subtree (**90, 100**) are greater than **80**. You should perform the same verification for all nodes in the tree. Similarly, you can confirm that the BST from the right-hand side of the diagram adheres to the rules.

However, two such BSTs significantly differ in their topology. Both have the same height, but the number of nodes is different—12 and 7. The one on the left seems to be fat, while the other is rather skinny. Which one is better? To answer to this question, let's think about the algorithm of searching a value in the tree. As an example, the process of searching for the value **43** is described and presented in the following diagram:

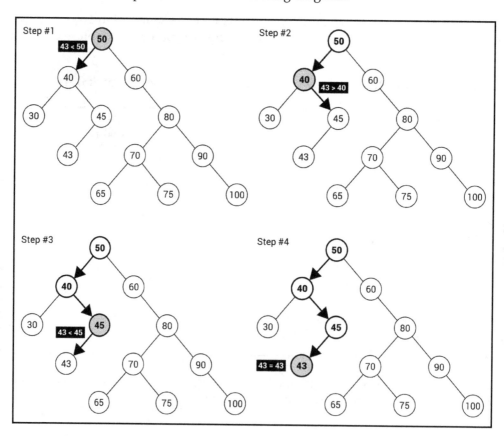

At the beginning, you take a value of the root node (that is, **50**) and check whether the given value (**43**) is smaller or greater. It is smaller, so you proceed to searching in the left subtree. Thus, you compare **43** with **40**. This time, the right subtree is chosen, because **43** is greater than **40**. Next, **43** is compared with **45** and the left subtree is chosen. Here, you compare **43** with **43**. Thus, the given value is found. If you take a look at the tree, you will see that only four comparisons are necessary and the impact on performance is obvious.

For this reason, it is clear than the shape of a tree has a great impact on the lookup performance. Of course, it is much better to have a fat tree with limited height than a skinny tree with bigger height. The performance boost is caused by making decisions as to whether searching should be continued in the left or right subtree, without the necessity of analyzing values of all nodes. If nodes do not have both subtrees, the positive impact on the performance will be limited. In the worst case, when each node contains only one child, the search time is even linear. However, in the ideal BST, the lookup time is the *O(log n)* operation.

 You can find more information about BSTs at
`https://en.wikipedia.org/wiki/Binary_search_tree`.

After this short introduction, let's proceed to the implementation in the C# language. At the end, you will see the example that shows how to use this data structure in practice.

Implementation

The implementation of a BST is more difficult than the previously-described variants of trees. For example, it requires you to prepare operations of insertion and removal of nodes from a tree, which do not break the rule regarding arrangement of elements in the BST. What is more, you need to introduce a mechanism for comparing nodes.

Node

Let's start with the class representing a single node in a tree. Fortunately, you can use the implementation of the class already described for the binary tree (`BinaryTreeNode`) as a base. The modified code is as follows:

```
public class BinaryTreeNode<T> : TreeNode<T>
{
    public BinaryTreeNode() => Children =
        new List<TreeNode<T>>() { null, null };

    public BinaryTreeNode<T> Parent { get; set; }

    public BinaryTreeNode<T> Left
    {
        get { return (BinaryTreeNode<T>)Children[0]; }
        set { Children[0] = value; }
    }

    public BinaryTreeNode<T> Right
    {
        get { return (BinaryTreeNode<T>)Children[1]; }
        set { Children[1] = value; }
    }

    public int GetHeight()
    {
        int height = 1;
        BinaryTreeNode<T> current = this;
        while (current.Parent != null)
        {
            height++;
            current = current.Parent;
        }
        return height;
    }
}
```

As a BST is a variant of a binary tree, each node has a reference to its left and right child node (or `null` if it does not exist), as well as to the parent node. A node stores also a value of a given type. As you can see in the preceding code, two members are added to the `BinaryTreeNode` class, namely the `Parent` property (of the `BinaryTreeNode` type) and the `GetHeight` method. They are moved and adjusted from the implementation of the `TreeNode` class. Its final code is as follows:

```
public class TreeNode<T>
{
    public T Data { get; set; }
    public List<TreeNode<T>> Children { get; set; }
}
```

The reason for the modification is to provide a developer with the simple way of accessing the parent node for a given node without casting from `TreeNode` to `BinaryTreeNode`.

Tree

The whole tree is represented by an instance of the `BinarySearchTree` class, which inherits from the `BinaryTree` generic class, as in the following code snippet:

```
public class BinarySearchTree<T> : BinaryTree<T>
    where T : IComparable
{
}
```

It is worth mentioning that a type of data, stored in each node, should be comparable. For this reason, it has to implement the `IComparable` interface. Such a requirement is necessary because the algorithm needs to know the relationships between values.

Of course, it is not the final version of the implementation of the `BinarySearchTree` class. You will see how to add new features, such as lookup, insertion, and removal of nodes, in the following sections.

Lookup

Let's take a look at the Contains method, which checks whether the tree contains a node with a given value. Of course, this method takes into account the BST rule regarding arrangement of nodes to limit the amount of comparisons. The code is as follows:

```
public bool Contains(T data)
{
    BinaryTreeNode<T> node = Root;
    while (node != null)
    {
        int result = data.CompareTo(node.Data);
        if (result == 0)
        {
            return true;
        }
        else if (result < 0)
        {
            node = node.Left;
        }
        else
        {
            node = node.Right;
        }
    }
    return false;
}
```

The method takes only one parameter, the value that should be found in the tree. Inside the method, the while loop exists. Within it, the searched value is compared with the value of the current node. If they are equal (the comparison returns 0 as the result), the value is found and the true Boolean value is returned to inform that the search is completed successfully. If the searched value is smaller than the value of the current node, the algorithm continues searching in the subtree with the left child of the current node as the root. Otherwise, the right subtree is used instead.

> The CompareTo method is provided by implementation of the IComparable interface from the System namespace. Such a method makes it possible to compare values. If they are equal, 0 is returned. If the object on which the method is called is bigger than the parameter, a value higher than 0 is returned. Otherwise, a value lower than 0 is returned.

The loop is executed until the node is found or there is no suitable child node to follow.

Insertion

The next necessary operation is insertion of a node into a BST. Such a task is a bit more complicated, because you need to find a place for adding a new element that will not violate the BST rules. Let's take a look at the code of the Add method:

```
public void Add(T data)
{
    BinaryTreeNode<T> parent = GetParentForNewNode(data);
    BinaryTreeNode<T> node = new BinaryTreeNode<T>()
        { Data = data, Parent = parent };

    if (parent == null)
    {
        Root = node;
    }
    else if (data.CompareTo(parent.Data) < 0)
    {
        parent.Left = node;
    }
    else
    {
        parent.Right = node;
    }

    Count++;
}
```

The method takes one parameter, a value that should be added to the tree. Within the method, you find a parent element (using the GetParentForNewNode auxiliary method), where a new node should be added as a child. Then, a new instance of the BinaryTreeNode class is created and the values of its Data and Parent properties are set.

In the following part of the method, you check whether the found parent element is equal to null. It means that there are no nodes in the tree and the new node should be added as the root, which is well visible in the line, where a reference to the node is assigned to the Root property. The next comparison checks whether the value for addition is smaller than the value of the parent node. In such a case, the new node should be added as the left child of the parent node. Otherwise, the new node is placed as the right child of the parent node. At the end, the number of elements stored in the tree is incremented.

Let's take a look at the auxiliary method for finding the parent element for a new node:

```
private BinaryTreeNode<T> GetParentForNewNode(T data)
{
    BinaryTreeNode<T> current = Root;
    BinaryTreeNode<T> parent = null;
    while (current != null)
    {
        parent = current;
        int result = data.CompareTo(current.Data);
        if (result == 0)
        {
            throw new ArgumentException(
                $"The node {data} already exists.");
        }
        else if (result < 0)
        {
            current = current.Left;
        }
        else
        {
            current = current.Right;
        }
    }

    return parent;
}
```

This method is named `GetParentForNewNode` and takes one parameter, the value of the new node. Within this method, you declare two variables representing the currently-analyzed node (`current`) and the parent node (`parent`). Such values are modified in the `while` loop until the algorithm finds a proper place for the new node.

In the loop, you store a reference to the current node as the potential parent node. Then, the comparisons are performed, as in the case of the previously-described code snippet. First, you check whether the value for addition is equal to the value of the current node. If so, an exception is thrown, because it is not allowed to add more than one element with the same value to the analyzed version of the BST. If the value for addition is smaller than the value of the current node, the algorithm continues searching for the place for the new node in the left subtree. Otherwise, the right subtree of the current node is used. At the end, the value of the `parent` variable is returned to indicate the found location for the new node.

Removal

Now you know how to create a new BST, add some nodes to it, as well as check whether a given value already exists in the tree. However, can you also remove an item from a tree? Of course! You will learn how to achieve this goal in this section.

The main method regarding removal of a node from the tree is named Remove and takes only one parameter, the value of the node that should be removed. The implementation of the Remove method is as follows:

```
public void Remove(T data)
{
    Remove(Root, data);
}
```

As you can see, the method just calls another method, also named Remove. The implementation of this method is more complicated and is as follows:

```
private void Remove(BinaryTreeNode<T> node, T data)
{
    if (node == null)
    {
        throw new ArgumentException(
            $"The node {data} does not exist.");
    }
    else if (data.CompareTo(node.Data) < 0)
    {
        Remove(node.Left, data);
    }
    else if (data.CompareTo(node.Data) > 0)
    {
        Remove(node.Right, data);
    }
    else
    {
        if (node.Left == null && node.Right == null)
        {
            ReplaceInParent(node, null);
            Count--;
        }
        else if (node.Right == null)
        {
            ReplaceInParent(node, node.Left);
            Count--;
        }
        else if (node.Left == null)
        {
```

```
            ReplaceInParent(node, node.Right);
            Count--;
        }
        else
        {
            BinaryTreeNode<T> successor =
                FindMinimumInSubtree(node.Right);
            node.Data = successor.Data;
            Remove(successor, successor.Data);
        }
    }
}
```

At the beginning, the method checks whether the current node (the `node` parameter) exists. If not, the exception is thrown. Then, the `Remove` method tries to find the node to remove. That is achieved by comparing the value of the current node with the value for removal and calling the `Remove` method recursively for either the left or right subtree of the current node. Such operations are performed in the conditional statements with conditions `data.CompareTo(node.Data) < 0` and `data.CompareTo(node.Data) > 0`.

The most interesting operations are performed in the following part of the method. Here, you need to handle four scenarios of node removal, namely:

- Removing a leaf node
- Removing a node with only a left child
- Removing a node with only a right child
- Removing a node with both left and right children

In the first case, you just update a reference to the deleted node in the parent element. Therefore, there will be no reference from the parent node to the deleted node and it cannot be reached while traversing the tree.

The second case is also simple, because you only need to replace a reference to the deleted node (in the parent element) with the node that is a left child of the deleted node. This scenario is shown in the following diagram, which presents how to remove node **80** with only the left child:

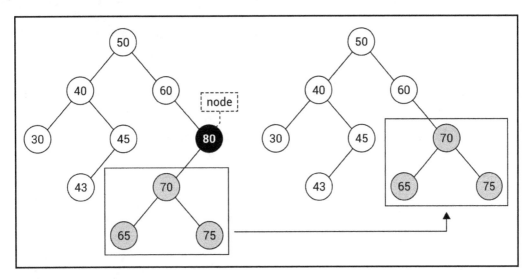

The third case is very similar to the second case. Thus, you just replace a reference to the deleted node (in the parent element) with the node that is a right child of the deleted node.

All those three cases are handled in the code in a similar way, by calling the auxiliary method (ReplaceInParent). It takes two parameters: the node for removal and the node that should replace it in the parent node. For this reason, if you want to remove a leaf node, you just pass null as the second parameter, because you do not want to replace the removed node with anything else. In the case of removing a node with only one child, you pass a reference to the left or right child. Of course, you also need to decrement the counter storing the number of elements located in the tree.

The related part of code is as follows (it differs for various cases):

```
ReplaceInParent(node, node.Left);
Count--;
```

Of course, the most complicated scenario is removal of a node with both child nodes. In such a case, you find a node with the minimum value in the right subtree of the node for removal. Then, you swap the value of the node for removal with the value of the found node. Finally, you just need to call the Remove method recursively for the found node. The relevant part of code is shown in the following code snippet:

```
BinaryTreeNode<T> successor = FindMinimumInSubtree(node.Right);
node.Data = successor.Data;
Remove(successor, successor.Data);
```

The important role is performed by the ReplaceInParent auxiliary method, the code for which is as follows:

```
private void ReplaceInParent(BinaryTreeNode<T> node,
    BinaryTreeNode<T> newNode)
{
    if (node.Parent != null)
    {
        if (node.Parent.Left == node)
        {
            node.Parent.Left = newNode;
        }
        else
        {
            node.Parent.Right = newNode;
        }
    }
    else
    {
        Root = newNode;
    }

    if (newNode != null)
    {
        newNode.Parent = node.Parent;
    }
}
```

The method takes two parameters: the node for removal (node) and the node that should replace it in the parent node (newNode). If the node for removal is not the root, you check whether it is the left child of the parent. If so, a proper reference is updated, that is, the new node is set as the left child of the parent node of the node for removal. In a similar way, the method handles the scenario when the node for removal is the right child of the parent. If the node for removal is the root, the node for replacing is set as the root.

At the end, you check whether the new node is not equal to `null`, that is, you are not removing a leaf node. In such a case, you set a value of the `Parent` property to indicate that the new node should have the same parent as the node for removal.

The last auxiliary method is named `FindMinimumInSubtree` and is as follows:

```
private BinaryTreeNode<T> FindMinimumInSubtree(
    BinaryTreeNode<T> node)
{
    while (node.Left != null)
    {
        node = node.Left;
    }
    return node;
}
```

The method takes only one parameter, namely the root of the subtree, where the minimum value should be found. Within the method, the `while` loop is used to get the leftmost element. When there is no left child, the current value of the `node` variable is returned.

The presented implementation of the BST is based on the code shown at https://en.wikipedia.org/wiki/Binary_search_tree.

The code looks quite simple, doesn't it? However, how does it work in practice? Let's take a look at a diagram depicting the removal of a node with two children:

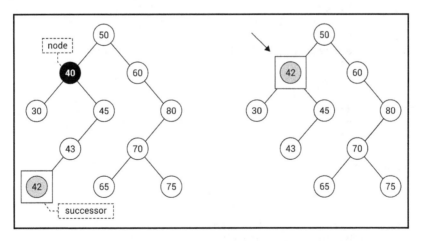

The diagram shows how to remove the node with **40** as the value. To do so, you need to find the successor, that is, the node with the minimum value in the right subtree of the node for removal. The successor is node **42**, which replaces node **40**.

Example – BST visualization

While reading the part regarding the BSTs, you have learned a lot about the data structure. As such, it is high time to create an example program to see this variant of trees in action. The application will show how to create a BST, add some nodes (both manually and using the previously-presented method for insertion), remove nodes, traverse the tree, and visualize the tree in the console.

Let's adjust the code of the Program class, as shown in the following block of code:

```
class Program
{
    private const int COLUMN_WIDTH = 5;

    public static void Main(string[] args)
    {
        Console.OutputEncoding = Encoding.UTF8;

        BinarySearchTree<int> tree = new BinarySearchTree<int>();
        tree.Root = new BinaryTreeNode<int>() { Data = 100 };
        tree.Root.Left = new BinaryTreeNode<int>()
            { Data = 50, Parent = tree.Root };
        tree.Root.Right = new BinaryTreeNode<int>()
            { Data = 150, Parent = tree.Root };
        tree.Count = 3;
        VisualizeTree(tree, "The BST with three nodes
            (50, 100, 150):");

        tree.Add(75);
        tree.Add(125);
        VisualizeTree(tree, "The BST after adding two nodes
            (75, 125):"); (...)

        tree.Remove(25);
        VisualizeTree(tree,
            "The BST after removing the node 25:"); (...)

        Console.Write("Pre-order traversal:\t");
        Console.Write(string.Join(", ", tree.Traverse(
            TraversalEnum.PREORDER).Select(n => n.Data)));
        Console.Write("\nIn-order traversal:\t");
```

```
Console.Write(string.Join(", ", tree.Traverse(
    TraversalEnum.INORDER).Select(n => n.Data)));
Console.Write("\nPost-order traversal:\t");
Console.Write(string.Join(", ", tree.Traverse(
    TraversalEnum.POSTORDER).Select(n => n.Data)));
}
```

At the beginning, a new tree (with nodes storing integer values) is prepared by creating a new instance of the `BinarySearchTree` class. It is configured manually by adding three nodes, together with indicating proper references for children and parent elements. The relevent part of code is as follows:

```
BinarySearchTree<int> tree = new BinarySearchTree<int>();
tree.Root = new BinaryTreeNode<int>() { Data = 100 };
tree.Root.Left = new BinaryTreeNode<int>()
    { Data = 50, Parent = tree.Root };
tree.Root.Right = new BinaryTreeNode<int>()
    { Data = 150, Parent = tree.Root };
tree.Count = 3;
```

Then, you use the `Add` method to add some nodes to the tree, and visualize the current state of the tree using the `VisualizeTree` method, as follows:

```
tree.Add(125);
VisualizeTree(tree, "The BST after adding two nodes (75, 125):");
```

The next set of operations is related to the removal of various nodes from the tree, together with visualization of particular changes. The code is as follows:

```
tree.Remove(25);
VisualizeTree(tree, "The BST after removing the node 25:");
```

At the end, all three traversal modes are presented. The part of code related to the pre-order approach is as follows:

```
Console.WriteLine("Pre-order traversal:\t");
Console.Write(string.Join(", ",
    tree.Traverse(TraversalEnum.PREORDER).Select(n => n.Data)));
```

Another interesting task is the development of the visualization of the tree in the console. Such a feature is really useful, because it allows a comfortable and fast way of observing the tree without the necessity of debugging the application in the IDE and expanding the following elements in the tooltip with the current values of variables. However, presenting the tree in the console is not a trivial task. Fortunately, you do not need to worry about it, because you will learn how to implement such a feature in this section.

First, let's take a look at the `VisualizeTree` method:

```
private static void VisualizeTree(
    BinarySearchTree<int> tree, string caption)
{
    char[][] console = InitializeVisualization(
        tree, out int width);
    VisualizeNode(tree.Root, 0, width / 2, console, width);
    Console.WriteLine(caption);
    foreach (char[] row in console)
    {
        Console.WriteLine(row);
    }
}
```

The method takes two parameters: an instance of the `BinarySearchTree` class representing the whole tree, and the caption that should be shown above the visualization. Within the method, the jagged array (with characters that should be presented in the console) is initialized using the `InitializeVisualization` auxiliary method. Then, you call the `VisualizeNode` recursive method to fill various parts of the jagged array with data regarding particular nodes existing in the tree. At the end, the caption and all rows from the buffer (represented by the jagged array) are written in the console.

The next interesting method is `InitializeVisualization`, which creates the afore mentioned jagged array, as presented in the following code snippet:

```
private static char[][] InitializeVisualization(
    BinarySearchTree<int> tree, out int width)
{
    int height = tree.GetHeight();
    width = (int)Math.Pow(2, height) - 1;
    char[][] console = new char[height * 2][];
    for (int i = 0; i < height * 2; i++)
    {
        console[i] = new char[COLUMN_WIDTH * width];
    }
    return console;
}
```

The jagged array contains the number of rows equal to the height of the tree multiplied by 2 to have space also for lines connecting nodes with parents. The number of columns is calculated according to the formula *width* * 2^{height} - 1, where *width* is the constant value COLUMN_WIDTH and *height* is the height of the tree. These values can be simpler to understand if you take a look at the result in the console:

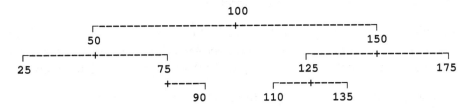

Here, the jagged array has 8 elements. Each is an array with 75 elements. Of course, you can understand it as a screen buffer with 8 rows and 75 columns.

In the VisualizeTree method, VisualizeNode is called. Are you interested to learn about how it works and how you can present not only the values of nodes, but also lines? If so, let's take a look at its code, which is as follows:

```
private static void VisualizeNode(BinaryTreeNode<int> node,
    int row, int column, char[][] console, int width)
{
    if (node != null)
    {
        char[] chars = node.Data.ToString().ToCharArray();
        int margin = (COLUMN_WIDTH - chars.Length) / 2;
        for (int i = 0; i < chars.Length; i++)
        {
            console[row][COLUMN_WIDTH * column + i + margin]
                = chars[i];
        }

        int columnDelta = (width + 1) /
            (int)Math.Pow(2, node.GetHeight() + 1);
        VisualizeNode(node.Left, row + 2, column - columnDelta,
            console, width);
        VisualizeNode(node.Right, row + 2, column + columnDelta,
            console, width);
        DrawLineLeft(node, row, column, console, columnDelta);
        DrawLineRight(node, row, column, console, columnDelta);
    }
}
```

The `VisualizeNode` method takes five parameters: the current node for visualization (node), the index of a row (row), the index of a column (column), the jagged array as the buffer (console), and the width (width). Within the method, there is a check for whether the current node exists. If it does, the value of the node is obtained as the char array, the margin is calculated, and the char array (with character-based representation of the value) is written in the buffer (the console variable).

In the following lines of code, the `VisualizeNode` method is called for left and right child nodes of the current node. Of course, you need to adjust the index of the row (by adding 2) and the index of the column (by adding or subtracting the calculated value).

At the end, the lines are drawn by calling the `DrawLineLeft` and `DrawLineRight` methods. The first is presented in the following code snippet:

```
private static void DrawLineLeft(BinaryTreeNode<int> node,
    int row, int column, char[][] console, int columnDelta)
{
    if (node.Left != null)
    {
        int startColumnIndex =
            COLUMN_WIDTH * (column - columnDelta) + 2;
        int endColumnIndex = COLUMN_WIDTH * column + 2;
        for (int x = startColumnIndex + 1;
            x < endColumnIndex; x++)
        {
            console[row + 1][x] = '-';
        }
        console[row + 1][startColumnIndex] = '\u250c';
        console[row + 1][endColumnIndex] = '+';
    }
}
```

The method also takes five parameters: the current node for which the line should be drawn (node), the index of a row (row), the index of a column (column), the jagged array as the buffer (console), and the delta value calculated in the `VisualizeNode` method (columnDelta). At the beginning, you check whether the current node contains a left child, because only then is it necessary to draw the left part of the line. If so, you calculate the start and end indices of columns, and fill the proper elements of the jagged array with dashes. At the end, the plus sign is added to the jagged array in the place where the drawn line will be connected with the right line of another element. Moreover, the Unicode character ⌐ (\u250c) is added on the other side of the line to create a user-friendly visualization.

In almost the same way, you can draw the right line for the current node. Of course, you need to adjust the code regarding calculating column start and end indices, and change a character used to present changing direction of the line. The final version of the code of the `DrawLineRight` method is as follows:

```
private static void DrawLineRight(BinaryTreeNode<int> node,
    int row, int column, char[][] console, int columnDelta)
{
    if (node.Right != null)
    {
        int startColumnIndex = COLUMN_WIDTH * column + 2;
        int endColumnIndex =
            COLUMN_WIDTH * (column + columnDelta) + 2;
        for (int x = startColumnIndex + 1;
            x < endColumnIndex; x++)
        {
            console[row + 1][x] = '-';
        }
        console[row + 1][startColumnIndex] = '+';
        console[row + 1][endColumnIndex] = '\u2510';
    }
}
```

That's all! You have written the whole code necessary to build the project, launch the program, and see it in action. Just after launching, you will see the first BST, as follows:

```
The BST with three nodes (50, 100, 150):
        100
    ┌----+----┐
 50          150
```

After adding the next two nodes, 75 and 125, the BST looks a bit different:

```
The BST after adding two nodes (75, 125):
            100
    ┌----------+----------┐
 50                      150
    +----┐           ┌----+
        75          125
```

Then, you perform the insertion operation for the next five elements. These operations have a very visible impact on the tree shape, as presented in the console:

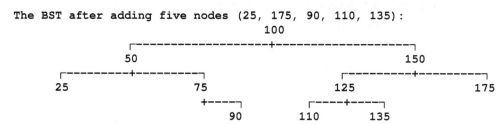

After adding 10 elements, the program shows an impact of removing a particular node on the shape of the tree. To start, let's remove the leaf node with 25 as the value:

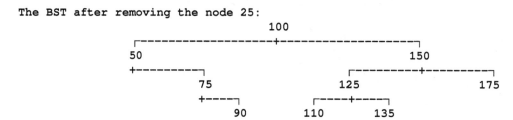

Then, the program checks removing a node with only one child node, namely the right one. What is interesting is that the right child also has a right child. However, the presented algorithm works properly in such conditions and you receive the following result:

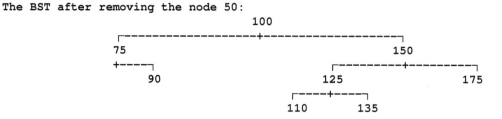

The last removal operation is the most complicated one because it requires you to remove the node with both children, and it also performs the role of the root. In such a case, the leftmost element from the right subtree of the root is found and replaces the node for removal, as shown in the final view of the tree:

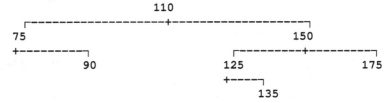

One more set of operations left—the traversal of the tree in three different modes: pre-order, in-order, and post-order. The application presents the following results:

```
Pre-order traversal:    110, 75, 90, 150, 125, 135, 175
In-order traversal:      75, 90, 110, 125, 135, 150, 175
Post-order traversal:    90, 75, 135, 125, 175, 150, 110
```

The created application looks quite impressive, doesn't it? You have created not only the implementation of the binary search tree from scratch, but also prepared the platform for its visualization in the console. Great job!

Let's take one more look at the results of the in-order approach. As you can see, it gives you the nodes sorted in the ascending order in the case of a binary search tree.

However, can you see a potential problem with the created solution? What about a scenario where you remove nodes only from the given area of the tree or when you insert the already-sorted values? It could mean that the fat tree, with proper breadth-depth ratio, could become a skinny one. In the worst case, it could even be depicted as a list, where all nodes have only one child. Do you have any idea how to solve the problem of unbalanced trees and keep them balanced all the time? If not, let's proceed to the next sections, where two variants of self-balancing trees are presented.

AVL trees

In this section, you will get to know one of the variants of **self-balancing trees**, which keeps the tree balanced all the time while adding and removing nodes. However, why is it so important? As already mentioned, the performance of the lookup time depends on the shape of the tree. In the case of improper organization of nodes, forming a list, the process of searching for a given value can be the $O(n)$ operation. With a correctly arranged tree, the performance can be significantly improved to $O(\log n)$.

Do you know that a BST can very easily become an **unbalanced tree**? Let's make a simple test of adding the following nine numbers to the tree, from 1 to 9. Then, you will receive the tree with the shape shown in the following diagram on the left. However, the same values can be arranged in another way, as a **balanced tree**, with significantly better breadth-depth ratio, which is shown on the right:

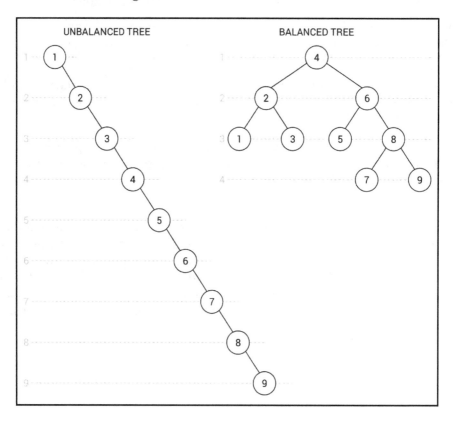

You know what unbalanced and balanced trees are, as well as the aim of self-balancing trees—but what is an AVL tree? How does it work? What rules should be taken into account while using this data structure?

An AVL tree is a binary search tree with the additional requirement that, for each node, the height of its left and right subtrees cannot differ by more than one. Of course, that rule must be maintained after adding and removing nodes from a tree. The important role is performed by **rotations**, used to fix incorrect arrangements of nodes.

While talking about the AVL trees, it is also crucial to indicate the performance of this data structure. In this case, both average and worst-case scenarios of insertion, removal, and lookup are *O(log n)*, so there is significant improvement in the worst-case scenarios in comparison with the binary search tree.

You can find more information about AVL trees at
`https://en.wikipedia.org/wiki/AVL_tree`.

After this short introduction, let's proceed to the implementation.

Implementation

The implementation of the AVL trees, including various rotations necessary to keep the balanced state of a tree, seems to be quite complicated. Fortunately, you do not need to create its implementation from scratch, because you can use one of the available NuGet packages, such as **Adjunct**, which will be used for creating our example.

More information about the Adjunct library can be found at:

- `http://adjunct.codeplex.com/`
- `https://www.nuget.org/packages/adjunct-System.DataStruc`
  `tures.AvlTree/`.

The package provides developers with a few classes that can be used while creating C#-based applications. Let's focus on the `AvlTree` generic class, which represents an AVL tree. The class is very simple to use, so you do not need to know all internal details of the AVL trees and you can easily benefit from its advantages.

For example, the `AvlTree` class is equipped with the `Add` method, which inserts a new node in a proper location in the tree. You can easily remove a node using the `Remove` method. What is more, you can get the height for a given node by calling the `Height` method. It is also possible to get the balance factor for a given node, using `GetBalanceFactor`, which is calculated as the difference between the height of the left and right subtrees.

Another important class is `AvlTreeNode`. It implements the `IBinaryTreeNode` interface and contains four properties representing the height of the node (`Height`), references to the left and right nodes (`Left` and `Right`, respectively), as well as the value stored in the node (`Value`) with a type specified while creating an instance of the class.

Example – keep the tree balanced

As mentioned in the introduction to the topic of AVL trees, there is a very simple test that can cause a BST tree to become unbalanced. You can just add ordered numbers to create a long and skinny tree. So, let's try to create an example of adding exactly the same set of data to an AVL tree, implemented using the `Adjunct` library.

The code placed in the `Main` method in the `Program` class is as follows:

```
AvlTree<int> tree = new AvlTree<int>();
for (int i = 1; i < 10; i++)
{
    tree.Add(i);
}

Console.WriteLine("In-order: "
    + string.Join(", ", tree.GetInorderEnumerator()));
Console.WriteLine("Post-order: "
    + string.Join(", ", tree.GetPostorderEnumerator()));
Console.WriteLine("Breadth-first: "
    + string.Join(", ", tree.GetBreadthFirstEnumerator()));

AvlTreeNode<int> node = tree.FindNode(8);
Console.WriteLine($"Children of node {node.Value} (height =
    {node.Height}): {node.Left.Value} and {node.Right.Value}.");
```

At the beginning, a new instance of the `AvlTree` class is created with indication that nodes will store integer values. Then, the `for` loop is used to add the following numbers (from 1 to 9) to the tree, using the `Add` method. After execution of the loop, the tree should contain 9 nodes, arranged according to the rules of AVL trees.

Moreover, you can traverse the tree using the regular methods: the in-order (`GetInorderEnumerator`), post-order (`GetPostorderEnumerator`), and breadth-first (`GetBreadthFirstEnumerator`) approaches. You have already learned about the first two, but what is **breadth-first traversal**? Its aim is to first visit all nodes on the same depth and then proceed to the next depth, until the maximum depth is reached.

When you run the application, you will receive the following results for the traversals:

```
In-order: 1, 2, 3, 4, 5, 6, 7, 8, 9
Post-order: 1, 3, 2, 5, 7, 9, 8, 6, 4
Breadth-first: 4, 2, 6, 1, 3, 5, 8, 7, 9
```

The last part of code shows the lookup feature of the AVL tree, using the `FindNode` method. It is used to get the `AvlTreeNode` instance representing a node with the given value. Then, you can easily get various data regarding the node, such as its height, as well as the values of left and right children, using the properties of the `AvlTreeNode` class. The part of the console output regarding the lookup feature is as follows:

```
Children of node 8 (height = 2): 7 and 9.
```

Easy, convenient, and without significant development effort—that quite precisely describes the process of applying one of the available packages to support AVL trees. By using it, you do not need to prepare complex code on your own and the number of possible problems can be significantly limited.

Red-black trees

A **Red-black tree**, also referred to as an **RBT**, is the next variant of the self-balancing binary search trees. As a variant of BSTs, this data structure requires that the standard BST rules be maintained. Moreover, the following rules must be taken into account:

- Each node must be colored either red or black. Thus, you need to add additional data for a node that stores a color.

- All nodes with values cannot be leaf nodes. For this reason, the NIL pseudo-nodes should be used as leaves in the tree, while all other nodes are internal ones. Moreover, all NIL pseudo-nodes must be black.
- If a node is red, both its children must be black.
- For any node, the number of black nodes on the route to a descendant leaf (that is, the NIL pseudo-node) must be the same.

The proper RBT is presented in the following diagram:

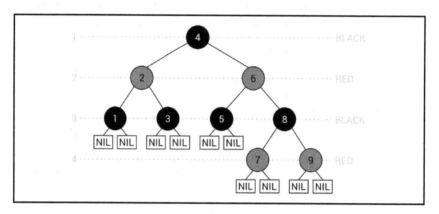

The tree consists of nine nodes, each colored red or black. It is worth mentioning the NIL pseudo-nodes, which are added as leaf nodes. If you again take a look at the set of rules listed afore, you can confirm that all such rules are maintained in this case.

Similarly to AVL trees, RBTs also must maintain the rules after adding or removing a node. In this case, the process of restoring the RBT properties is even more complicated, because it involves both **recoloring** and **rotations**. Fortunately, you do not need to know and understand the internal details, which are quite complex, to benefit from this data structure and apply it in your projects.

While talking about this variant of self-balancing BSTs, it is also worth noting the performance. In both average and worst-case scenarios, insertion, removal, and lookup are *O(log n)* operations, so they are the same as in the case of the AVL trees and much better in worst-case scenarios in comparison with the BSTs.

You can find more information about RBTs at
`https://en.wikipedia.org/wiki/Red-black_tree`.

You have already learned some basic information about RBTs, so let's proceed to the implementation using one of the available libraries.

Implementation

If you want to use an RBT in your application, you can either implement it from scratch or use one of the available libraries, such as `TreeLib`, which you can easily install using the **NuGet Package Manager**. This library supports a few kinds of trees, among which the RBTs exist.

You can find more information about the library at
`http://programmatom.github.io/TreeLib/` and
`https://www.nuget.org/packages/TreeLib`.

As the library provides developers with many classes, it is a good idea to take a look at those related to RBTs. The first class is named `RedBlackTreeList` and represents an RBT. It is a generic class, so you can easily specify a type of data stored in each node.

The class contains a set of methods, including `Add` for inserting a new element to the tree, `Remove` for deleting a node with a particular value, `ContainsKey` for checking whether the tree contains a given value, and `Greatest` and `Least` for returning the maximum and minimum values stored in the tree. Moreover, the class is equipped with a few variants of iterating through the nodes, including the enumerator.

Example – RBT-related features

As in the case of AVL trees, let's prepare the example for RBTs, using the external library. The simple program will show how to create a new tree, add elements, remove a particular node, and benefit from other features of the library.

Let's take a look at the following fragments of the code, which should be added to the Main method in the Program class. The first part is as follows:

```
RedBlackTreeList<int> tree = new RedBlackTreeList<int>();
for (int i = 1; i <= 10; i++)
{
    tree.Add(i);
}
```

Here, a new instance of the RedBlackTreeList class is created. It is indicated that the nodes will store integer values. Then, the for loop is used to add 10 numbers (ordered from 1 to 10) to the tree, using the Add method. After execution, the properly-arranged RBT with 10 elements should be ready.

In the next line, the Remove method is used to delete the node with the value equal to 9:

```
tree.Remove(9);
```

The following lines of code check whether the tree contains a node with the value equal to 5. The returned Boolean value is then used to present the message in the console:

```
bool contains = tree.ContainsKey(5);
Console.WriteLine(
    "Does value exist? " + (contains ? "yes" : "no"));
```

The next part of the code shows how to use the Count property, as well as the Greatest and Least methods. Such features allow the calculation of the total number of elements in the tree, as well as the minimum and maximum values stored within it. The relevant lines of code are as follows:

```
uint count = tree.Count;
tree.Greatest(out int greatest);
tree.Least(out int least);
Console.WriteLine(
    $"{count} elements in the range {least}-{greatest}");
```

While using a tree data structure, you could need some way of getting values of nodes. You can achieve this goal using the GetEnumerable method, as follows:

```
Console.WriteLine(
    "Values: " + string.Join(", ", tree.GetEnumerable()));
```

Another way of iterating through nodes in the tree involves the `foreach` loop, as presented in the following code snippet:

```
Console.Write("Values: ");
foreach (EntryList<int> node in tree)
{
    Console.Write(node + " ");
}
```

As you can see, using the `TreeLib` library is really simple and you can add it to your application in just a few minutes. However, what is the result shown in the console after launching the program? Let's see:

```
Does value exist? yes
9 elements in the range 1-10
Values: 1, 2, 3, 4, 5, 6, 7, 8, 10
Values: 1 2 3 4 5 6 7 8 10
```

It is worth noting that `TreeLib` is not the only package that supports RBTs, so it is a good idea to take a look at various solutions and choose the one that the best suits your needs.

You have reached the end of the part of the chapter regarding self-balancing binary search trees. Now, let's proceed to the last part, which is related to heaps. What are they and why are they located in the chapter about trees? You will learn answers to these and many other questions very soon!

Binary heaps

A **heap** is another variant of a tree, which exists in two versions: **min-heap** and **max-heap**. For each of them, an additional property must be satisfied:

- **For min-heap**: The value of each node must be greater than or equal to the value of its parent node
- **For max-heap**: The value of each node must be less than or equal to the value of its parent node

These rules perform a very important role, because they dictate that the root node always contains the smallest (in the min-heap) or the largest (in the max-heap) value. For this reason, it is a convenient data structure for implementing a priority queue, described in `Chapter 3`, *Stacks and Queues*.

Heaps come in many variants, including **binary heaps**, which are the topic of this section. In this case, a heap must comply to one of the previously-mentioned rules (depending on the kind: min-heap or max-heap) and it must adhere to the **complete binary tree** rule, which requires that each node cannot contain more than two children, as well as all levels of a tree must be fully filled, except the last one, which must be filled from left to right and can have some empty space on the right.

Let's take a look at the following two binary heaps:

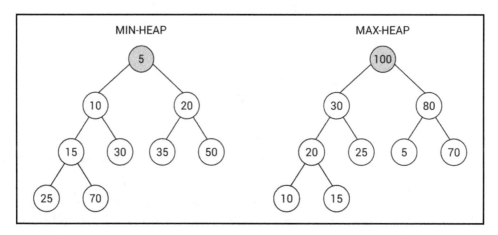

You can easily check whether both heaps adhere to all the rules. As an example, let's verify the heap property for the node with value equal to **20** from the min-heap variant (shown on the left). The node has two children with values **35** and **50**, which are both greater than **20**. In the same way, you can check the remaining nodes in the heap. The binary tree rule is also maintained, as each node contains at most two children. The last requirement is that each level of the tree is fully filled, except the last one which does not need to be fully filled, but must contain nodes from left to right. In the min-heap example, three levels are fully filled (with one, two, and four nodes), while the last level contains two nodes (**25** and **70**), placed on the two leftmost positions. In the same way, you can confirm that the max-heap (shown on the right) is configured properly.

At the end of this short introduction to the topic of heaps, and especially to binary heaps, it is worth mentioning the broad range of applications. As already mentioned, this data structure is a convenient way of implementing the priority queue with the operation of inserting a new value and removing the smallest (in the min-heap) or the largest value (in the max-heap). Moreover, a heap is used in the heap sort algorithm, which is described in the example that follows. The data structure has also many other applications, such as in graph algorithms.

You can find more information about binary heaps at
https://en.wikipedia.org/wiki/Binary_heap.

Are you ready to take a look at the implementation of heaps? If so, let's proceed to the next section, where one of the available libraries supporting heaps is presented.

Implementation

A binary heap can be implemented either from scratch or you can use some of the already-available implementations. One of the solutions is named `Hippie` and can be installed to the project using the **NuGet Package Manager**. The library contains implementation of a few variants of heaps, including binary, binomial, and Fibonacci heaps, which are presented and described in this chapter of the book.

You can find more information about the library at
https://github.com/pomma89/Hippie and
https://www.nuget.org/packages/Hippie.

The library contains a few classes, such as the `MultiHeap` generic class, which is common for various variants of heaps, including binary ones. However, if the same class is used for binary, binomial, and Fibonacci heaps, how can you choose which type of heap you want to use? You can use the static methods from the `HeapFactory` class to solve this problem. As an example, a binary heap can be created using the `NewBinaryHeap` method, as follows:

```
MultiHeap<int> heap = HeapFactory.NewBinaryHeap<int>();
```

The `MultiHeap` class is equipped with a few properties, such as `Count` for getting the total number of elements in the heap and `Min` for retrieving the minimum value. Moreover, the available methods allow adding a new element (`Add`), removing a particular item (`Remove`), removing the minimum value (`RemoveMin`), removing all elements (`Clear`), checking whether the given value exists in the heap (`Contains`), and merging two heaps (`Merge`).

Example – heap sort

As an example of the binary heap, implemented using the `Hippie` library, the heap sort algorithm is presented and described below. The C#-based implementation, which should be added to the `Main` method in the `Program` class, is as follows:

```
List<int> unsorted = new List<int>() { 50, 33, 78, -23, 90, 41 };
MultiHeap<int> heap = HeapFactory.NewBinaryHeap<int>();
unsorted.ForEach(i => heap.Add(i));
Console.WriteLine("Unsorted: " + string.Join(", ", unsorted));

List<int> sorted = new List<int>(heap.Count);
while (heap.Count > 0)
{
    sorted.Add(heap.RemoveMin());
}
Console.WriteLine("Sorted: " + string.Join(", ", sorted));
```

As you can see, the implementation is very simple and short. At the beginning, you create a list with unsorted integer values as the input for the algorithm. Then, a new binary heap is prepared and you add each input value to the heap. At this stage, the elements from the input list are written in the console.

In the following part of the code, a new list is created. It will contain the sorted values and therefore it will contain the result of the algorithm. Then, the `while` loop is used to remove the minimum value from the heap in each iteration. The loop is executed until there are no elements in the heap. At the end, the sorted list is shown in the console.

The heap sort algorithm has $O(n * log(n))$ time complexity.

When you build the project and run the application, you will see the following result:

```
Unsorted: 50, 33, 78, -23, 90, 41
Sorted: -23, 33, 41, 50, 78, 90
```

As already mentioned, binary heaps are not the only variant of heaps. Among others, a binomial heap is one of the very interesting approaches, which is the topic of the next section.

Binomial heaps

Another kind of heap is a **binomial heap**. This data structure consists of a set of **binomial trees** with different orders. The binomial tree with order *0* is just a single node. You can construct the tree with order *n* using two binomial trees with order *n-1*. One of them should be attached as the left-most child of the parent of the first tree. It does sound a bit complicated, but the following diagram should remove any confusion:

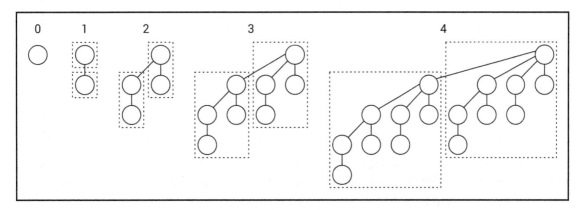

As already mentioned, the binomial tree with order **0** is only a single node, as shown on the left. The tree with order **1** consists of two trees with order **0** (marked with the dashed border) connected to each other. In the case of the tree with order **2**, two trees with order **1** are used. The second is attached as the left-most child of the parent of the first tree. In the same way, you can configure the binomial trees with the following orders.

However, how can you know how many binomial trees should be located in the binomial heap, as well as how many nodes should they contain? The answer could be a bit surprising, because you need to prepare the binary representation of the number of nodes. As an example, let's create a binomial heap with **13** elements. The number **13** has the following binary representation: **1101**, namely $1*2^0 + 0*2^1 + 1*2^2 + 1*2^3$.

You need to get zero-based positions of the set bits, that is, **0, 2,** and **3** in this example. Such positions indicate orders of binomial trees that should be configured:

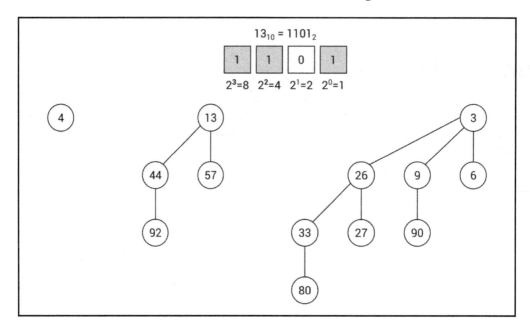

Moreover, there cannot be more than one binomial tree with the same order (such as two trees with order **2**) in the binomial heap. Is it also worth noting that each binomial tree must maintain the min-heap property.

You can find more information about binomial heaps at https://en.wikipedia.org/wiki/Binomial_heap.

The implementation of the binomial heap is significantly more complicated than the binary heap. For this reason, it may be a good idea to use one of the available implementations instead of writing your own from scratch. As stated in the case of binary heaps, the Hippie library is a solution that supports various variants of heaps, including binomial.

It could be surprising, but the only difference in the code, in comparison with the example of the binary heap, is modification of the line where a new instance of the `MultiHeap` class is created. For supporting a binomial heap, you need to use the `NewBinomialHeap` method from the `HeapFactory` class, as follows:

```
MultiHeap<int> heap = HeapFactory.NewBinomialHeap<int>();
```

No more changes are necessary! Now you can perform the remaining operations, such as insertion or removal of elements, in the exact same way as in the case of the binary heap.

You have already learned about two kinds of heaps, namely binary and binomial ones. In the next section, the Fibonacci heap is briefly described.

Fibonacci heaps

A **Fibonacci heap** is an interesting variant of heaps, which in some ways is similar to a binomial heap. First of all, it also consists of many trees, but there are no constraints regarding the shape of each tree, so it is much more flexible than the binomial heap. Moreover, it is allowed to have more than one tree with exactly the same shape in the heap.

An example of a Fibonacci heap is as follows:

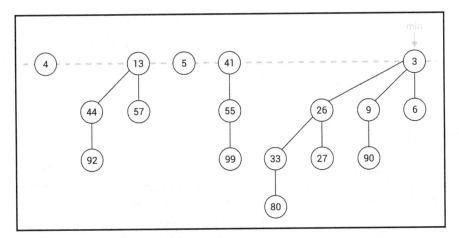

One of the important assumptions is that each tree is a min-heap. Thus, the minimum value in the whole Fibonacci heap is certainly a root node in one of the trees. Moreover, the presented data structure supports performing various operations in the *lazy* way. That means that it does not perform additional complex operations unless it is really necessary. For example, it can add a new node just as a new tree with only one node.

 You can find more information about Fibonacci heaps at
https://en.wikipedia.org/wiki/Fibonacci_heap.

Similarly to the binomial heap, the implementation of the Fibonacci heap is also not a trivial task and requires good understanding of the internal details of this data structure. For this reason, if you need to use Fibonacci heaps in your application, it may be a good idea to use one of the available implementations instead of writing your own from scratch. As stated previously, the `Hippie` library is a solution that supports many variants of heaps, including Fibonacci ones.

It is worth mentioning that the only difference in the code, in comparison with the binary and binomial heaps, is modification of the line where a new instance of the `MultiHeap` class is created. For supporting a Fibonacci heap, you need to use the `NewFibonacciHeap` method from the `HeapFactory` class, as follows:

```
MultiHeap<int> heap = HeapFactory.NewFibonacciHeap<int>();
```

That's all! You have just read a brief introduction to the topic of Fibonacci heaps, as another variant of a heap and, therefore, another kind of a tree. That was the last subject in this chapter, so it is time to proceed to the summary.

Summary

The current chapter is the longest so far in the book. However, it contains a lot of information about variants of trees. Such data structures perform very important role in many algorithms and it is good to learn more about them, as well as to know how to use them in your applications. For this reason, this chapter contains not only short theoretical introductions, but also diagrams, explanations, and code samples.

At the beginning, the concept of a tree was described. As a reminder, a tree consists of nodes, including one root. The root does not contain a parent node, while all other nodes do. Each node can have any number of child nodes. The child nodes of the same node can be named siblings, while a node without children is named a leaf.

Various variants of trees follow this structure. The first one described in the chapter is a binary tree. In this case, a node can contain at most two children. However, the rules for BSTs are even more strict. For any node in such trees, the values of all nodes in its left subtree must be smaller than the value of the node, while the values of all nodes in its right subtree must be greater than the value of the node. BSTs have a very broad range of applications and provide developers with significant improvements of the lookup performance. Unfortunately, it is possible to easily make a tree unbalanced while adding sorted values to the tree. Therefore, the positive impact on the performance can be limited.

To solve this problem, you can use some kind of self-balancing tree, which remains balanced all the time while adding or removing nodes. In this chapter, two variants of self-balancing trees were presented: AVL trees and RBTs. The first kind has the additional requirement that, for each node, the height of its left and right subtrees cannot differ by more than one. The RBT is a bit more complex, because it introduces the concept of coloring nodes, either to red or black, as well as the NIL pseudo-nodes. Moreover, it is required that if a node is red, both its children must be black, and for any node, the number of black nodes on the route to a descendant leaf must be the same. As you have seen while analyzing such data structures, their implementation is significantly more difficult. Thus, the additional libraries, available to download using the NuGet Package Manager, were presented.

The remaining part of the chapter was related to heaps. As a reminder, a heap is another variant of a tree, which exists in two versions, min-heap and max-heap. It is worth noting that the value of each node must be greater than or equal to (for min-heaps) or less than or equal to (for max-heaps) the value of its parent node. The heaps exist in many variants, including binary, binomial, and Fibonacci ones. All of these kinds were briefly presented in the chapter, together with information about using the implementation from one of the NuGet packages.

Let's proceed to graphs, which are the subject of the next chapter!

6
Exploring Graphs

In the previous chapter, you got to know trees. However, did you know that such data structures also belong to graphs? But what is a graph and how you can use it in your applications? You can find answers to these and many other questions in this chapter!

At the beginning, the basic information about graphs will be presented, including an explanation of nodes and edges. Moreover, you will see the difference between directed and undirected edges, as well as between weighted and unweighted ones. As graphs are data structures that are commonly used in practice, you will also see some applications, such as for storing the data of friends in social media or finding a road in a city. Then, the topic of graph representation will be covered, namely using an adjacency list and matrix.

After this short introduction, you will learn how to implement a graph in the C# language. This task involves the declaration of a few classes, such as regarding nodes and edges. The whole necessary code will be described in detail in the chapter.

Moreover, you will also have a chance to read the description of two modes of graph traversal, namely depth-first and breadth-first search. For both of them, the C# code and a detailed description will be shown.

The next part will present the subject of minimum spanning trees, as well as two algorithms for their creation, namely Kruskal's and Prim's. Such algorithms will be presented as textual description, C#-based code snippets, as well as easy-to-understand illustrations. Moreover, the example real-world application will be provided.

Another interesting graph-related problem is the coloring of nodes, which will be taken into account in the following part of the chapter. At the end, the topic of finding the shortest path in a graph will be analyzed using Dijkstra's algorithm. Of course, the example real-world application will be shown as well, together with the C#-based implementation.

As you can see, the topic of graphs involves many interesting problems and only some of them will be mentioned in the book. However, the chosen subjects are suitable for the presentation of various graph-related aspects in the context of C#-based implementation. Are you ready to dive into the topic of graphs? If so, start reading this chapter!

In this chapter, the following topics will be covered:

- Concept of graphs
- Applications
- Representation
- Implementation
- Traversal
- Minimum spanning tree
- Coloring
- Shortest path

Concept of graphs

Let's start with the question *what is a graph?* Broadly speaking, a graph is a data structure that consists of **nodes** (also called **vertices**) and **edges**. Each edge connects two nodes. A graph data structure does not require any specific rules regarding connections between nodes, as shown in the following diagram:

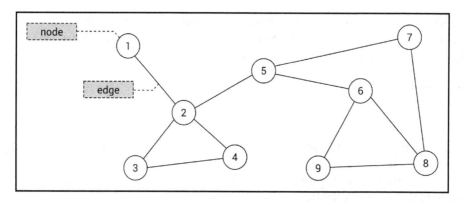

The afore mentioned concept seems very simple, doesn't it? Let's try to analyze the preceding graph to eliminate any doubts. It contains nine nodes with numbers between **1** and **9** as values. Such nodes are connected by 11 edges, such as between nodes **2** and **4**. Moreover, a graph can contain **cycles**, for example, with nodes indicated by **2, 3**, and **4**, as well as separate groups of nodes, which are not connected together. However, what about the topic of parent and child nodes, which you know from learning about trees? As there are no specific rules about connections in a graph, such concepts are not used in this case.

A graph can also contain **self-loops**. Each is an edge that connects a given node with itself. However, such a topic is out of the scope of this book and is not taken into account in examples shown in this chapter.

Some more comments are necessary for edges in a graph. In the preceding diagram, you can see a graph where all nodes are connected with **undirected edges**, that is, **bidirectional edges**. They indicate that it is possible to travel between nodes in both directions, for example, from the node **2** to **3** and from the node **3** to **2**. Such edges are presented graphically as straight lines. When a graph contains undirected edges, it is an **undirected graph**.

However, what about a scenario when you need to indicate that traveling between nodes is possible only in one direction? In such a case, you can use **directed edges**, that is, **unidirectional edges**, which are presented graphically as straight lines with arrows indicating the direction of an edge. If a graph contains directed edges, it can be named a **directed graph**.

An example directed graph is presented in the following diagram on the right, while an undirected one is shown on the left:

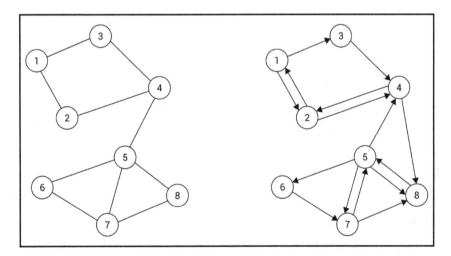

Just as a short explanation, the directed graph (shown on the right in the preceding diagram) contains eight nodes connected by 15 unidirectional edges. For example, they indicate that it is possible to travel between the node **1** and **2** in both directions, but it is allowed to travel from the node **1** to **3** only in one direction, so it is impossible to reach the node **1** from **3** directly.

The division between undirected and directed edges is not the only one. You can also specify **weights** (also referred to as **costs**) for particular edges to indicate the cost of traveling between nodes. Of course, such weights can be assigned to both undirected and directed edges. If weights are provided, an edge is named a **weighted edge** and the whole graph a **weighted graph**. Similarly, if no weights are provided, **unweighted edges** are used in a graph that can be called an **unweighted graph**.

The example weighted graphs with undirected (on the left) and directed (on the right) edges are presented in the following diagram:

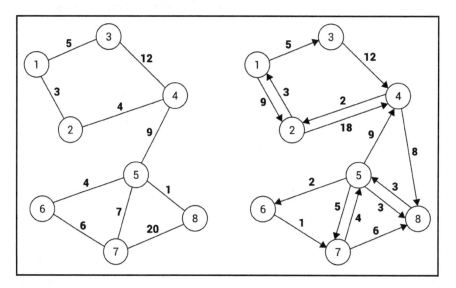

The graphical presentation of a weighted edge only shows the addition of the weight of an edge next to the line. For example, the cost of traveling from the node **1** to **2**, as well as from the node **2** to **1**, is equal to **3** in the case of the undirected graph, shown on the left in the preceding diagram. The situation is a bit more complicated in the case of the directed graph (on the right). Here, you can travel from the node **1** to **2** with a cost equal to **9**, while traveling in the opposite direction (from the node **2** to **1**) is much cheaper and costs only **3**.

Applications

After the short introduction, you know some basic information about graphs, especially regarding nodes and various kinds of edges. However, why is the topic of graphs so important and why does it take up a whole chapter in this book? Could you use this data structure in your applications? The answer is obvious: yes! The graphs are commonly used while solving various algorithmic problems and have numerous real-world applications. Two examples are shown in the following diagrams.

To start with, let's think about a structure of friends available in social media. Each user has many contacts, but they also have many friends, and so on. What data structure should you choose to store such data? The graph is one of the simplest answers. In such a scenario, the nodes represent contacts, while edges depict relationships between people. As an example, let's take a look at the following diagram of an undirected and unweighted graph:

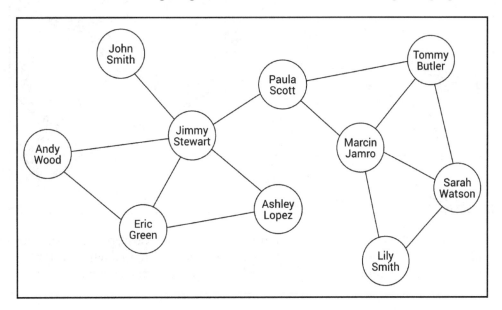

As you can see, **Jimmy Stewart** has five contacts, namely **John Smith, Andy Wood, Eric Green, Ashley Lopez,** and **Paula Scott**. In the meantime, **Paula Scott** has two other friends: **Marcin Jamro** and **Tommy Butler**. With the usage of a graph as a data structure, you can easily check whether two people are friends or whether they have a common contact.

Another common application of graphs involves the problem of searching for the shortest path. Let's imagine a program that should find a path between two points in the city, taking into account the time necessary for driving particular roads. In such a case, you can use a graph to present a map of a city, where nodes depict intersections and edges represent roads. Of course, you should assign weights to edges to indicate the time necessary for driving a given road. The topic of searching the shortest path can be understood as finding the list of edges from the source to the target node, with the minimum total cost. The diagram of a city map, based on a graph, is shown here:

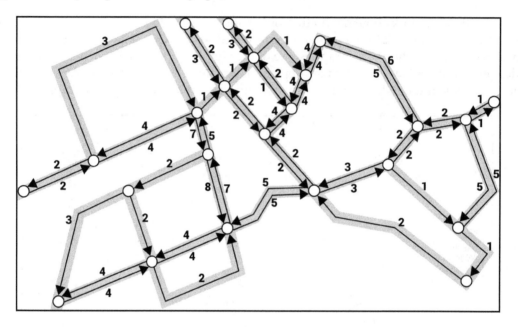

As you can see, the directed and weighted graph was chosen. The application of directed edges makes it possible to support both two-way and one-way roads, while weighted edges allow for specifying the time necessary to travel between two intersections.

Representation

Now you know what a graph is and when it can be used, but how you can represent it in the memory of a computer? There are two popular approaches to solve this problem, namely using an **adjacency list** and an **adjacency matrix**. Both are described in detail in the following sections.

Adjacency list

The first approach requires you to extend the data of a node by specifying a list of its neighbors. Thus, you can easily get all neighbors of a given node just by iterating through the adjacency list of a given node. Such a solution is space-efficient, because you only store the data of adjacent edges. Let's take a look at the following diagram:

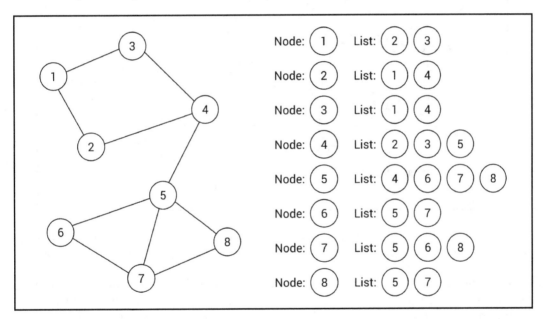

The example graph contains 8 nodes and 10 edges. For each node, a list of adjacent nodes (that is, neighbors) is created, as shown on the right-hand side of the diagram. For example, the node **1** has two neighbors, namely the nodes **2** and **3**, while the node **5** has four neighbors, namely the nodes **4, 6, 7**, and **8**. As you can see, the representation based on the adjacency list for an undirected and unweighted graph is really straightforward, as well as easy to use, understand, and implement.

However, how does the adjacency list work in the case of a directed graph? The answer is obvious, because the list assigned to each node just shows adjacent nodes that can be reached from the given node. The example diagram is shown as follows:

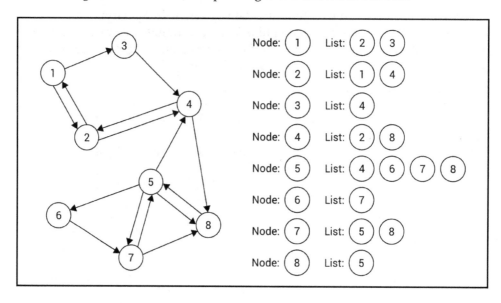

Let's take a look at the node **3**. Here, the adjacency list contains only one element, that is, the node **4**. The node **1** is not included, because it cannot be reached directly from the node **3**.

A bit more clarification may be necessary in the case of a weighted graph. In such a case, it is also necessary to store weights for particular edges. You can achieve this goal by extending data stored in the adjacency list, as shown in the following diagram:

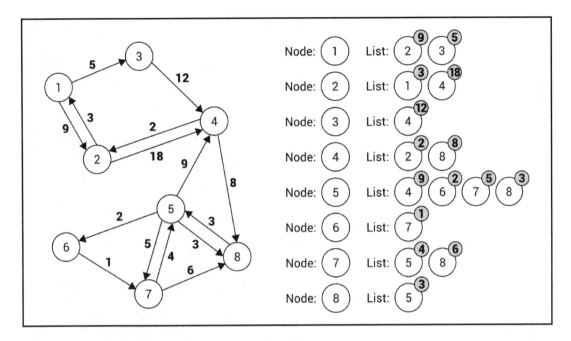

The adjacency list for the node **7** contains two elements, namely regarding an edge to the node **5** (with a weight equal to **4**) and to the node **8** (with a weight equal to **6**).

Adjacency matrix

Another approach to graph representation involves the adjacency matrix, which uses the two-dimensional array to show which nodes are connected by edges. The matrix contains the same number of rows and columns, which is equal to the number of nodes. The main idea is to store information about a particular edge in an element at a given row and column in the matrix. The index of the row and the column depends on the nodes connected with the edge. For example, if you want to get information about an edge between nodes with indices 1 and 5, you should check the element in the row with an index equal to 1 and in the column with an index set to 5.

Such a solution provides you with a fast way of checking whether two particular nodes are connected by an edge. However, it may require you to store significantly more data than the adjacency list, especially if the graph does not contain many edges between nodes.

To start, let's analyze the basic scenario of an undirected and unweighted graph. In such a case, the adjacency matrix may store only Boolean values. The `true` value placed in the element at `i` row and `j` column indicates that there is a connection between a node with an index equal to `i` and the node with index `j`. If it sounds complicated, take a look at the following example:

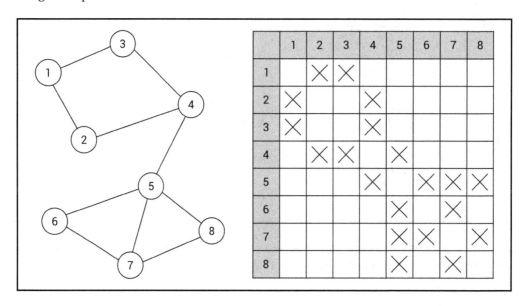

Here, the adjacency matrix contains 64 elements (for eight rows and eight columns), because there are eight nodes in the graph. The values of many elements in the array are set to `false`, which is represented by missing indicators. The remaining are marked with crosses, representing `true` values. For example, such a value in the element at the fourth row and third column means that there is an edge between the node **4** and **3**, as shown in the preceding diagram of the graph.

TIP

As the presented graph is undirected, the adjacency matrix is symmetric. If there is an edge between nodes i and j, there is also an edge between nodes j and i.

The next example involves a directed and unweighted graph. In such a case, the same rules can be used, but the adjacency matrix does not need to be symmetric. Let's take a look at the following diagram of the graph, presented together with the adjacency matrix:

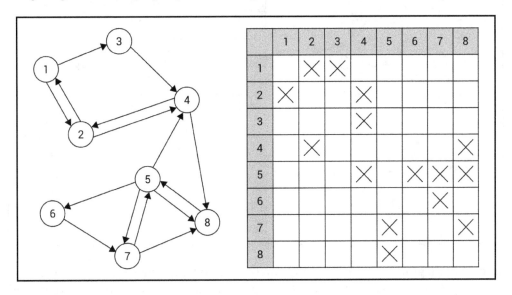

Within the shown adjacency matrix you can find data of 15 edges, represented by 15 elements with `true` values, indicated by crosses in the matrix. For example, the unidirectional edge from the node **5** to **4** is shown as the cross at the fifth row and fourth column.

In both previous examples, you have learnt how to present an unweighted graph using an adjacency matrix. However, how you can store the data of the weighted graph, either undirected or directed? The answer is very simple—you just need to change the type of data stored in particular elements in the adjacency matrix from Boolean to numeric. Thus, you can specify the weight of edges, as shown in the following diagram:

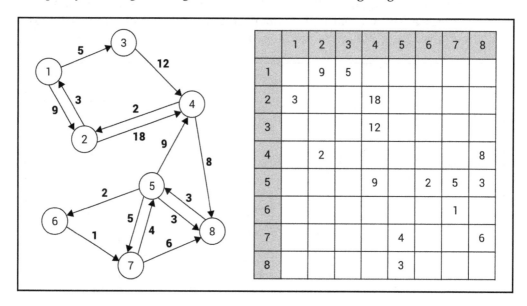

	1	2	3	4	5	6	7	8
1		9	5					
2	3			18				
3				12				
4		2						8
5				9		2	5	3
6							1	
7					4			6
8					3			

The preceding diagram and the adjacency matrix are self-explanatory. However, to eliminate any doubt, let's take a look at the edge between the node **5** and **6** with the weight set to **2**. Such an edge is represented by the element at the fifth row and sixth column. The value of the element is equal to the cost of traveling between such nodes.

Implementation

You have already got to know some basic information about graphs, including nodes, edges, and two methods of representation, namely using an adjacency list and matrix. However, how you can use such a data structure in your applications? In this section, you will learn how to implement a graph using the C# language. To make your understanding of the presented content easier, two examples are provided.

Node

To start with, let's take a look at the code of the generic class representing a single node in a graph. Such a class is named `Node` and its code is shown as follows:

```
public class Node<T>
{
    public int Index { get; set; }
    public T Data { get; set; }
    public List<Node<T>> Neighbors { get; set; }
        = new List<Node<T>>();
    public List<int> Weights { get; set; } = new List<int>();

    public override string ToString()
    {
        return $"Node with index {Index}: {Data},
            neighbors: {Neighbors.Count}";
    }
}
```

The class contains four properties. As all of these elements perform important roles in the code snippets shown in this chapter, let's analyze them in detail:

- The first property (`Index`) stores an index of a particular node in a collection of nodes in a graph to simplify the process of accessing a particular element. Thus, it is possible to easily get an instance of the `Node` class, representing a particular node, by using an index.
- The next property is named `Data` and just stores some data in the node. It is worth mentioning that a type of such data is consistent with the type specified while creating an instance of the generic class.
- The `Neighbors` property represents the adjacency list for a particular node. Thus, it contains references to the `Node` instances representing adjacent nodes.
- The last property is named `Weights` and stores weights assigned to adjacent edges. In the case of a weighted graph, the number of elements in the `Weights` list is the same as the number of neighbors (`Neighbors`). If a graph is unweighted, the `Weights` list is empty.

Apart from the properties, the class contains the overridden `ToString` method, which returns the textual representation of the object. Here, the string in the format "`Node with index [index]: [data], neighbors: [count]`" is returned.

Edge

As mentioned in the short introduction to the topic of graphs, a graph consists of nodes and edges. As a node is represented by an instance of the `Node` class, the `Edge` generic class can be used to represent an edge. The suitable part of code is as follows:

```
public class Edge<T>
{
    public Node<T> From { get; set; }
    public Node<T> To { get; set; }
    public int Weight { get; set; }

    public override string ToString()
    {
        return $"Edge: {From.Data} -> {To.Data},
            weight: {Weight}";
    }
}
```

The class contains three properties, namely representing nodes adjacent to the edge (`From` and `To`), as well as the weight of the edge (`Weight`). Moreover, the `ToString` method is overridden to present some basic information about the edge.

Graph

The next class is named `Graph` and represents a whole graph, with either directed or undirected edges, as well as either weighted or unweighted edges. The implementation consists of various fields and methods, which are described in details as follows.

Let's take a look at the basic version of the `Graph` class:

```
public class Graph<T>
{
    private bool _isDirected = false;
    private bool _isWeighted = false;
    public List<Node<T>> Nodes { get; set; }
        = new List<Node<T>>();
}
```

The class contains two fields indicating whether edges are directed (`_isDirected`) and weighted (`_isWeighted`). Moreover, the `Nodes` property is declared, which stores a list of nodes existing in the graph.

The class also contains the constructor, as follows:

```
public Graph(bool isDirected, bool isWeighted)
{
    _isDirected = isDirected;
    _isWeighted = isWeighted;
}
```

Here, only values of the _isDirected and _isWeighted private fields are set, according to the values of parameters passed to the constructor.

The next interesting member of the Graph class is the indexer that takes two indices, namely indices of two nodes, to return an instance of the Edge generic class representing an edge between such nodes. The implementation is shown in the following code snippet:

```
public Edge<T> this[int from, int to]
{
    get
    {
        Node<T> nodeFrom = Nodes[from];
        Node<T> nodeTo = Nodes[to];
        int i = nodeFrom.Neighbors.IndexOf(nodeTo);
        if (i >= 0)
        {
            Edge<T> edge = new Edge<T>()
            {
                From = nodeFrom,
                To = nodeTo,
                Weight = i < nodeFrom.Weights.Count
                    ? nodeFrom.Weights[i] : 0
            };
            return edge;
        }

        return null;
    }
}
```

Within the indexer, you get instances of the Node class representing two nodes (nodeFrom and nodeTo), according to the indices. As you want to find an edge from the first node (nodeFrom) to the second one (nodeTo), you need to try to find the second node in the collection of neighbor nodes of the first node, using the IndexOf method. If such a connection does not exist, the IndexOf method returns a negative value and null is returned by the indexer. Otherwise, you create a new instance of the Edge class and set the values of its properties, including From and To. If the data regarding the weight of particular edges are provided, the value of the Weight property of the Edge class is set as well.

Now you know how to store the data of nodes in the graph, but how can you add a new node? To do so, the AddNode method is implemented, as follows:

```
public Node<T> AddNode(T value)
{
    Node<T> node = new Node<T>() { Data = value };
    Nodes.Add(node);
    UpdateIndices();
    return node;
}
```

Within this method, you create a new instance of the Node class and set a value of the Data property, according to the value of the parameter. Then, the newly-created instance is added to the Nodes collection, and the UpdateIndices method (described later) is called to update the indices of all nodes stored in the collection. At the end, the Node instance, representing the newly-added node, is returned.

You can remove the existing node as well. This operation is performed by the RemoveNode method, shown in the following code snippet:

```
public void RemoveNode(Node<T> nodeToRemove)
{
    Nodes.Remove(nodeToRemove);
    UpdateIndices();
    foreach (Node<T> node in Nodes)
    {
        RemoveEdge(node, nodeToRemove);
    }
}
```

The method takes one parameter, namely an instance of the node that should be removed. First, you remove it from the collection of nodes. Then, you update the indices of the remaining nodes. At the end, you iterate through all nodes in the graph to remove all edges that are connected with the node that has been removed.

As you already know, a graph consists of nodes and edges. Thus, the implementation of the Graph class should provide developers with the method for adding a new edge. Of course, it should support various variants of edges, either directed, undirected, weighted, or unweighted. The proposed implementation is shown as follows:

```
public void AddEdge(Node<T> from, Node<T> to, int weight = 0)
{
    from.Neighbors.Add(to);
    if (_isWeighted)
    {
        from.Weights.Add(weight);
    }

    if (!_isDirected)
    {
        to.Neighbors.Add(from);
        if (_isWeighted)
        {
            to.Weights.Add(weight);
        }
    }
}
```

The AddEdge method takes three parameters, namely two instances of the Node class representing nodes connected by the edge (from and to), as well as the weight of the connection (weight), which is set to 0 by default.

In the first line within the method, you add the Node instance representing the second node to the list of neighbor nodes of the first one. If the weighted graph is considered, a weight of the afore mentioned edge is added as well.

The following part of the code is taken into account only when the graph is undirected. In such a case, you need to automatically add an edge in the opposite direction. To do so, you add the Node instance representing the first node to the list of neighbor nodes of the second one. If the edges are weighted, a weight of the afore mentioned edge is added to the Weights list as well.

The process of removing an edge from the graph is supported by the RemoveEdge method. The code is as follows:

```
public void RemoveEdge(Node<T> from, Node<T> to)
{
    int index = from.Neighbors.FindIndex(n => n == to);
    if (index >= 0)
    {
        from.Neighbors.RemoveAt(index);
        if (_isWeighted)
        {
            from.Weights.RemoveAt(index);
        }
    }
}
```

The method takes two parameters, namely two nodes (from and to), between which there is an edge that should be removed. To start, you try to find the second node in the list of neighbor nodes of the first one. If it is found, you remove it. Of course, you should also remove the weight data, if the weighted graph is considered.

The last public method is named GetEdges and makes it possible to get a collection of all edges available in the graph. The proposed implementation is as follows:

```
public List<Edge<T>> GetEdges()
{
    List<Edge<T>> edges = new List<Edge<T>>();
    foreach (Node<T> from in Nodes)
    {
        for (int i = 0; i < from.Neighbors.Count; i++)
        {
            Edge<T> edge = new Edge<T>()
            {
                From = from,
                To = from.Neighbors[i],
                Weight = i < from.Weights.Count
                    ? from.Weights[i] : 0
            };
            edges.Add(edge);
        }
    }
    return edges;
}
```

To start with, a new list of edges is initialized. Then, you iterate through all nodes in the graph, using the `foreach` loop. Within it, you use the `for` loop to create instances of the `Edge` class. The number of instances should be equal to the number of neighbors of the current node (the `from` variable in the `foreach` loop). In the `for` loop, the newly-created instance of the `Edge` class is configured by setting values of its properties, namely the first node (the `from` variable, that is, the current node from the `foreach` loop), the second node (to the currently-analyzed neighbor), and the weight. Then, the newly-created instance is added to the collection of edges, represented by the `edges` variable. At the end, the result is returned.

In various methods, you use the `UpdateIndices` method. The code is as follows:

```
private void UpdateIndices()
{
    int i = 0;
    Nodes.ForEach(n => n.Index = i++);
}
```

The method just iterates through all nodes in the graph and updates the values of the `Index` property to the consecutive number, starting from 0. It is worth noting that the iteration is performed using the `ForEach` method, instead of `foreach` or a `for` loop.

Now you know how to create a basic implementation of a graph. The next step is to apply it to represent some example graphs, as shown in the two following sections.

Example – undirected and unweighted edges

Let's try to use the previous implementation to create the undirected and unweighted graph, according to the following diagram:

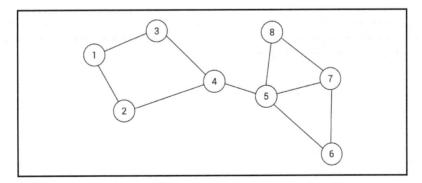

As you can see, the graph contains 8 nodes and 10 edges. You can configure the example graph in the Main method in the Program class. The implementation starts with the following line of code, which initializes a new undirected graph (with false as the value of the first parameter) and an unweighted graph (with false as the value of the second parameter):

```
Graph<int> graph = new Graph<int>(false, false);
```

Then, you add the necessary nodes, and store references to them as new variables of the Node<int> type, as follows:

```
Node<int> n1 = graph.AddNode(1);
Node<int> n2 = graph.AddNode(2);
Node<int> n3 = graph.AddNode(3);
Node<int> n4 = graph.AddNode(4);
Node<int> n5 = graph.AddNode(5);
Node<int> n6 = graph.AddNode(6);
Node<int> n7 = graph.AddNode(7);
Node<int> n8 = graph.AddNode(8);
```

At the end, you only need to add edges between nodes, according to the preceding diagram of the graph. The necessary code is presented as follows:

```
graph.AddEdge(n1, n2);
graph.AddEdge(n1, n3);
graph.AddEdge(n2, n4);
graph.AddEdge(n3, n4);
graph.AddEdge(n4, n5);
graph.AddEdge(n5, n6);
graph.AddEdge(n5, n7);
graph.AddEdge(n5, n8);
graph.AddEdge(n6, n7);
graph.AddEdge(n7, n8);
```

That's all! As you can see, configuration of a graph is very easy using the proposed implementation of this data structure. Now, let's proceed to a slightly more complex scenario with directed and weighted edges.

Example – directed and weighted edges

The next example involves the directed and weighted graph, as follows:

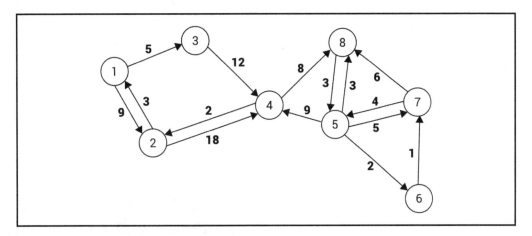

The implementation is very similar to the one described in the previous section. However, some modifications are necessary. To start with, different values of the parameters of the constructor are used, namely `true` instead of `false` to indicate that a directed and weighted variant of edges is being considered. The suitable line of code is as follows:

```
Graph<int> graph = new Graph<int>(true, true);
```

The part regarding adding nodes is exactly the same as in the previous example:

```
Node<int> n1 = graph.AddNode(1);
Node<int> n2 = graph.AddNode(2);
Node<int> n3 = graph.AddNode(3);
Node<int> n4 = graph.AddNode(4);
Node<int> n5 = graph.AddNode(5);
Node<int> n6 = graph.AddNode(6);
Node<int> n7 = graph.AddNode(7);
Node<int> n8 = graph.AddNode(8);
```

Some changes are easily visible in the lines of code regarding the addition of edges. Here, you specify directed edges together with their weights, as follows:

```
graph.AddEdge(n1, n2, 9);
graph.AddEdge(n1, n3, 5);
graph.AddEdge(n2, n1, 3);
graph.AddEdge(n2, n4, 18);
graph.AddEdge(n3, n4, 12);
graph.AddEdge(n4, n2, 2);
graph.AddEdge(n4, n8, 8);
graph.AddEdge(n5, n4, 9);
graph.AddEdge(n5, n6, 2);
graph.AddEdge(n5, n7, 5);
graph.AddEdge(n5, n8, 3);
graph.AddEdge(n6, n7, 1);
graph.AddEdge(n7, n5, 4);
graph.AddEdge(n7, n8, 6);
graph.AddEdge(n8, n5, 3);
```

You have just completed the basic implementation of a graph, shown in two examples. So, let's proceed to another topic, namely traversing a graph.

Traversal

One of the useful operations performed on a graph is its **traversal**, that is, visiting all of the nodes in some particular order. Of course, the afore mentioned problem can be solved in various ways, such as using **depth-first search** (**DFS**) or **breadth-first search** (**BFS**) approaches. It is worth mentioning that the traversal topic is strictly connected with the task of searching for a given node in a graph.

Depth-first search

The first graph traversal algorithm described in this chapter is named DFS. Its steps, in the context of the example graph, are as follows:

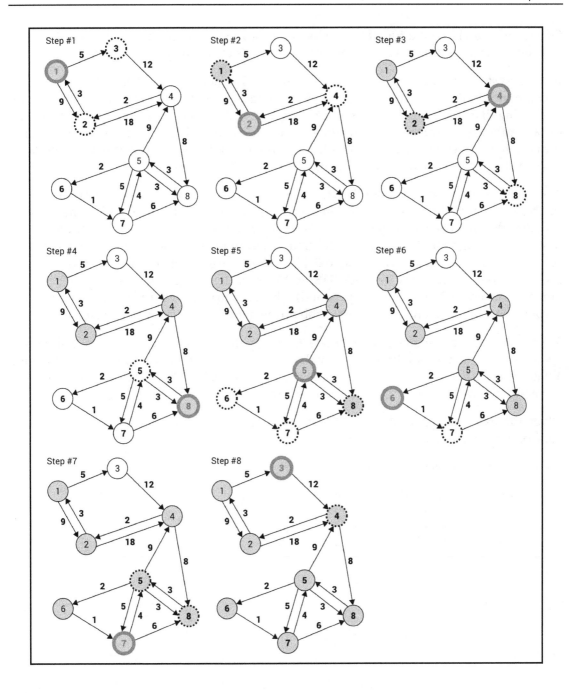

Of course, it can be a bit difficult to understand how the DFS algorithm operates just by looking at the preceding diagram. For this reason, let's try to analyze its stages.

In the first step, you see the graph with eight nodes. The node **1** is marked with a gray background (indicating that the node has been already visited), as well as with a red border (indicating that it is the node that is currently being visited). Moreover, an important role in the algorithm is performed by the neighbor nodes (shown as circles with dashed borders) of the current one. When you know the roles of particular indicators, it is clear that in the first step, the node **1** is visited. It has two neighbors (the nodes **2** and **3**).

Then, the first neighbor (the node **2**) is taken into account and the same operations are performed, that is, the node is visited and the neighbors (the nodes **1** and **4**) are analyzed. As the node **1** has been already visited, it is skipped. In the next step (shown as **Step** #3), the first suitable neighbor of the node **2** is taken into account—the node **4**. It has two neighbors, namely the node **2** (already visited) and **8**. Next, the node **8** is visited (**Step** #4) and, according to the same rules, the node **5** (**Step** #5). It has four neighbors, namely the nodes **4** (already visited), **6**, **7**, and **8** (already visited). Thus, in the next step, the node **6** is taken into account (**Step** #6). As it has only one neighbor (the node **7**), it is visited next (**Step** #7).

Then, you check the neighbors of the node **7**, namely the nodes **5** and **8**. Both have already been visited, so you return to the node with an unvisited neighbor. In the example, the node **1** has one unvisited node, namely the node **3**. When it is visited (**Step** #8), all nodes are traversed and no further operations are necessary.

Given this example, let's try to create the implementation in the C# language. To start, the code of the DFS method (in the Graph class) is presented as follows:

```
public List<Node<T>> DFS()
{
    bool[] isVisited = new bool[Nodes.Count];
    List<Node<T>> result = new List<Node<T>>();
    DFS(isVisited, Nodes[0], result);
    return result;
}
```

The important role is performed by the isVisited array. It has exactly the same number of elements as the number of nodes and stores values indicating whether a given node has already been visited. If so, the true value is stored, otherwise false. The list of traversed nodes is represented as a list in the result variable. What is more, another variant of the DFS method is called here, passing three parameters, namely a reference to the isVisited array, the first node to analyze, as well as the list for storing results.

The code of the afore mentioned variant of the DFS method is presented as follows:

```
private void DFS(bool[] isVisited, Node<T> node,
    List<Node<T>> result)
{
    result.Add(node);
    isVisited[node.Index] = true;

    foreach (Node<T> neighbor in node.Neighbors)
    {
        if (!isVisited[neighbor.Index])
        {
            DFS(isVisited, neighbor, result);
        }
    }
}
```

The shown implementation is very simple. At the beginning, the current node is added to the collection of traversed nodes and the element in the isVisited array is updated. Then, you use the foreach loop to iterate through all neighbors of the current node. For each of them, if it is not already visited, the DFS method is called recursively.

 You can find more information about DFS at
https://en.wikipedia.org/wiki/Depth-first_search.

To finish, let's take a look at the code that can be placed in the Main method in the Program class. Its main parts are presented in the following code snippet:

```
Graph<int> graph = new Graph<int>(true, true);
Node<int> n1 = graph.AddNode(1); (...)
Node<int> n8 = graph.AddNode(8);
graph.AddEdge(n1, n2, 9); (...)
graph.AddEdge(n8, n5, 3);
List<Node<int>> dfsNodes = graph.DFS();
dfsNodes.ForEach(n => Console.WriteLine(n));
```

Here, you initialize a directed and weighted graph. To start traversing the graph, you just need to call the DFS method, which returns a list of Node instances. Then, you can easily iterate through elements of the list to print some basic information about each node. The result is shown as follows:

```
Node with index 0: 1, neighbors: 2
Node with index 1: 2, neighbors: 2
Node with index 3: 4, neighbors: 2
Node with index 7: 8, neighbors: 1
Node with index 4: 5, neighbors: 4
Node with index 5: 6, neighbors: 1
Node with index 6: 7, neighbors: 2
Node with index 2: 3, neighbors: 1
```

That's all! As you can see, the algorithm tries to go as deep as possible and then goes back to find the next unvisited neighbor that can be traversed. However, the presented algorithm is not the only approach to the problem of graph traversal. In the next section, you will see another method, together with a basic example and its implementation.

Breadth-first search

In the previous section, you learnt the DFS approach. Now you will see another solution, namely BFS. Its main aim is to first visit all neighbors of the current node and then proceed to the next level of nodes.

If the previous description sounds a bit complicated, take a look at this diagram, which depicts the steps of the BFS algorithm:

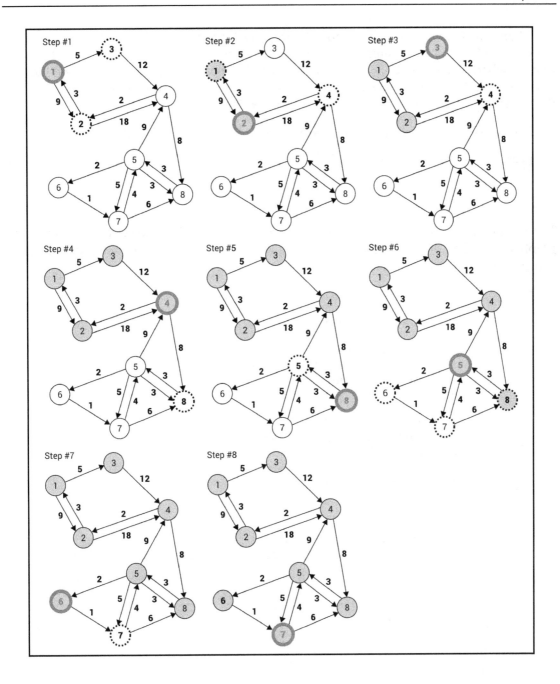

The algorithm starts by visiting the node **1** (**Step #1**). It has two neighbors, namely the nodes **2** and **3**, which are visited next (**Step #2** and **Step #3**). As the node **1** does not have more neighbors, the neighbors of its first neighbor (the node **2**) are considered. As it has only one neighbor (the node **4**), it is visited in the next step. According to the same method, the remaining nodes are visited in this order: **8, 5, 6, 7**.

It sounds very simple, doesn't it? Let's take a look at the implementation:

```
public List<Node<T>> BFS()
{
    return BFS(Nodes[0]);
}
```

The BFS public method is added to the Graph class and is used just to start the traversal of a graph. It calls the private BFS method, passing the first node as the parameter. Its code is shown as follows:

```
private List<Node<T>> BFS(Node<T> node)
{
    bool[] isVisited = new bool[Nodes.Count];
    isVisited[node.Index] = true;

    List<Node<T>> result = new List<Node<T>>();
    Queue<Node<T>> queue = new Queue<Node<T>>();
    queue.Enqueue(node);
    while (queue.Count > 0)
    {
        Node<T> next = queue.Dequeue();
        result.Add(next);

        foreach (Node<T> neighbor in next.Neighbors)
        {
            if (!isVisited[neighbor.Index])
            {
                isVisited[neighbor.Index] = true;
                queue.Enqueue(neighbor);
            }
        }
    }

    return result;
}
```

The important role in the code is performed by the `isVisited` array, which stores Boolean values indicating whether particular nodes have been visited already. Such an array is initialized at the beginning of the `BFS` method, and the value of the element related to the current node is set to `true`, which indicates that the node has been visited.

Then, the list for storing traversed nodes (`result`) and the queue for storing nodes that should be visited in the following iterations (`queue`) are created. Just after the initialization of the queue, the current node is added into it.

The following operations are performed until the queue is empty: you get the first node from the queue (the `next` variable), add it to the collection of visited nodes, and iterate through the neighbors of the current node. For each of them, you check whether it has already been visited. If not, it is marked as visited by setting a proper value in the `isVisited` array, and the neighbor is added to the queue for analysis in one of the next iterations of the `while` loop.

> You can find more information about the BFS algorithm and its implementation at
> `https://www.geeksforgeeks.org/breadth-first-traversal-for-a-grap h/`.

At the end, the list of the visited nodes is returned. If you want to test the described algorithm, you can place the following code in the `Main` method in the `Program` class:

```
Graph<int> graph = new Graph<int>(true, true);
Node<int> n1 = graph.AddNode(1); (...)
Node<int> n8 = graph.AddNode(8);
graph.AddEdge(n1, n2, 9); (...)
graph.AddEdge(n8, n5, 3);
List<Node<int>> bfsNodes = graph.BFS();
bfsNodes.ForEach(n => Console.WriteLine(n));
```

The code initializes the graph, adds proper nodes and edges, and calls the `BFS` public method to traverse the graph according to the BFS algorithm. The last line is responsible for iterating through the result to present the data of the nodes in the console:

```
Node with index 0: 1, neighbors: 2
Node with index 1: 2, neighbors: 2
Node with index 2: 3, neighbors: 1
Node with index 3: 4, neighbors: 2
Node with index 7: 8, neighbors: 1
Node with index 4: 5, neighbors: 4
Node with index 5: 6, neighbors: 1
Node with index 6: 7, neighbors: 2
```

You have just learnt two algorithms for traversing a graph, namely DFS and BFS. To make your understanding of such topics easier, this chapter contains detailed descriptions, diagrams, and examples. Now, let's proceed to the next section to get to know another important topic, namely a minimum spanning tree, which has many real-world applications.

Minimum spanning tree

While talking about graphs, it is beneficial to introduce the subject of a **spanning tree**. What is it? A spanning tree is a subset of edges that connects all nodes in a graph without cycles. Of course, it is possible to have many spanning trees within the same graph. For example, let's take a look at the following diagram:

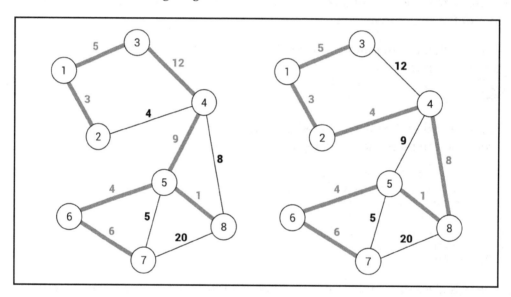

On the left-hand side is a spanning tree that consists of the following edges: (**1**, **2**), (**1**, **3**), (**3**, **4**), (**4**, **5**), (**5**, **6**), (**6**, **7**), and (**5**, **8**). The total weight is equal to 40. On the right-hand side, another spanning tree is shown. Here, the following edges are taken into account: (**1**, **2**), (**1**, **3**), (**2**, **4**), (**4**, **8**), (**5**, **8**), (**5**, **6**), and (**6**, **7**). The total weight is equal to 31.

However, neither of the preceding spanning trees is the **minimum spanning tree** (**MST**) of this graph. What does it mean that a spanning tree is *minimum*? The answer is really simple: it is a spanning tree with the minimum cost from all spanning trees available in the graph. You can get the MST by replacing the edge (**6, 7**) with (**5, 7**). Then, the cost is equal to 30. It is also worth mentioning that the number of edges in a spanning tree is equal to the number of nodes minus one.

Why is the topic of the MST so important? Let's imagine a scenario when you need to connect many buildings to a telecommunication cable. Of course, there are various possible connections, such as from one building to another, or using a hub. What is more, environmental conditions can have a serious impact on the cost of the investment due to the necessity of crossing a road or even a river. Your task is to successfully connect all buildings to the telecommunication cable with the lowest possible cost. How should you design the connections? To answer this question, you just need to create a graph, where nodes represent connectors and edges indicate possible connections. Then, you find the MST, and that's all!

The afore mentioned problem of connecting many buildings to the telecommunication cable is presented in the example at the end of the section regarding the MST.

The next question is how you can find the MST? There are various approaches to solve this problem, including the application of Kruskal's or Prim's algorithms, which are presented and explained in the following sections.

Kruskal's algorithm

One of the algorithms for finding the MST was discovered by Kruskal. Its operation is very simple to explain. The algorithm takes an edge with the minimum weight from the remaining ones and adds it to the MST, only if adding it does not create a cycle. The algorithm stops when all nodes are connected.

Let's take a look at the diagram that presents the steps of finding the MST using **Kruskal's algorithm**:

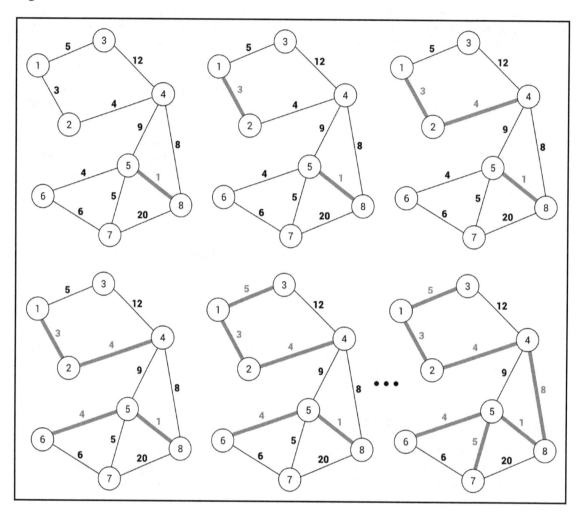

In the first step, the edge (**5, 8**) is chosen, because it has the minimum weight, namely **1**. Then, the edges (**1, 2**), (**2, 4**), (**5, 6**), (**1, 3**), (**5, 7**), and (**4, 8**) are selected. It is worth noting that before taking the (**4, 8**) edge, the (**6, 7**) one is considered, due to lower weight. However, adding it to the MST will introduce a cycle formed by (**5, 6**), (**6, 7**), and (**5, 7**) edges. For this reason, such an edge is ignored and the algorithm chooses the edge (**4, 8**). At the end, the number of edges in the MST is 7. The number of nodes is equal to **8**, so it means that the algorithm can stop operating and the MST is found.

Let's take a look at the implementation. It involves the `MinimumSpanningTreeKruskal`
method, which should be added to the `Graph` class. The proposed code is as follows:

```
public List<Edge<T>> MinimumSpanningTreeKruskal()
{
    List<Edge<T>> edges = GetEdges();
    edges.Sort((a, b) => a.Weight.CompareTo(b.Weight));
    Queue<Edge<T>> queue = new Queue<Edge<T>>(edges);

    Subset<T>[] subsets = new Subset<T>[Nodes.Count];
    for (int i = 0; i < Nodes.Count; i++)
    {
        subsets[i] = new Subset<T>() { Parent = Nodes[i] };
    }

    List<Edge<T>> result = new List<Edge<T>>();
    while (result.Count < Nodes.Count - 1)
    {
        Edge<T> edge = queue.Dequeue();
        Node<T> from = GetRoot(subsets, edge.From);
        Node<T> to = GetRoot(subsets, edge.To);
        if (from != to)
        {
            result.Add(edge);
            Union(subsets, from, to);
        }
    }

    return result;
}
```

The method does not take any parameters. To start, a list of edges is obtained by calling the
`GetEdges` method. Then, the edges are sorted in ascending order by weight. Such a step is
crucial, because you need to get an edge with the minimum cost in the following iterations
of the algorithm. In the next line, a new queue is created and `Edge` instances are enqueued,
using the constructor of the `Queue` class.

In the next block of code, an array with data of subsets is created. By default, each node is
added to a separate subset. It is the reason why the number of elements in the `subsets`
array is equal to the number of nodes. The subsets are used to check whether an addition of
an edge to the MST causes the creation of a cycle.

Then, the list for storing edges from the MST is created (`result`). The most interesting part of code is the `while` loop, which iterates until the correct number of edges is found in the MST. Within the loop, you get the edge with the minimum weight, just by calling the `Dequeue` method on the `Queue` instance. Then, you check whether no cycles were introduced by adding the found edge to the MST. In such a case, the edge is added to the target list and the `Union` method is called to union two subsets.

While analyzing the previous method, the `GetRoot` one is mentioned. Its aim is to update parents for subsets, as well as return the root node of the subset, as follows:

```
private Node<T> GetRoot(Subset<T>[] subsets, Node<T> node)
{
    if (subsets[node.Index].Parent != node)
    {
        subsets[node.Index].Parent = GetRoot(
            subsets,
            subsets[node.Index].Parent);
    }

    return subsets[node.Index].Parent;
}
```

The last private method is named `Union` and performs the union operation (by a rank) of two sets. It takes three parameters, namely an array of `Subset` instances and two `Node` instances, representing root nodes for subsets on which the union operation should be performed. The suitable part of code is as follows:

```
private void Union(Subset<T>[] subsets, Node<T> a, Node<T> b)
{
    if (subsets[a.Index].Rank > subsets[b.Index].Rank)
    {
        subsets[b.Index].Parent = a;
    }
    else if (subsets[a.Index].Rank < subsets[b.Index].Rank)
    {
        subsets[a.Index].Parent = b;
    }
    else
    {
        subsets[b.Index].Parent = a;
        subsets[a.Index].Rank++;
    }
}
```

In the previous code snippets, you can see the `Subset` class, but what does it look like? Let's take a look at its declaration:

```
public class Subset<T>
{
    public Node<T> Parent { get; set; }
    public int Rank { get; set; }

    public override string ToString()
    {
        return $"Subset with rank {Rank}, parent: {Parent.Data}
            (index: {Parent.Index})";
    }
}
```

The class contains properties representing the parent node (`Parent`), as well as the rank of the subset (`Rank`). The class has also overridden the `ToString` method, which presents some basic information about the subset in textual form.

 The presented code is based on the implementation shown at `https://www.geeksforgeeks.org/greedy-algorithms-set-2-kruskals-m inimum-spanning-tree-mst/`. You can also find more information about Kruskal's algorithm there.

Let's take a look at the usage of the `MinimumSpanningTreeKruskal` method:

```
Graph<int> graph = new Graph<int>(false, true);
Node<int> n1 = graph.AddNode(1); (...)
Node<int> n8 = graph.AddNode(8);
graph.AddEdge(n1, n2, 3); (...)
graph.AddEdge(n7, n8, 20);
List<Edge<int>> mstKruskal = graph.MinimumSpanningTreeKruskal();
mstKruskal.ForEach(e => Console.WriteLine(e));
```

First, you initialize an undirected and weighted graph, as well as add nodes and edges. Then, you call the `MinimumSpanningTreeKruskal` method to find the MST using Kruskal's algorithm. At the end, you use the `ForEach` method to write the data of each edge from the MST in the console.

Prim's algorithm

Another solution to solve the problem of finding the MST is **Prim's algorithm**. It uses two sets of nodes which are disjointed, namely the nodes located in the MST and the nodes that are not placed there yet. In the following iterations, the algorithm finds an edge with the minimum weight that connects a node from the first group with a node from the second group. The node of the edge, which is not already in the MST, is added to this set.

The preceding description sounds quite simple, doesn't it? Let's see it in action by analyzing the diagram presenting the steps of finding the MST using Prim's algorithm:

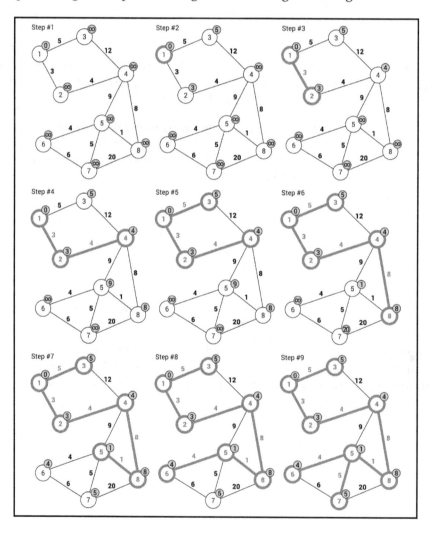

Let's take a look at the additional indicators added next to the nodes in the graph. They present the minimum weight necessary to reach such a node from any of its neighbors. By default, the starting node has such a value set to **0**, while all others are set to infinity.

In **Step #2**, the starting node is added to the subset of nodes forming the MST and the distance to its neighbors is updated, namely **5** for reaching the node **3** and **3** for reaching the node **2**.

In the next step (that is **Step #3**), the node with the minimum cost is chosen. In this case, the node **2** is selected, because the cost is equal to **3**. Its competitor (namely the node **3**) has a cost equal to **5**. Next, you need to update the cost of reaching the neighbors of the current node, namely the node **4** with the cost set to **4**.

The next chosen node is obviously the node **4**, because it does not exist in the MST set and has the lowest reaching cost (**Step #4**). In the same way, you choose the next edges in the following order: (**1, 3**), (**4, 8**), (**8, 5**), (**5, 6**), and (**5, 7**). Now, all nodes are included in the MST and the algorithm can stop its operation.

Given this detailed description of the steps of the algorithm, let's proceed to the C#-based implementation. The majority of operations are performed in the `MinimumSpanningTreePrim` method, which should be added to the `Graph` class:

```
public List<Edge<T>> MinimumSpanningTreePrim()
{
    int[] previous = new int[Nodes.Count];
    previous[0] = -1;

    int[] minWeight = new int[Nodes.Count];
    Fill(minWeight, int.MaxValue);
    minWeight[0] = 0;

    bool[] isInMST = new bool[Nodes.Count];
    Fill(isInMST, false);

    for (int i = 0; i < Nodes.Count - 1; i++)
    {
        int minWeightIndex = GetMinimumWeightIndex(
            minWeight, isInMST);
        isInMST[minWeightIndex] = true;

        for (int j = 0; j < Nodes.Count; j++)
        {
            Edge<T> edge = this[minWeightIndex, j];
            int weight = edge != null ? edge.Weight : -1;
            if (edge != null
```

```
                    && !isInMST[j]
                    && weight < minWeight[j])
            {
                    previous[j] = minWeightIndex;
                    minWeight[j] = weight;
            }
        }
    }

    List<Edge<T>> result = new List<Edge<T>>();
    for (int i = 1; i < Nodes.Count; i++)
    {
        Edge<T> edge = this[previous[i], i];
        result.Add(edge);
    }
    return result;
}
```

The MinimumSpanningTreePrim method does not take any parameters. It uses three auxiliary node-related arrays that assign additional data to the nodes of the graph. The first, namely previous, stores indices of the previous node, from which the given node can be reached. By default, values of all elements are equal to 0, except the first one, which is set to −1. The minWeight array stores the minimum weight of the edge for accessing the given node. By default, all elements are set to the maximum value of the int type, while the value for the first element is set to 0. The isInMST array indicates whether the given node is already in the MST. To start with, values of all elements should be set to false.

The most interesting part of code is located in the for loop. Within it, the index of the node from the set of nodes not located in the MST, which can be reached with the minimum cost, is found. Such a task is performed by the GetMinimumWeightIndex method. Then, another for loop is used. Within it, you get an edge that connects nodes with the index minWeightIndex and j. You check whether the node is not already located in the MST and whether the cost of reaching the node is smaller than the previous minimum cost. If so, values of node-related elements in the previous and minWeight arrays are updated.

The remaining part of the code just prepares the final results. Here, you create a new instance of the list with the data of edges that form the MST. The for loop is used to get the data of the following edges and to add them to the result list.

While analyzing the code, the `GetMinimumWeightIndex` private method is mentioned. Its code is as follows:

```
private int GetMinimumWeightIndex(int[] weights, bool[] isInMST)
{
    int minValue = int.MaxValue;
    int minIndex = 0;

    for (int i = 0; i < Nodes.Count; i++)
    {
        if (!isInMST[i] && weights[i] < minValue)
        {
            minValue = weights[i];
            minIndex = i;
        }
    }

    return minIndex;
}
```

The `GetMinimumWeightIndex` method just finds an index of the node, which is not located in the MST and can be reached with the minimum cost. To do so, you use the `for` loop to iterate through all nodes. For each of them, you check whether the current node is not located in the MST and whether the cost of reaching it is smaller than the already-stored minimum value. If so, values of the `minValue` and `minIndex` variables are updated. At the end, the index is returned.

The presented code is based on the implementation shown at
`https://www.geeksforgeeks.org/greedy-algorithms-set-5-prims-mini`
`mum-spanning-tree-mst-2/`. You can also find more information about Prim's algorithm there.

What is more, the auxiliary `Fill` method is used. It just sets the values of all elements in the array to the value passed as the second parameter. The code of the method is as follows:

```
private void Fill<Q>(Q[] array, Q value)
{
    for (int i = 0; i < array.Length; i++)
    {
        array[i] = value;
    }
}
```

Let's take a look at the usage of the `MinimumSpanningTreePrim` method:

```
Graph<int> graph = new Graph<int>(false, true);
Node<int> n1 = graph.AddNode(1); (...)
Node<int> n8 = graph.AddNode(8);
graph.AddEdge(n1, n2, 3); (...)
graph.AddEdge(n7, n8, 20);
List<Edge<int>> mstPrim = graph.MinimumSpanningTreePrim();
mstPrim.ForEach(e => Console.WriteLine(e));
```

First, you initialize an undirected and weighted graph, as well as add nodes and edges. Then, you call the `MinimumSpanningTreePrim` method to find the MST using Prim's algorithm. At the end, you use the `ForEach` method to write the data of each edge from the MST in the console.

Example – telecommunication cable

As mentioned in the introduction to the topic of the MST, this problem has some important real-world applications, such as for creating a plan of connections between buildings to supply all of them with a telecommunication cable with the smallest cost. Of course, there are various possible connections, such as from one building to another or using a hub. What is more, environmental conditions can have serious impact on the cost of the investment due to the necessity of crossing a road or even a river. For example, let's create the program that solves this problem in the context of the set of buildings, as shown in the following diagram:

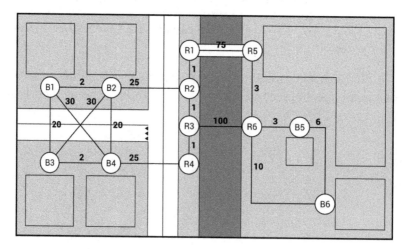

As you can see, the estate community consists of 12 buildings, including blocks of flats and kiosks located by the river. The buildings are located on two sides of a small river with only one bridge. Moreover, two roads exist. Of course, there are different costs of connections between various points, depending both on the distance and the environmental conditions. For example, the direct connection between two buildings (**B1** and **B2**) has a cost equal to **2**, while using the bridge (between **R1** and **R5**) involves a cost equal to **75**. If you need to cross the river without a bridge (between **R3** and **R6**), the cost is even higher and equal to **100**.

Your task is to find the MST. Within this example, you will apply both Kruskal's and Prim's algorithms to solve this problem. To start, let's initialize the undirected and weighted graph, as well as add nodes and edges, as follows:

```
Graph<string> graph = new Graph<string>(false, true);
Node<string> nodeB1 = graph.AddNode("B1"); (...)
Node<string> nodeR6 = graph.AddNode("R6");
graph.AddEdge(nodeB1, nodeB2, 2); (...)
graph.AddEdge(nodeR6, nodeB6, 10);
```

Then, you just need to call the `MinimumSpanningTreeKruskal` method to use Kruskal's algorithm to find the MST. When the results are obtained, you can easily present them in the console, together with the presentation of the total cost. The suitable part of code is shown in the following block:

```
Console.WriteLine("Minimum Spanning Tree - Kruskal's Algorithm:");
List<Edge<string>> mstKruskal =
    graph.MinimumSpanningTreeKruskal();
mstKruskal.ForEach(e => Console.WriteLine(e));
Console.WriteLine("Total cost: " + mstKruskal.Sum(e => e.Weight));
```

The results presented in the console are shown here:

```
Minimum Spanning Tree - Kruskal's Algorithm:
Edge: R4 -> R3, weight: 1
Edge: R3 -> R2, weight: 1
Edge: R2 -> R1, weight: 1
Edge: B1 -> B2, weight: 2
Edge: B3 -> B4, weight: 2
Edge: R6 -> R5, weight: 3
Edge: R6 -> B5, weight: 3
Edge: B5 -> B6, weight: 6
Edge: B1 -> B3, weight: 20
Edge: B2 -> R2, weight: 25
Edge: R1 -> R5, weight: 75
Total cost: 139
```

If you visualize such results on the map, the following MST is found:

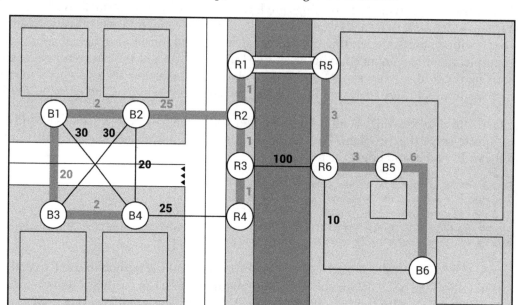

In a similar way, you can apply Prim's algorithm:

```
Console.WriteLine("nMinimum Spanning Tree - Prim's Algorithm:");
List<Edge<string>> mstPrim = graph.MinimumSpanningTreePrim();
mstPrim.ForEach(e => Console.WriteLine(e));
Console.WriteLine("Total cost: " + mstPrim.Sum(e => e.Weight));
```

The obtained results are as follows:

```
Minimum Spanning Tree - Prim's Algorithm:
Edge: B1 -> B2, weight: 2
Edge: B1 -> B3, weight: 20
Edge: B3 -> B4, weight: 2
Edge: R6 -> B5, weight: 3
Edge: B5 -> B6, weight: 6
Edge: R2 -> R1, weight: 1
Edge: B2 -> R2, weight: 25
Edge: R2 -> R3, weight: 1
Edge: R3 -> R4, weight: 1
Edge: R1 -> R5, weight: 75
Edge: R5 -> R6, weight: 3
Total cost: 139
```

That's all! You have just completed the example relating to the real-world application of the MST. Are you ready to proceed to another graph-related subject, which is named coloring?

Coloring

The topic of finding the MST is not the only graph-related problem. Among others, **node coloring** exists. Its aim is to assign colors (numbers) to all nodes to comply with the rule that there cannot be an edge between two nodes with the same color. Of course, the number of colors should be as low as possible. Such a problem has some real-world applications, such as for coloring a map, which is the topic of the example shown later.

Did you know that the nodes of each planar graph can be colored with no more than four colors? If you are interested in this topic, take a look at the **four-color theorem** (http://mathworld.wolfram.com/Four-ColorTheorem.html). The implementation of the coloring algorithm shown in this chapter is simple and in some cases could use more colors than really necessary.

Let's take a look at the following diagram:

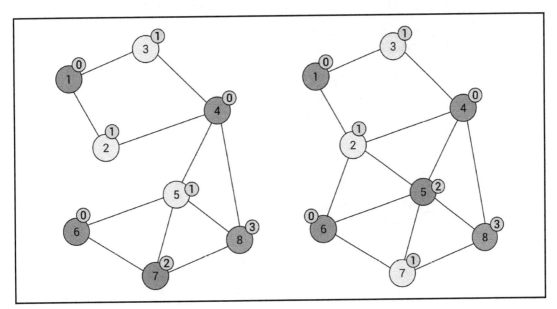

The first diagram (shown on the left) presents a graph that is colored using four colors: red (index equal to **0**), green (**1**), blue (**2**), and violet (**3**). As you can see, there are no nodes with the same colors connected by an edge. The graph shown on the right depicts the graph with two additional edges, namely (**2, 6**) and (**2, 5**). In such a case, the coloring has changed, but the number of colors remains the same.

The question is, how can you find colors for nodes to comply with the afore mentioned rule? Fortunately, the algorithm is very simple and its implementation is presented here. The code of the `Color` method, which should be added to the `Graph` class, is as follows:

```
public int[] Color()
{
    int[] colors = new int[Nodes.Count];
    Fill(colors, -1);
    colors[0] = 0;

    bool[] availability = new bool[Nodes.Count];
    for (int i = 1; i < Nodes.Count; i++)
    {
        Fill(availability, true);

        int colorIndex = 0;
        foreach (Node<T> neighbor in Nodes[i].Neighbors)
        {
            colorIndex = colors[neighbor.Index];
            if (colorIndex >= 0)
            {
                availability[colorIndex] = false;
            }
        }

        colorIndex = 0;
        for (int j = 0; j < availability.Length; j++)
        {
            if (availability[j])
            {
                colorIndex = j;
                break;
            }
        }

        colors[i] = colorIndex;
    }

    return colors;
}
```

The `Color` method uses two auxiliary node-related arrays. The first is named `colors` and stores indices of colors chosen for particular nodes. By default, values of all elements are set to -1, except the first one, which is set to 0. It means that the color of the first node is automatically set to the first color (for example, red). The other auxiliary array (`availability`) stores information about the availability of particular colors.

The most crucial part of the code is the `for` loop. Within it, you reset the availability of colors by setting `true` as the value of all elements within the `availability` array. Then, you iterate through the neighbor nodes of the current node to read their colors and mark such colors as unavailable by setting `false` as a value of a particular element in the `availability` array. The last inner `for` loop just iterates through the `availability` array and finds the first available color for the current node.

 The presented code is based on the implementation shown at `https://www.geeksforgeeks.org/graph-coloring-set-2-greedy-algori thm/`. What is more, you can find more information about the coloring problem there.

What is more, the auxiliary `Fill` method is used with exactly the same code, as explained in one of the previous examples. It just sets the values of all elements in the array to the value passed as the second parameter. The code of the method is as follows:

```
private void Fill<Q>(Q[] array, Q value)
{
    for (int i = 0; i < array.Length; i++)
    {
        array[i] = value;
    }
}
```

Let's take a look at the usage of the `Color` method:

```
Graph<int> graph = new Graph<int>(false, false);
Node<int> n1 = graph.AddNode(1); (...)
Node<int> n8 = graph.AddNode(8);
graph.AddEdge(n1, n2); (...)
graph.AddEdge(n7, n8);

int[] colors = graph.Color();
for (int i = 0; i < colors.Length; i++)
{
    Console.WriteLine($"Node {graph.Nodes[i].Data}: {colors[i]}");
}
```

Here, you create a new undirected and unweighted graph, add nodes and edges, and call the `Color` method to perform the node coloring. As a result, you receive an array with indices of colors for particular nodes. Then, you present the results in the console:

```
Node 1: 0
Node 2: 1
Node 3: 1
Node 4: 0
Node 5: 1
Node 6: 0
Node 7: 2
Node 8: 3
```

After this short introduction you are ready to proceed to the real-world application, namely for coloring the voivodeship map, which is presented next.

Example – voivodeship map

Let's create a program that represents the map of voivodeships in Poland as a graph, and color such areas so that two voivodeships with common borders do not have the same color. Of course, you should limit the number of colors.

To start, let's think about the graph representation. Here, nodes represent particular voivodeships, while edges represent common borders between voivodeships.

The map of Poland with the graph already colored is shown in the following diagram:

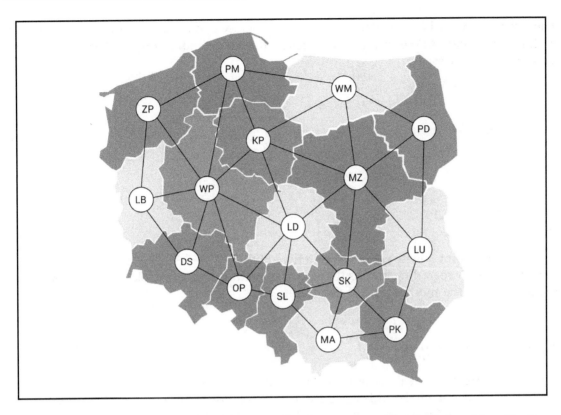

Your task is just to color nodes in the graph using the already-described algorithm. To do so, you create the undirected and unweighted graph, add nodes representing voivodeships, and add edges to indicate common borders. The code is as follows:

```
Graph<string> graph = new Graph<string>(false, false);
Node<string> nodePK = graph.AddNode("PK"); (...)
Node<string> nodeOP = graph.AddNode("OP");
graph.AddEdge(nodePK, nodeLU); (...)
graph.AddEdge(nodeDS, nodeOP);
```

Then, the `Color` method is called on the `Graph` instance and the color indices for particular nodes are returned. At the end, you just present the results in the console. The suitable part of code is as follows:

```
int[] colors = graph.Color();
for (int i = 0; i < colors.Length; i++)
{
    Console.WriteLine($"{graph.Nodes[i].Data}: {colors[i]}");
}
```

Part of the results is presented as follows:

```
PK: 0
LU: 1  (...)
OP: 2
```

You have just learnt how to color nodes in the graph! However, this is not the end of the interesting topics regarding graphs that are presented within this book. Now, let's proceed to searching for the shortest path in the graph.

Shortest path

A graph is a great data structure for storing the data of various maps, such as cities and the distances between them. For this reason, one of the obvious real-world applications of graphs is searching for the **shortest path** between two locations, which takes into account a specific cost, such as the distance, the necessary time, or even the amount of fuel required.

There are several approaches to the topic of searching for the shortest path in a graph. However, one of the common solutions is **Dijkstra's algorithm**, which makes it possible to calculate distance from a starting node to all nodes located in the graph. Then, you can easily get not only the cost of connection between two nodes, but also find nodes that are between the start and end nodes.

Dijkstra's algorithm uses two auxiliary node-related arrays, namely for storing an identifier of the previous node—the node from which the current node can be reached with the smallest overall cost, as well as the minimum distance (cost), which is necessary for accessing the current node. What is more, it uses the queue for storing nodes that should be checked. During the consecutive iterations, the algorithm updates the minimum distances to particular nodes in the graph. At the end, the auxiliary arrays contain the minimum distance (cost) to reach all the nodes from the chosen starting node, as well as information on how to reach each node using the shortest path.

Before proceeding to the example, let's take a look at the following diagram presenting two various shortest paths found using Dijkstra's algorithm. The left-hand side shows the path from the node **8** to **1**, while the right-hand side shows the path from the node **1** to **7**:

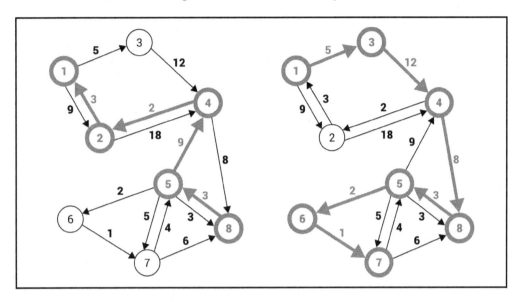

It is high time that you see some C# code, which can be used to implement Dijkstra's algorithm. The main role is performed by the `GetShortestPathDijkstra` method, which should be added to the `Graph` class. The code is as follows:

```
public List<Edge<T>> GetShortestPathDijkstra(
    Node<T> source, Node<T> target)
{
    int[] previous = new int[Nodes.Count];
    Fill(previous, -1);

    int[] distances = new int[Nodes.Count];
    Fill(distances, int.MaxValue);
    distances[source.Index] = 0;

    SimplePriorityQueue<Node<T>> nodes =
        new SimplePriorityQueue<Node<T>>();
    for (int i = 0; i < Nodes.Count; i++)
    {
        nodes.Enqueue(Nodes[i], distances[i]);
    }

    while (nodes.Count != 0)
```

```
    {
        Node<T> node = nodes.Dequeue();
        for (int i = 0; i < node.Neighbors.Count; i++)
        {
            Node<T> neighbor = node.Neighbors[i];
            int weight = i < node.Weights.Count
                ? node.Weights[i] : 0;
            int weightTotal = distances[node.Index] + weight;

            if (distances[neighbor.Index] > weightTotal)
            {
                distances[neighbor.Index] = weightTotal;
                previous[neighbor.Index] = node.Index;
                nodes.UpdatePriority(neighbor,
                    distances[neighbor.Index]);
            }
        }
    }

    List<int> indices = new List<int>();
    int index = target.Index;
    while (index >= 0)
    {
        indices.Add(index);
        index = previous[index];
    }

    indices.Reverse();
    List<Edge<T>> result = new List<Edge<T>>();
    for (int i = 0; i < indices.Count - 1; i++)
    {
        Edge<T> edge = this[indices[i], indices[i + 1]];
        result.Add(edge);
    }
    return result;
}
```

The GetShortestPathDijkstra method takes two parameters, namely source and target nodes. To start, it creates two node-related auxiliary arrays for storing the indices of previous nodes, from which the given node can be reached with the smallest overall cost (previous), as well as for storing the current minimum distances to the given node (distances). By default, the values of all elements in the previous array are set to −1, while in the distances array they are set to the maximum value of the int type. Of course, the distance to the source node is set to 0. Then, you create a new priority queue, and enqueue the data of all nodes. The priority of each element is equal to the current distance to such a node.

It is worth noting that the example uses the `OptimizedPriorityQueue` package from NuGet. More information about this package is available at `https://www.nuget.org/packages/OptimizedPriorityQueue` and in the *Priority queues* section in `Chapter 3`, *Stacks and Queues*.

The most interesting part of the code is the `while` loop which is executed until the queue is empty. Within the `while` loop, you get the first node from the queue and iterate through all of its neighbors using the `for` loop. Inside such a loop, you calculate the distance to a neighbor by taking the sum of the distance to the current node and the weight of the edge. If the calculated distance is smaller than the currently-stored value, you update the values regarding the minimum distance to the given neighbor, as well as the index of the previous node, from which you can reach the neighbor. It is worth noting that the priority of the element in the queue should be updated as well.

The remaining operations are used to resolve the path using the values stored in the `previous` array. To do so, you save indices of the following nodes (in the opposite direction) in the `indices` list. Then, you reverse it to achieve the order from the source node to the target one. At the end, you just create the list of edges to present the result in the form suitable for returning from the method.

 The presented and described implementation is based on the pseudocode shown at `https://en.wikipedia.org/wiki/Dijkstra%27s_algorithm`. You can find some additional information about Dijkstra's algorithm there.

Let's take a look at the usage of the `GetShortestPathDijkstra` method:

```
Graph<int> graph = new Graph<int>(true, true);
Node<int> n1 = graph.AddNode(1); (...)
Node<int> n8 = graph.AddNode(8);
graph.AddEdge(n1, n2, 9); (...)
graph.AddEdge(n8, n5, 3);
List<Edge<int>> path = graph.GetShortestPathDijkstra(n1, n5);
path.ForEach(e => Console.WriteLine(e));
```

Here, you create a new directed and weighted graph, add nodes and edges, and call the `GetShortestPathDijkstra` method to search the shortest path between two nodes, namely between the nodes 1 and 5. As a result, you receive a list of edges forming the shortest path. Then, you just iterate through all edges and present the results in the console:

```
Edge: 1 -> 3, weight: 5
Edge: 3 -> 4, weight: 12
Edge: 4 -> 8, weight: 8
Edge: 8 -> 5, weight: 3
```

After this short introduction, together with the simple example, let's proceed to the more advanced and interesting application related to game development. Let's go!

Example – game map

The last example shown in this chapter involves the application of Dijkstra's algorithm for finding the shortest path in a game map. Let's imagine that you have a board with various obstacles. For this reason, the player can use only part of the board to move. Your task is to find the shortest path between two places located on the board.

To start, let's represent the board as a two-dimensional array where a given position on the board can be available for movement or not. The suitable part of code should be added to the `Main` method in the `Program` class, as follows:

```
string[] lines = new string[]
{
    "001110000011111000001111",
    "001110000011111000001111",
    "001110000011111000001111",
    "000000000011100000011111",
    "000000111000000000011111",
    "000100111001110000011111",
    "111111111111110111111100",
    "111111111111110111111101",
    "111111111111110111111100",
    "000000000000000111111110",
    "000000000000000111111100",
    "000111111001100000001101",
    "000111111001100000001100",
    "000110000000000111111110",
    "111110000000000111111100",
    "111110001100110010010001",
    "111110001100110001000100"
};
bool[][] map = new bool[lines.Length][];
for (int i = 0; i < lines.Length; i++)
{
    map[i] = lines[i]
        .Select(c => int.Parse(c.ToString()) == 0)
        .ToArray();
}
```

To improve the readability of code, the map is represented as an array of `string` values. Each row is presented as text, with the number of characters equal to the number of columns. The value of each character indicates the availability of the point. If it is equal to 0, the position is available. Otherwise, it is not. The `string`-based map representation should be then converted into the Boolean two-dimensional array. Such a task is performed by a few lines of code, as shown in the preceding snippet.

The next step is the creation of the graph, as well as adding the necessary nodes and edges. The suitable part of code is presented as follows:

```
Graph<string> graph = new Graph<string>(false, true);
for (int i = 0; i < map.Length; i++)
{
    for (int j = 0; j < map[i].Length; j++)
    {
        if (map[i][j])
        {
            Node<string> from = graph.AddNode($"{i}-{j}");

            if (i > 0 && map[i - 1][j])
            {
                Node<string> to = graph.Nodes.Find(
                    n => n.Data == $"{i - 1}-{j}");
                graph.AddEdge(from, to, 1);
            }

            if (j > 0 && map[i][j - 1])
            {
                Node<string> to = graph.Nodes.Find(
                    n => n.Data == $"{i}-{j - 1}");
                graph.AddEdge(from, to, 1);
            }
        }
    }
}
```

First, you initialize a new undirected and weighted graph. Then, you use two `for` loops to iterate through all places on the board. Within such loops, you check whether the given place is available. If so, you create a new node (`from`). Then, you check whether the node placed immediately above the current one is also available. If so, a suitable edge is added with the weight equal to 1. In a similar way you check whether the node placed on the left of the current one is available and add an edge, if necessary.

Now you just need to get the `Node` instances representing the source and the target nodes. You can do it by using the `Find` method and providing the textual representation of the node, such as `0-0` or `16-24`. Then, you just call the `GetShortestPathDijkstra` method. In this case, the algorithm will try to find the shortest path between the node in the first row and column and the node in the last row and column. The code is as follows:

```
Node<string> source = graph.Nodes.Find(n => n.Data == "0-0");
Node<string> target = graph.Nodes.Find(n => n.Data == "16-24");
List<Edge<string>> path = graph.GetShortestPathDijkstra(
    source, target);
```

The last part of code is related to the presentation of the map in the console:

```
Console.OutputEncoding = Encoding.UTF8;
for (int row = 0; row < map.Length; row++)
{
    for (int column = 0; column < map[row].Length; column++)
    {
        ConsoleColor color = map[row][column]
            ? ConsoleColor.Green : ConsoleColor.Red;
        if (path.Any(e => e.From.Data == $"{row}-{column}"
            || e.To.Data == $"{row}-{column}"))
        {
            color = ConsoleColor.White;
        }

        Console.ForegroundColor = color;
        Console.Write("\u25cf ");
    }
    Console.WriteLine();
}
Console.ForegroundColor = ConsoleColor.Gray;
```

To start, you set the proper encoding in the console to be able to present Unicode characters as well. Then, you use two `for` loops to iterate through all places on the board. Inside such loops, you choose a color that should be used to represent a point in the console, either green (the point is available) or red (unavailable). If the currently-analyzed point is a part of the shortest path, the color is changed to white. At the end, you just set a proper color and write the Unicode character representing a bullet. When the program execution exits both loops, the default console color is set.

When you run the application, you will see the following result:

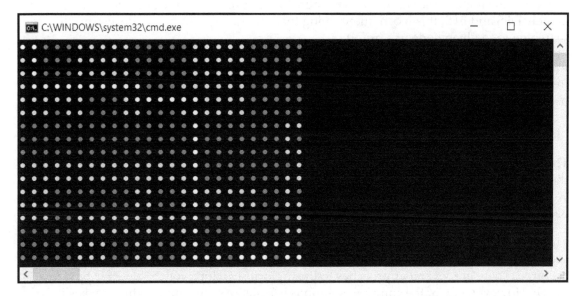

Great work! Now, let's proceed to a short summary to conclude the topics you have learnt about while reading the current chapter.

Summary

You have just completed the chapter related to one of the most important data structures available while developing applications, namely graphs. As you have learnt, a graph is a data structure that consists of nodes and edges. Each edge connects two nodes. What is more, there are various variants of edges in a graph, such as undirected and directed, as well as unweighted and weighted. All of them have been described and explained in detail, together with diagrams and code samples. Two methods of graph representation, namely using an adjacency list and an adjacency matrix, have been explained as well. Of course, you have also learnt how to implement a graph using the C# language.

While talking about graphs, is also important to present some real-world applications, especially due to the common use of such a data structure. For example, the chapter contains the description of the structure of friends available in social media or the problem of searching for the shortest path in a city.

Among the topics in this chapter, you have got to know how to traverse a graph, that is, visit all of the nodes in some particular order. Two approaches have been presented, namely DFS and BFS. It is worth mentioning that the traversal topic can be also applied for searching for a given node in a graph.

In one of the other sections, the subject of a spanning tree, as well as a minimum spanning tree, was introduced. As a reminder, a spanning tree is a subset of edges that connects all nodes in a graph without cycles, while a MST is a spanning tree with the minimum cost from all spanning trees available in the graph. There are a few approaches to finding the MST, including the application of Kruskal's or Prim's algorithms.

Then, you learnt solutions for the next two popular graph-related problems. The first was the coloring of nodes, where you needed to assign colors (numbers) to all nodes to comply with the rule that there cannot be an edge between two nodes with the same color. Of course, the number of colors should have been as low as possible.

The other problem was searching for the shortest path between two nodes, which took into account a specific cost, such as the distance, the necessary time, or even the amount of fuel required. There are several approaches to the topic of searching for the shortest path in a graph. However, one of the common solutions is Dijkstra's algorithm, which makes it possible to calculate the distance from a starting node to all nodes located in the graph. This topic has been presented and explained within this chapter.

Now, it is the high time to proceed to the overall summary to take a look at all of the data structures and algorithms that have been presented in the book so far. Let's turn the page and proceed to the last chapter!

Summary 7

While reading many pages of this book, you have learned a lot about various data structures and algorithms that you can use while developing applications in the C# language. Arrays, lists, stacks, queues, dictionaries, hash sets, trees, heaps, and graphs, as well as accompanying algorithms—it's quite a broad range of subjects, isn't it? Now it is high time to summarize this knowledge, as well as to remind you about some specific applications for particular structures.

First, you will see a brief classification of data structures, divided into two groups, namely linear and non-linear. Then, the topic of diversity of applications of various data structures is taken into account. You will see a short summary of each described data structure, as well as information about some problems which can be solved with the use of a particular data structure.

Are you ready to start reading the last chapter? If so, let's enjoy it and see how many topics you have learned while reading all the previous chapters. Let's go!

In this chapter, the following topics will be covered:

- Classification of data structures
- Diversity of applications

Classification of data structures

As you have seen while reading the book, there are many data structures with many configuration variants. Thus, choosing a proper data structure is not an easy task, which could have a significant impact on the performance of the developed solution. Even the topics mentioned in this book form quite a long list of described data structures. For this reason, it is a good idea to classify them in some way.

Within this chapter, the described data structures are grouped into linear and non-linear categories. Each element in a linear data structure can be logically adjacent to the following or the previous element. In the case of a nonlinear data structure, a single element can be logically adjacent to numerous others, not necessarily only one or two. They can be freely distributed throughout the memory.

Let's take a look at the following diagram, which shows the classification of data structures according to the mentioned criteria:

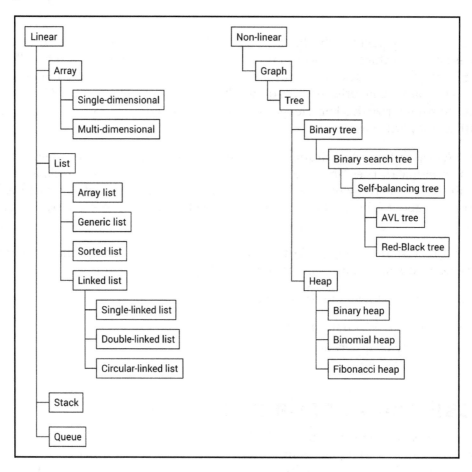

As you can see, the group of linear data structures contains arrays, lists, stacks, and queues. Of course, you should also take care of various subtypes of the mentioned data structures, such as three variants of a linked list, which is a subtype of a list.

In the case of non-linear data structures, a graph performs the most important role, because it also includes a tree subtype. Moreover, trees include binary trees and heaps, while a binary search tree is a subtype of a binary tree. In the same way, you can describe the relationships of other data structures presented and explained in this book.

Diversity of applications

Do you remember all of the data structures shown in the book? Due to the high number of described topics, it is a good idea to take a look at the following data structures once more, together with their associated algorithms, just in the form of a brief summary with information about some real-world applications.

Arrays

Let's start with arrays, which is one of the two main topics in the first chapter. You can use this data structure to store many variables of the same type, such as int, string, or a user-defined class. The important assumption is that the number of elements in an array cannot be changed after initialization. Moreover, arrays belong to random access data structures, which means that you can use indices to get access to the first, the middle, the *n*-th, or the last element from the array. You can benefit from a few variants of arrays, namely single-dimensional, multi-dimensional, and jagged arrays, also referred to as an array of arrays.

All of these variants are shown in the following diagram:

SINGLE-DIMENSIONAL	MULTI-DIMENSIONAL	JAGGED ARRAY

SINGLE-DIMENSIONAL

| 9 array[0] |
| -11 array[1] |
| 6 array[2] |
| -12 array[3] |
| 1 array[4] |

MULTI-DIMENSIONAL

9 array[0,0]	5 array[0,1]	-9 array[0,2]
-11 array[1,0]	4 array[1,1]	0 array[1,2]
6 array[2,0]	115 array[2,1]	3 array[2,2]
-12 array[3,0]	-9 array[3,1]	71 array[3,2]
1 array[4,0]	-6 array[4,1]	-1 array[4,2]

JAGGED ARRAY

array[0]

9 array[0][0]	5 array[0][1]	-9 array[0][2]

array[1]

0 array[1][0]	-3 array[1][1]	12 array[1][2]	51 array[1][3]	-3 array[1][4]

array[2]

NULL

array[3]

54 array[3][0]

There are a lot of applications of arrays and, as a developer, you have probably used this data structure many times. In this book, you have seen how you can use it to store various data, such as the names of months, the multiplication table, or even a map of a game. In the last case, you created a two-dimensional array with the same size as a map, where each element specifies a certain type of terrain, for example, grass or a wall.

There are many algorithms that perform various operations on arrays. However, one of the most common tasks is sorting an array to arrange its elements in the correct order, either ascending or descending. This book focuses on four algorithms, namely selection sort, insertion sort, bubble sort, as well as quick sort.

Lists

The next group of data structures, described in the first chapter, is related to lists. They are similar to arrays, but make it possible to dynamically increase the size of the collection if necessary. In the following diagram, you can see a few variants of a list, namely single-linked, double-linked, and circular-linked, respectively:

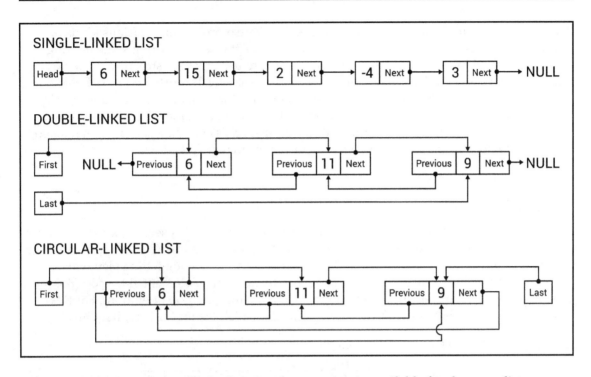

It is worth mentioning that the built-in implementation is available for the array list (ArrayList), as well as its generic (List) and sorted (SortedList) variants. The latter can be understood as a collection of key-value pairs, always sorted by keys.

A short comment may be beneficial for a single-linked, double-linked, and circular-linked list. The first data structure makes it possible to easily navigate from one element to the next using the Next property. However, it can be further expanded by adding the Previous property to allow navigating in forward and backward directions, forming the double-linked list. In the circular-linked list, the Previous property of the first node navigates to the last one, while the Next property links the last node to the first. It is worth noting that there is a built-in implementation of the double-linked list (LinkedList), and you can quite easily extend the double-linked list to behave as the circular-linked list.

There are a lot of applications for the lists to solve diverse problems in various kinds of applications. In this book, you have seen how to utilize the list for storing some floating point values and calculating the average value, how to use this data structure to create a simple database of people, and how to develop an automatically sorted address book. Moreover, you have prepared a simple application that allows a user to read the book by changing the pages, as well as the game, in which the user spins the wheel with random power. The wheel rotates slower and slower until it stops. Then, the user can spin it again, from the previous stop position, which illustrates the circular-linked list.

Stacks

The third chapter of this book focuses on stacks and queues. In this section, let's take a look at a stack, which is a representative of limited access data structures. This name means that you cannot access every element from the structure, and the way of getting elements is strictly specified. In the case of a stack, you can only add a new element at the top (the push operation) and get an element by removing it from the top (the pop operation). For this reason, a stack is consistent with the LIFO principle, which means Last-In First-Out.

The diagram of a stack is shown as follows:

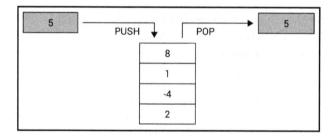

Of course, a stack has many real-world applications. One of the mentioned examples is related to a pile of many plates, each placed on top of the other. You can only add a new plate at the top of the pile, and you can only get a plate from the top of the pile. You cannot remove the seventh plate without taking the previous six from the top, and you cannot add a plate to the middle of the pile. You have also seen how to use a stack to reverse a word and how to apply it for solving the mathematical game Tower of Hanoi.

Queues

Another leading subject of the third chapter is a queue. While using this data structure, you can only add new elements at the end of the queue (the enqueue operation) and only remove the element from the queue from the beginning of the queue (the dequeue operation). For this reason, this data structure is consistent with the FIFO principle, which stands for First-In First-Out.

The diagram of a queue is shown as follows:

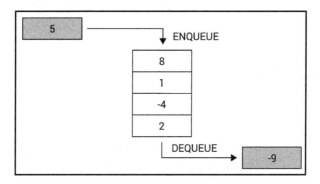

It is also possible to use a priority queue, which extends the concept of a queue by setting the priority for each element. Thus, the Dequeue operation returns the element with the highest priority, which has been added earliest to the queue.

There are many real-world applications of a queue. For example, a queue can be used to represent a line of people waiting in a shop at a checkout. New people stand at the end of the line, and the next person is taken to the checkout from the beginning of the line. You are not allowed to choose a person from the middle and serve them. Moreover, you have seen a few examples of the solution of a call center, where there are many callers (with different client identifiers) and one consultant, many callers and many consultants, as well as many callers (with different plans, either standard or priority support) and only one consultant, who answers the waiting calls.

Dictionaries

The topic of the fourth chapter is related to dictionaries and sets. First, let's take a look at a dictionary, which allows mapping keys to values and performing fast lookups. A dictionary uses a hash function and can be understood as a collection of pairs, each consisting of a key and a value. There are two built-in versions of a dictionary, namely non-generic (`Hashtable`) and generic (`Dictionary`). The sorted variant of a dictionary (`SortedDictionary`) is available, as well.

The mechanism of the hash table is presented in the following diagram:

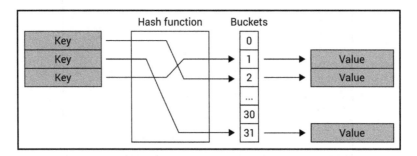

Due to the great performance of the hash table, such a data structure is frequently used in many real-world applications, such as for associative arrays, database indices, or cache systems. Within this book, you have seen how to create the phone book to store entries where a person's name is a key and a phone number is a value. Among other examples, you have developed an application that helps employees of shops to find the location of where a product should be placed, and you have applied the sorted dictionary to create the simple encyclopedia, where a user can add entries and show its full content.

Sets

Another data structure is a set, which is a collection of distinct objects without duplicated elements and without any particular order. Therefore, you can only get to know whether a given element is in the set or not. The sets are strictly connected with mathematical models and operations, such as union, intersection, subtraction, and symmetric difference.

The exemplary sets, storing data of various types, are shown as follows:

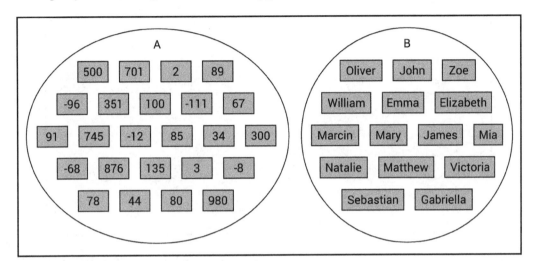

While developing applications in the C# language, you can benefit from high-performance, set-related operations provided by the `HashSet` class. As an example, you have seen how to create a system that handles one-time promotional coupons and allows you to check whether the scanned one has been already used. Another example is the reporting service for the system of a SPA center with four swimming pools. By using sets, you have calculated statistics, such as the number of visitors to a pool, the most popular pool, and the number of people who visited at least one pool.

Trees

The next topic is about trees, which are data structures that consist of nodes with one root. The root contains no parent node, while all other nodes do. Moreover, each node can have any number of child nodes. The child nodes of the same node can be called siblings, while a node without children is called a leaf.

Generally speaking, each node in a tree can contain any number of children. However, in the case of binary trees, a node cannot contain more than two children, that is, it can contain no child nodes, or only one or two, but there are no rules about relations between the nodes. If you want to use a binary search tree (BST), the next rule is introduced. It states that, for any node, values of all nodes in its left subtree must be smaller than its value, and that the values of all nodes in its right subtree must be greater than its value.

The exemplary BSTs are shown in the following diagram:

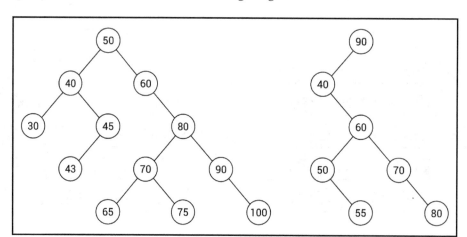

Another group of trees is called the self-balancing trees, which keeps a tree balanced all the time while adding and removing nodes. Their application is very important, because it allows you to form the correctly arranged tree, which has a positive impact on performance. There are various variants of the self-balancing trees, but AVL and Red-Black Trees (RBTs) are ones of the most popular. Both have been briefly described in this book.

While talking about trees, it is also beneficial to present a few approaches on how you can traverse a tree. In this book, you have learned pre-order, in-order, and post-order variants.

A tree is a data structure that is perfect for the representation of various data, such as the structure of a company, divided into a few departments, where each has its own structure. You have also seen an example where a tree is used to arrange a simple quiz consisting of a few questions and answers, which are shown depending on the previously taken decisions.

Heaps

A heap is another variant of a tree, which exists in two versions, namely min-heap and max-heap. For each of them, the additional property must be satisfied. For the min-heap, the value of each node must be greater than or equal to the value of its parent node. For the max-heap, the value of each node must be less than or equal to the value of its parent node. The mentioned rule performs the crucial role of ensuring that the root node always contains the smallest (in the min-heap) or the largest (in the max-heap) value. For this reason, it is a very convenient data structure for implementing a priority queue.

The heaps exist in many variants, including binary heaps, which must also maintain the complete binary tree rule, that is, each node cannot contain more than two children, and that all levels of a tree must be fully filled, except the last one, which can be filled from left to right with some empty space on the right.

The exemplary heaps are shown as follows:

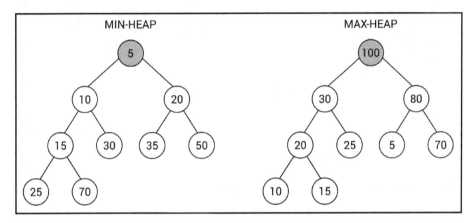

Of course, a binary heap is not the only one that is available. Among others, binomial heaps and Fibonacci heaps exist. All three variants have been described in this book.

One of the interesting applications of a heap is the sorting algorithm, named heap sort.

Graphs

The previous chapter is related to graphs, as a very popular data structure with a broad range of real-world applications. As a reminder, a graph is a data structure that consists of nodes and edges. Each edge connects two nodes. Moreover, there are a few variants of edges in a graph, such as undirected and directed, as well as unweighted and weighted. A graph can be represented either as an adjacency list or as an adjacency matrix.

All of these topics have been described in this book, together with the problem of graph traversal, finding the minimum spanning tree, node coloring, and finding the shortest path in a graph.

The exemplary graphs are shown in the following diagram:

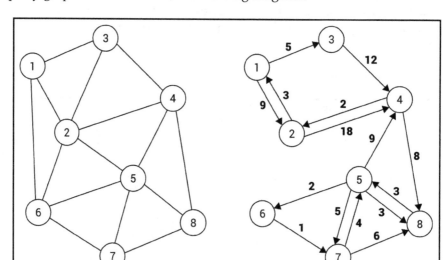

A graph data structure is commonly used in various applications, and it is a great way to represent diverse data, such as the structure of friends available on a social media site. Here, the nodes can represent contacts, while edges represent relations between people. Thus, you can easily check whether two contacts know each other or how many people should be involved to arrange a meeting between two particular people.

Another common application of graphs involves the problem of finding a path. As an example, you can use a graph to find a path between two points in the city, taking into account distance or time necessary for driving. You can use a graph to represent a map of a city, where nodes are intersections and edges represent roads. Of course, you should assign weights to edges to indicate the necessary distance or time for driving a given road.

There are many other applications related to graphs. For instance, the minimum spanning tree can be used to create a plan of connections between buildings to supply all of them with a telecommunication cable with the smallest cost, as explained in the previous chapter.

The node coloring problem has been used for coloring voivodeships on a map of Poland according to the rule that two voivodeships that have common borders cannot have the same color. Of course, the number of colors should be limited.

Another example shown in this book involves Dijkstra's algorithm for finding the shortest path in a game map. The task is to find the shortest path between two places on a board, taking into account various obstacles.

The last word

You have just reached the end of the last chapter of the book. First, the classification of data structures has been presented, taking into account linear and non-linear data structures. In the first group, you can find arrays, lists, stacks, and queues, while the second group involves graphs, trees, heaps, as well as their variants. In the following part of this chapter, the diversity of applications of various data structures has been taken into account. You have seen a short summary of each described data structure, as well as information about some problems which can be solved with the use of a particular data structure, such as a queue or a graph. To make the content easier to understand, as well as to remind you of the various topics from the previous chapters, the summary has been equipped with illustrations of data structures.

In the introduction to this book, I invited you to start your adventure with data structures and algorithms. While reading the following chapters, writing hundreds of lines of code and debugging, you had a chance to familiarize yourself with various data structures, starting with arrays and lists, through stacks, queues, dictionaries, and hash sets, ending with trees, heaps, and graphs. I hope that this book is only the first step into your long, challenging, and successful adventure with data structures and algorithms.

I would like to thank you for reading this book. If you have any questions or problems regarding the described content, please do not hesitate to contact me directly using the contact information shown at `http://jamro.biz`. I would like to wish you all the best in your career as a software developer, and I hope that you have many successful projects!

Other Books You May Enjoy

If you enjoyed this book, you may be interested in these other books by Packt:

C# 7 and .NET Core 2.0

Dirk Strauss, Jas Rademeyer

ISBN: 978-1-78839-619-6

- How to incorporate Entity Framework Core to build ASP .NET Core MVC applications
- Get hands-on experience with SignalR, and NuGet packages
- Working with MongoDB in your ASP.NET Core MVC application
- Get hands-on experience with .NET Core MVC, Middleware, Controllers, Views, Layouts, Routing, and OAuth
- Implementing Azure Functions and learn what Serverless computing means
- See how .NET Core enables cross-platform applications that run on Windows, macOS and Linux
- Running a .NET Core MVC application with Docker Compose

C# 7.1 and .NET Core 2.0 – Modern Cross-Platform Development - Third Edition

Mark J. Price

ISBN: 978-1-78839-807-7

- Build cross-platform applications using C# 7.1 and .NET Core 2.0
- Explore ASP.NET Core 2.0 and learn how to create professional websites, services, and applications
- Improve your application's performance using multitasking
- Use Entity Framework Core and LINQ to query and manipulate data
- Master object-oriented programming with C# to increase code reuse and efficiency
- Familiarize yourself with cross-device app development using the Universal Windows Platform
- Protect and manage your files and data with encryption, streams, and serialization
- Get started with mobile app development using Xamarin.Forms
- Preview the nullable reference type feature of C# 8

Leave a review - let other readers know what you think

Please share your thoughts on this book with others by leaving a review on the site that you bought it from. If you purchased the book from Amazon, please leave us an honest review on this book's Amazon page. This is vital so that other potential readers can see and use your unbiased opinion to make purchasing decisions, we can understand what our customers think about our products, and our authors can see your feedback on the title that they have worked with Packt to create. It will only take a few minutes of your time, but is valuable to other potential customers, our authors, and Packt. Thank you!

Index

CPSIA information can be obtained
at www.ICGtesting.com
Printed in the USA
LVHW101722031220
673319LV00010B/654